doing a *successful* research project

Doing a *successful* research project

Using qualitative or quantitative methods

Martin Brett Davies

www.palgrave.com/sociology/davies/

First published 2007 by
PALGRAVE MACMILLAN

Palgrave Macmillan in the UK is an imprint of Macmillian Publishers Limited, registered in England, company number 785998, of Houndmills, Basingstoke, Hampshire RG21 6XS.

Palgrave Macmillan in the US is a division of St Martin's Press LLC, 175 Fifth Avenue, New York, NY 10010.

Palgrave Macmillan is the global academic imprint of the above companies and has companies and representatives throughout the world.

Palgrave® and Macmillan® are registered trademarks in the United States, the United Kingdom, Europe and other countries.

ISBN-13: 978–1–4039–9379–3
ISBN-10: 1–4039–9379–3

This book is printed on paper suitable for recycling and made from fully managed and sustained forest sources. Logging, pulping and manufacturing processes are expected to conform to the environmental regulations of the country of origin.

A catalogue record for this book is available from the British Library.

A catalog record for this book is available from the Library of Congress.

Library of Congress Catalogue Card Number : 2006050218

10 9 8 7 6
16 15 14 13 12 11 10

Printed in China

For Jane, Emily and Beth

Contents

Preface

This book has a simple aim: it is to help you, the reader, to undertake a research project successfully, carry it to a satisfactory conclusion on schedule, and do it to the highest standard of which you are capable.

There are other volumes on bookshop and library shelves that may engage you in more theoretical or intellectual discussion. This book has an unashamedly practical bias – all I want is for you to succeed in your project.

If, like me, you eventually become fascinated by 'research methodology' as a subject in its own right, you'll be able, like M Poirot, to exercise your little grey cells to your heart's content. But, in this book, I assume that you have a particular task to pursue within the framework of a course of study, and that you've been given a time limit by which you must complete your work and submit a dissertation or research report.

Whether you plan to use qualitative methods, quantitative methods or a mixture of the two, if you follow my guidelines carefully, you *will* succeed.

Don't make the mistake of despising the simple approach. If I've learnt one thing over the years (and it's made me a better researcher now than when I did my PhD), it is that 'keeping it simple' is the key to the clever handling of complex research data.

I can't expect you to know exactly what I mean by that until you've learnt it for yourself, but in the course of completing your first project, you'll begin to get a sense of the relevance of my advice. Never make your project more complicated than it needs to be. Social and psychological reality is quite complex enough without the researcher making it worse by trying to cover too much ground in too little time.

Good luck – but, always remember: the best researchers make their own luck.

MARTIN BRETT DAVIES

Acknowledgements

Over the years, I have learnt many things about research methods from teachers, supervisors, colleagues and students; to them I am for ever indebted; much of what they taught me is deeply embedded in the pages that follow. I would especially place on record my gratitude to Marie Jahoda at Brunel University and to Ian Sinclair when we were Home Office colleagues.

I am grateful to the following for specific help with aspects of this book: Joanna Austin, Rose Barton, Susan Clark, Abigail Cooke, Louisa Doggett, Emily Edwards, Jane Edwards, Nick Gould, Catherine Gray, David Howe, Jo Kensit, Georgina Key, Helen Macdonald, Maresa Malhotra, Jamie Murdock, Caitlin Notley, Ali Pickard, Emily Salz, Gill Schofield, Jeanne Schofield, Natalie Start, Clare Symms, Emma Tarrington, Emma Tipple-Gooch, Liz Trinder, Kay Verdon, Kate Wallis and Fiona Watts.

Thank you, too, to Palgrave Macmillan's seven anonymous peer reviewers whose critical comments have greatly improved the quality of the final manuscript.

And a special thank you to Holly for foot-warming companionship.

CHAPTER 1

So you're going to do a research project

The dominance of research findings in our lives

Look in the pages of your newspaper any day of the week and you will find stories or snippets that draw on the findings of research projects. Some will report the outcome of large-scale controlled experiments into the use of pharmaceutical products and their value for a variety of health conditions; others will present the results of surveys into public opinion; and yet others will be descriptive accounts of what people say or do of the 'Isn't that interesting?' genre.

1. **A pint is more popular than the pulpit** In a survey carried out by InnSpired, a company that owns more than 1000 pubs, it was found that nearly two-thirds of British adults believe that the pub has more to offer the community than the church. Just 15 per cent have faith that it is the other way round. In answer to the question, 'Why do you go to your local pub?', respondents said:

To get drunk	6%
To socialise and meet friends	62%
To get out of the house	2%
I don't go to pubs	23%
Other	3%

From *The Times*, 10 November 2004, p. 32.

2. **For a longer life, look on the bright side** Researchers in the Netherlands investigated death rates among people who described themselves as optimists and pessimists. Out of 1000 men and women aged 65 to 85 enrolled into the investigation, those who were highly optimistic lived longer.

From the *Eastern Daily Press*, 2 November 2004, p. 5.

3. **Not so super markets** A postal survey of 1094 readers carried out by the BBC *Good Food* magazine showed that just 18 per cent enjoyed shopping in supermarkets; 45 per cent said they hated it. The nine worst things about supermarket shopping were identified as:
   1. Changes to food and aisle layout
   2. Running out of basics
   3. When they stop stocking favourite items
   4. Long queues
   5. Trolleys with dodgy wheels
   6. Picking the 'wrong' queue
   7. Grumpy till assistants
   8. The person in front of the queue running off to get another item
   9. Staff who don't know where things are.
   From the *Eastern Daily Press*, 6 July 2005, p. 6.

4. **Work eats into lunch breaks** Workers are taking less than half an hour for lunch because of spiralling pressures and one in five has no meal break at all, new research has revealed. A growing number of office staff eat a sandwich at their desk, but then snack on biscuits and sweets throughout the afternoon. Cake, doughnuts and chocolate are the favourite snacks of many workers, with just seven per cent preferring healthy options such as fruit. The poll of 500 office staff by recruitment firm Jobs@Pertemps showed that time taken for lunch has fallen by a quarter over the past five years. One in 10 people who eat in the afternoon said they were still hungry, while half wanted a 'sweet fix' to give them more energy.
   Reported on Yahoo!, 17 November 2004.

5. **National variations in happiness** There are some very dissatisfied people in Portugal. According to a survey from the pollsters Harris, a far higher proportion of the Portuguese are unhappy with their lives than anywhere else in Europe or the United States. Americans are the most content. While 58 per cent of those questioned in the US said that they were 'very satisfied' with their lives, only 3 per cent of Portuguese were so upbeat. Thirty-three per cent of Britons were 'very satisfied'.
   From *The Times*, 23 July 2005, p. 57.

6. **Adverts make young adults drink more** In a survey of 4000 Americans aged between 15 and 26, Leslie Snyder and a team of researchers at the University of Connecticut found that each additional alcohol advert seen each month was associated with a 1 per cent increase in the average number of drinks consumed. This finding contradicts industry claims that alcohol advertising only encourages brand switching.
From *The Times*, 3 January 2006, p. 15.

7. **Why do burglars do what they do?** In a Home Office research survey, 70 burglars gave reasons for their first and most recent burglaries:

	The first	The most recent
Influence of friends	25	10
Funding drug use	18	34
Boredom	14	0
Problems with parents	7	0
Buying luxuries	5	2
Funding alcohol use	4	6
Buying essentials	4	3
Saw an easy target	2	0
Coerced by others (not friends)	1	0
Responsibility for children	0	3

From 'Decision making by House Burglars: Offenders' Perspectives', Home Office, October 2004, quoted in *The Times Public Agenda*, 9 November 2004, p. 3.

8. **Turning a blind eye to cheating** Seven out of ten Britons believe infidelity is forgivable, making them the most laidback Europeans when it comes to affairs. A survey commissioned by the *Wall Street Journal Europe* on attitudes to sex and romance covering 20 European nations found, in contrast, more than half of Swedes believed that having an affair was unforgivable. Overall, women were less accepting of affairs than men.
Eastern Daily Press, 1 July 2005, p. 6.

Many of the studies reported in the media are health-related, partly because of the sheer volume of research that is funded and carried out in clinical settings, but also because almost everybody takes a keen interest in their own fitness and well-being.

Published accounts of research are often about what we eat and drink, the way we work, how we spend our leisure time, the goods that we buy and the shape and contents of the homes we live in. Research is used by political parties and pressure groups to help further their cause. And if influential organisations find that their researchers have come up with conclusions that conflict with their established interests, the findings may be partially or wholly suppressed – or the resulting press release issued on Christmas Eve.

Becoming a researcher

This book is designed to guide first-time researchers faced with the job of preparing a report or dissertation based on an empirical investigation.

By 'doing research' in your project, you will become, however modestly, a member of the scientific or policy development community – aiming to measure, to understand, perhaps to evaluate. Whether you had realised it or not, this draws you into a circle of professional people with developed expertise and places an obligation upon you to do it to a high standard.

I shall draw on, describe and suggest how you can use research methodologies derived from social science and psychology. Social research (in some contexts, called psychosocial research) is a mature and broad subject area, with its origins and development stretching over more than a century. It embraces the whole of empirical sociology and anthropology, together with the 'social' end of economics, geography and psychology. It has both pure and applied dimensions: some have used research tools to try and explain or understand the nature of human behaviour in its social context; others have sought to deliver findings that will have an impact on political, commercial or administrative practice.

Different disciplines use different research emphases. For example, mainstream psychology relies heavily on often quite complex statistical procedures; in sociology, the student may have to take on board epistemological arguments to the effect, for instance, that 'there is no such thing as facts' – everything is contingent upon who is perceiving it; in management or business studies, sociology and psychology operate alongside economics, accountancy and organisation theory, with a particular focus on sales, efficiency and staff relations; and in political science and social administration, policy development and programme evaluation are often the target.

Your subject-specific teachers and your own course reading will have prepared the ground for you to fit your research and its objectives into a relevant framework. Research can be concerned with theory development, the exploration of psychological or social reality, obtaining the answer to a stated question, the provision of policy-related information, or the evaluation or audit of an aspect of current practice. No matter what its aim, the rules governing research design and methodology are much the same, and this book will provide you with a generally applicable guide to the things you need to take into account.

Social research methods are drawn on by academics, managers and practitioners, students and career researchers in many fields of enquiry and employment. Here are twelve examples of the sort of questions to which answers might be sought:

- **Architecture, planning and housing design:** What things do people look for when they are buying a house? What do they like and dislike twelve months after moving in?

- **Childcare:** What are the patterns of (a) violent behaviour and (b) collaborative behaviour in a play group for the under-5s?

- **Consumer attitudes:** What different factors influence men and women in their choice of a car?

- **Crime and the penal system:** To what extent have people in different residential areas been the victims of a crime? To what extent do they admit to having committed a crime?

- **Diversity training:** What is the difference between expressed prejudice, unexpressed prejudice and discriminatory behaviour in any named professional group?

- **The environment:** What factors encourage and discourage people from recycling practices? How do people's practices change over time?

- **Information management:** How do students organise their literature surveys when preparing an essay? If they are given guidance, does this improve their performance?

- **Healthcare:** What do nurses, doctors, therapists and social workers each think about the attitudes and professional practices of the other professions?

- **Political opinion:** How do people's political opinions vary according to their age, gender, employment and financial position?

- **School teaching:** Twelve months after qualifying, what do school teachers say about their first year in post?

- **Sports science:** What kinds of training regimes are preferred by sports players? What kinds of training regimes have the most positive impact on their performance?

- **The travel industry:** What do people most like or dislike about air travel? Or about a named hotel or package holiday?

As we shall see, some of these questions are easier to answer than others. Some are much more difficult than may appear to be the case at first sight. Taken together, they would be likely to involve the use of all the various methods that I shall describe.

The basic rules

Sadly, despite the growing number of students who learn about social research methods and carry out a project under supervision, the quality of the finished product is often a disappointment. Students know, at the end of the process, how much time and effort have gone into it and they find it hard to understand why the project's findings are not all that they had hoped for. This is sometimes caused by the student's own overambitious expectations, but it is also often a result of the researcher not recognising that every part of the research task involves tricks of the trade that have to be learnt and patiently acted upon.

I shall introduce you to some of these as we work through each chapter. Even more fundamentally, though, it is the primary argument of this book that there are some very basic rules that must be followed if students are to emerge with a high-quality and successful report:

- Above all, **keep it simple**. Too many students are encouraged to believe that the best work involves complex methodological theories. It does not.

- **Don't try and do too much**. Entry-level students often want to explore too many questions at once. Be realistic about the scale of what you can do in the time available and about the conclusions you can draw from the data you have gathered.

- Good research requires an acceptance of the fact that, at every stage, there are good and bad ways of proceeding. **The cardinal virtue is patience**. You can't and mustn't rush it or try to take shortcuts.

- **Planning is crucial**. You must plan each step carefully if you want your project to be carried out to the highest standard of which you are capable.

Qualitative and quantitative research methods

No matter what field of study you are working in, if you are carrying out research into people's opinions, feelings, experiences or behaviour, you will be following one of two distinct paths. One owes its identity to the scientific tradition; the second is reflective or experiential in nature. Both paths use some of the same research skills although not always in the same order. Both deliver useful and informative results when they are well done, but each serves a rather different purpose. They are usually referred to as *quantitative research* and *qualitative research*.

Two quotations pinpoint the differences of ethos that characterise the two methodological approaches.

In respect of quantitative research:
The purpose of research is to discover answers to questions through the application of scientific procedures. These procedures have been developed in order to increase the likelihood

that the information gathered will be relevant to the question asked and will be reliable and unbiased. To be sure, there is no guarantee that any given research undertaking actually will produce relevant, reliable and unbiased information. But scientific research procedures are more likely to do so than any other method. (Selltiz et al, 1965, p. 2)

In respect of qualitative research:
Qualitative research is a situated activity that locates the observer in the world. It consists of a set of interpretive, material practices that make the world visible. These practices transform the world. They turn the world into a series of representations, including field notes, interviews, conversations, photographs, recordings and memos to the self. At this level, qualitative research involves an interpretive, naturalistic approach to the world. This means that qualitative researchers study things in their natural settings, attempting to make sense of, or to interpret, phenomena in terms of the meanings people bring to them. (Denzin and Lincoln, 2003, p. 4)

The distinction between quantitative and qualitative methods has been the subject of extensive discussion in academic circles. Some scholars say that it isn't so much a question of the researcher deciding which route to go down, but what kind of knowledge he or she is seeking to make, uncover or construct. Other theorists have suggested that the distinction is misleading and should be avoided. In practice, however, the labels are common currency in most social research circles.

The two approaches differ from each other in their style, language and stated objectives. Both are supported by a large and complex literature employing contrasting systems of terminology and analytical sophistication. Both have inspired the development of dedicated computer software programs. In Parts 2 and 3 of this book I will describe them in some detail.

Deciding which of the two research methods to use in a student project is often partly determined by the ethos of a particular course and the preference of its teacher. Students, too, may have an inclination. Some are drawn to the qualitative research approach by practical considerations: they see it as smaller scale, more manageable in a limited time frame, and offering the temptation of 'doing research' without having to 'do sums' or learn about statistics. Ideologically, there is an undeniable tendency for qualitative methods to be perceived as more human and even, perhaps, more in tune with contemporary social thinking.

On the other hand, quantitative research employs the same scientific principles and techniques that have made the modern world what it is, and it offers the tempting idea that its findings have a certain 'definiteness' about them, which make it possible for conclusions to be drawn to a specifiable level of probability. There is a satisfying neatness about quantitatively derived results that allows the author to feel that a rounded task has been completed.

The debate between the respective advocates of the two methodologies mirrors longstanding discussions in philosophy about the nature of knowledge. Is there such a thing as objective truth? Is all knowledge relative to the person through whose eyes it is perceived?

The primary task for the student researcher is to decide which route to go down, and, having chosen it, to be clear what conclusions can and cannot be drawn from the findings obtained. The two routes are not mutually exclusive; mixed methods can be employed, and students are often tempted by the roundedness of such an approach. You should, however, take account of the fact that there are workload and timescale implications in such a choice.

If you asked me to recommend just one book on …
general research methodology from a sociological perspective
it would be:

Robson, Colin (2002)
Real World Research, 2nd edn, Oxford, Blackwell

Are you ready to be a good project manager?

Managing a research project from start to finish is very different from writing an essay. Even though your first project will probably be modest in scale, it will still have a number of different strands to it, and, for a successful end-result, you will need to handle each of them competently. It's what experienced researchers mean when they talk about their work being like that of a juggler – keeping several balls in the air at the same time.

It's not that any of the elements present insuperable difficulties. It's just that you need to be clear about each one of them in advance. They overlap in time terms – that's the juggling bit – but they are separately identifiable, and the researcher's skill consists of being able to manage each of them in an efficient and effective manner.

ten steps to get you off to a good start

1. You need a supervisor
Even professional researchers with years of experience find that their work benefits from access to another person who can challenge and encourage their thinking. For students or beginning researchers, the absence of a good supervisor, providing face-to-face, one-to-one feedback is a major handicap. In busy university departments, you may need to use your initiative to secure guidance specific to your needs. Even a 10-minute conversation in the corridor with an experienced researcher can make all the difference – provided you've identified beforehand the issues to focus on.

2. You should expect to talk things over with your peers
This can be done either in an organised class group or informally and it's an excellent way of improving your performance. Some groups of students, enthused by the research process, organise their own get-togethers with each other so that they can share their experiences and offer supportive criticism. Doing this takes you across the divide from 'being a student' into something close to the working world of the professional researcher.

3. Accept that criticisms may be useful
In discussion with your supervisor or with colleagues, you should be prepared to invite, not just appreciative remarks, but tough observations, critical reactions and awkward questions. You may not find it easy to hear negative comments (even when you've invited others to give you an opinion), but such responses may warn you either that your research question isn't

ten steps to get you off to a good start *continued*

as sharp and as focused as it might be or that the design lacks tightness and discipline. At the planning stage, you must learn to tolerate and value bracing remarks and resist being too defensive in response. Of course, you don't *have* to accept or act on what other people suggest, but you should always think carefully about it before you reject their thoughts out of hand.

4. **Start out with a clear understanding of resource issues**
   - How much time are you realistically going to be able to devote to your project?
   - Are there likely to be any costs involved, and can you meet them?
   - Limitations of time, money and logistics mean that you will be restricted so far as geography is concerned: you must reconcile yourself to the fact that your study will be specific to a particular time and place – and your design and the conclusions you draw will need to take account of that.

5. **Don't firm up your project plan too soon**
   In the very early stages of planning, don't commit yourself precipitately to the nature, shape or title of your project. Before you've even begun, you may well have some ideas of what you want to do. But it is wrong to have *too fixed* a commitment to a particular way forward. It's fine to have an idea (and much better than not having one), but you must leave some flexibility for thinking it through in practice during the planning, preparatory, exploratory and pilot stages.

6. **But you do need to settle on a research topic**
   If you have absolutely no idea what you might do, then you should begin to think about topics that could motivate you. Many students tend to choose subjects either close to their hearts (typically, for example, with gender, age-related or ethnic identity implications) or they look to the course teacher for guidance. That, certainly, is what teachers are there for, and, if you are really stuck, you may need to press your claims for some personal attention. Alternatively, you could set up an informal brainstorming group session with colleagues.

ten steps to get you off to a good start *continued*

7. You should pre-plan your working systems

You can do this gradually while you are settling on your topic and methodology:

- Some researchers advocate the value of keeping a detailed research diary in which to note everything that occurs in chronological order; if you like that idea, you should start it right away.

- Others recommend the use of a flexible wall chart, which maps out the progress of your study so far and outlines the timing of future stages. You can use a blackboard, white-board, flip chart or computer file. Again, it is perfectly feasible to start this before you know where you will end up; indeed, it will help your thinking process from the very beginning.

- If your project is going to involve the use of hardware of various kinds – audio recorders with free-standing micro-phones, video equipment or significant quantities of stationery – you need to be sure that these will be available when you need them.

8. Make sure you stick to the requirements of your course

Different courses employ different styles of research methods teaching. This book tries to cover the full range, but it is important that you aim to plan your research project in such a way that it conforms to the methodological approaches that you have been taught. They may be highly specific, requiring you, for example, to gather data that will require statistical analysis or to deliver detailed transcripts from three focus groups that present problems of linguistic content analysis for you to solve. It would be a brave or foolhardy student who ignored such specific requirements.

9. Stay in touch with your favourite textbooks

Even with the help of this book, there will be times during your project when you will need to refer to other relevant text-books – either in your discipline or in research methodology. Make sure that you have them easily to hand. They will give

ten steps to get you off to a good start *continued*

you ideas about topic, method and procedure, and they will work creatively with you as you move through the various stages of your project.

10. Plan your timetable

You should draw up a project timetable as soon as possible; you can always adapt it and update it as go along. It should allow for all the various stages that are outlined in this book. It isn't just your own time that you need to take into account. You will find that the process of gaining access and obtaining permission for your work can take far longer than you might initially have anticipated, and those elements should be built in to your timetable.

Are you on message?

Doing research is different from any other kind of student exercise. In order to assume the mantle of a successful researcher, there are certain operational principles that you must embrace.

One of the hardest lessons for you to learn will be that, whatever method you use, you are not going to make a groundbreaking contribution to the subject. Not because you are not clever, but because that isn't how research – whether scientific or reflective – works.

Of course, the work that you do will have originality – partly because of the way you have designed it, and partly because, by definition, the doing of research means that you will be gathering original data. The way that you analyse it and write it up will also be unique.

The aim of the exercise is to enable you to demonstrate that:

1. You've learnt how to plan a research project
2. You've organised it from beginning to end
3. You've successfully gathered data
4. You've analysed that data
5. You've produced a good quality report based on your data.

That is what 'doing research' requires and if you do it all in style, your teacher will give you a good mark.

Often students are disappointed at what they think is the 'obviousness' of their findings. They have lived with their work for three, six or twelve months, and they feel that their conclusions don't measure up proportionately to the effort they have put into it. But if you absorb the lessons taught in this book, you will become mentally tuned in to the idea that a successful research project is equivalent to a single brick in the wall of knowledge and understanding. As long as the brick is the right shape, contains all the right ingredients, has been properly baked and expertly laid, you should feel, not disappointment, but pride in a job well done.

Like most people, I was an overambitious researcher when I began, and, because of that, my early work was not as good as it should have been. I was reminded of this when, recently, a student doing a university Business Management course complained that 'Nobody told me how much trouble I would have with a five-stage research project, incorporating three methods (focus groups, interviews and mail questionnaires) and with a three-month deadline'. The end result was submission of the report 18 months late, a very poor quality piece of work and a deep sense of disappointment for the student.

How could she have avoided that? There are two linked imperatives that I think would have helped my student friend in the planning stage and while doing the main body of work:

- **Aim for specificity of focus:** Research is not about the totality of life. It requires you to detach one element from reality, gather evidence about it (whether scientifically or reflectively) and describe what you have found. When you first identify a topic, you will find that your mind goes off in all directions. That's entirely natural and is initially helpful, but, once you are embarked on your project, you need to aim for a clear-cut sense of direction. In a single, time-limited project, you can't cover all aspects of everything. Keep the focus tight. Don't let it drift. Get a clear idea of where the evidence is leading you.

- **Ask a good question:** One of the best ways of achieving specificity of focus is to ask a good question. In scientific research, you should organise things so that you get to the starting block with 'a good question' clearly in your mind; in a reflective or exploratory study, the 'good question' that you start with may evolve and take on a different shape in the course of your project.

The nature of research

A true understanding of the nature of research can only come from *doing* it. Research is like playing a musical instrument or being a plumber or making a speech: you can't really get good at it just by reading books.

Definitions of research are legion, but three can be employed to embrace most projects that will involve student researchers:

- Research is a process of gathering data in a strictly organised manner. It is roughly equivalent to a newspaper editor saying to a journalist, 'Go away and research it'. The end-product of the data-gathering process may vary along a continuum from simple description to reflection and interpretation. The emphasis is on structured investigation, exploration or discovery. In some contexts, theoretical constructs mean that the process is far from simple.

- Research is a process of testing a stated idea or assertion (the hypothesis) to see if the evidence supports it or not. This may involve putting in place experimental practices and comparing them with other controlled or current practices, but it can also employ simple data-gathering procedures.

- Research is a process of engaging in planned or unplanned interactions with or interventions in parts of the real world, and reporting on what happens and what they seem to mean. Field trials are one example of this approach; 'action research' is another.

One of these definitions should match what you expect to be doing. If you can link your chosen approach with a commitment to specificity of focus and the identification of a good question, then you will be well on your way to success. Because research is incremental, it only works – or only works successfully – if the researcher thinks clearly about the task being embarked upon, engages in relevant prior reading and makes a commitment to careful planning.

exercise

The approach outlined in this book will encourage you at the outset to think about and acknowledge the complexity of even the simplest of questions, such as:
- Why do people like to drive cars?
- Why do vegetarians become vegetarians?
- Why do people spray walls with graffiti?
- When (and why) do people decide to move home/have a baby/change jobs/emigrate?
- How often do people have sex?

Questions like these are all inherently interesting, but they are fraught with methodological problems. If, right now, you pause and think about those problems and how, or whether, you could overcome them, you will learn valuable lessons relevant to your own research planning task.

Often, in organisational settings, a senior manager will ask a professional researcher to come up with the answer to questions like:

- Why is this product not selling?
- Do people look at (or read) this advertising leaflet?
- Are the workers in this office happy?
- Are they efficient?
- Why are people filling in this form badly?

The researcher's task is to recast such questions into a format that leads to useful answers.

Your aim, as an aspirant researcher venturing forth in pursuit of a successful project report, must be to settle upon a question that is realistically answerable and will enable you to make a modest contribution to your discipline's knowledge base. You will have learnt a valuable lesson about the incremental nature of research activity, and, no less important, you will have passed an important part of your course with flying colours.

2 Let's make a start

To complete a successful research project, you must prepare yourself, metaphorically speaking, to practise the art of juggling with several balls in the air at the same time. The art of achieving this is to keep clearly in your mind (or preferably on paper) the full sequence of events that you will be responsible for. As I suggested at the end of Chapter 1, the mantras of asking a good question and achieving specificity of focus are the magic keys that will make it all possible.

Choosing a topic and turning it into a question

One of the reasons why 'doing a project' is so exciting is because the exercise is personal to you. It is very different from being given an essay title or an exam question designed to test your knowledge in a predetermined area. Even if your course teacher suggests an acceptable topic, there will be plenty of scope for you to introduce your own ideas and stamp your identity upon it.

To some, it can seem almost like a personal voyage of exploration. You may well have been thinking about a suitable research field during earlier stages of your course and while you've been learning about research methods, but it is wise not to close down any options until you are ready to begin. Commonly, students are inspired by their experience of a particular taught unit or an admired teacher or by a new interest that has been stimulated by the degree programme.

What do you do if you can't think of a topic that appeals to you?

Talk it over with a teacher. Share your anxieties with colleague-students or friends. Browse through your textbooks and lecture notes. Find out what previous years' students have done and see if one of their titles gives you an idea. Approach the problem logically by thinking about:

The subject matter of your degree programme
↓
An interesting course unit
↓
An attractive field within that unit
↓
A topic that interests you

You may be trying to be too clever – aiming to come up with a topic unique in the history of the universe, something that will have people swooning with admiration at your originality and intellectual precociousness. Don't do it. It's safer – and likely to lead to a better mark – to settle on an ordinary, middle-of-the-road topic that will lend itself to a nicely organised process of project management. That's the clever way of proceeding and I've often noticed that the top-of-the-class students tend to recognise this fact only too well. You can always let your cleverness shine through during the stages of design, analysis and write-up.

Don't make things more difficult for yourself than they need to be.

What do you do if you have a string of possible topics, each of which seems tempting?

This is a common problem, but your own motivation and the practicality of your choice should be the determining factors. In my supervision class, in weeks 1 and 2 when I sit in a circle with the students and invite them to tell me their topic ideas, I inwardly groan when one of them insists on spelling out five or six possibilities. There is no quick solution to this, and students tend to resist it if the teacher tries to decide for them. Although we talk about it in class, time constraints (and the interests of the other students) press upon us, and 'come and see me afterwards' is all I can say. Together, we then try to assess which topic will sustain the student's interest the most (motivation) and which one will present the fewest problems (practicalities).

How do you move from a topic to a question?

This is a crucial stage in the development of your research-mindedness, and it marks the beginning of the logical process of thought that enables you to emerge at the end with presentable findings. The process has two stages. The first stage is straightforward: you just turn your topic into question format. We saw some examples of this in Chapter 1. It's the next stage that is trickier.

How do you move from your first idea of a question to a feasible research question?

You need to get this right because it counteracts any tendency towards too broad a focus and it sets your agenda within manageable limits. The best way of succeeding is to subject your proposed research question to a rigorous process of interrogation. A good supervisor will do it for you, but, with the following checklist, you can perfectly well do it yourself:

- Is your question too general for a small, time-limited study?
- Is it more suitable for a doctoral thesis, or even a book?
- Have you achieved specificity of focus?
- Is it possible that your question is more complex than it looks?
- If you are intending to carry out an 'evaluation' or gauge the 'effectiveness' of something, is that a realistic goal?
- Is it a question that lends itself to a predetermined structure (even, perhaps, enabling you to use an existing research instrument or measuring scale) or does it require exploratory/reflective analysis?
- Does the question fall within the agenda of the course?
- Have you thought about the likely cost to you?
- Might there be any problems of access to your research population?
- Will your project need the agreement of an ethics or governance committee? If so, is it likely that they will approve your choice?
- Do you need permission to use an intended research instrument?

How specific does the 'specificity of focus' need to be?

One of the things that a career researcher will tell you is that the more you research a subject, the more intrigued you become by specific aspects of it, and this leads you naturally to ask highly focused questions.

But at the beginning stage, the degree of specificity may vary from discipline to discipline, from methodology to methodology and from teacher to teacher. The focus is often tightest in those subjects that are close to the natural sciences – psychology, geography, environmental science and subjects allied to medicine, for example. It is less so in sociology, social administration and related fields.

But, no matter what the subject, I recommend the value of adopting the principle of 'specificity of focus' for two reasons:

- Most undergraduate or Masters-level student projects have to be completed within a short time frame or alongside other course units. It is simply not possible for a student researcher to handle diffuse material within broadly defined boundaries in a way that leads to high-quality results.
- However bright you are, however good you have become at essay-writing, and whatever teaching you have received in research methods, you still need to learn the art and craft of real-world research, step by step. By achieving specificity of focus, you will be able to practise and demonstrate your abilities at every stage of the project without losing sight of your goal.

Practicalities

Let's assume you have jumped the first hurdle and have a question that feels doable and has been approved by your supervisor. The next step is to work out how best to find an answer to your question.

First, you must take account of some of the practical realities that will determine how you might proceed.

The value of your project for your degree and career

The most important thing to bear in mind is that your completed project report will contribute significantly to your degree or diploma grade. It will tend to get mentioned in academic references that are written about you and may well be discussed by prospective employers when they interview you for a job. A student's research-based dissertation is widely recognised as something very special in the educational process and three things follow from that:

1. You would be wise to follow the methodological ethos of your course; don't be too stubborn or bloody-minded about 'doing your own thing' if it is in blatant conflict with what your course teacher recommends.

2. Do the very best that you can – and that means giving the task your full concentration throughout the period of time that is allowed.

3. Recognise that the research project task *in itself* may be relevant to your future career. People know you can write essays (all students can – more or less), but your dissertation will give you the opportunity to learn and demonstrate skills in project-planning, negotiation, interviewing strangers, data analysis (perhaps including statistical manipulation), software usage including spreadsheets and databases, and the presentation of numerical findings or analytical interpretations within a carefully constructed report.

Your own preference

Subject to whatever guidance you are given by course teachers, your own feeling for a preferred methodology may come into play. You should be wary, however, of allowing this to override your professional and academic judgement in determining the right methodology to use in order to get an appropriate answer to your research question.

Time constraints

You must be realistic. You would be well advised, for example, not to plan to use a lengthy interview schedule with 500 school children even if you have ease of access because you are working in the class-room. One hundred 5-minute structured survey interviews or twelve 45-minute reflective conversations will be more realistic and, provided they have been well designed, they will give you more than enough material to demonstrate your skills as a research analyst. For ease of access, you could plan to base your study on encounters with students on campus or with members of the public in the city centre or in an airport lounge where people are 'killing time' and are often only too pleased to talk to someone. A common shock for students doing a qualitative research study is the discovery that having collected (let us say) twelve 70-minute audio tapes of one-to-one interviews, the time needed just to listen to them will be 14 hours nonstop, while the time needed to transcribe and subject them to detailed analysis will extend to many hundreds of hours. It is essential that you think about this beforehand rather than halfway through your project when submission deadlines are looming.

Resource issues

The resource issues may simply be a matter of money: for example, imagine that you have committed yourself to carry out a study in ten garden centres or six tourist resorts; you've got to get there, perhaps on a number of occasions, and you will need to budget for it. Logistics can be problematic. For example, I supervised a student who aimed to interview shoppers using the all-night supermarket; she wanted to find out why they were there in the middle of the night; but only after she'd set about the business of data collection did she realise that she hadn't the means of getting there at 2 o'clock in the morning because of her reliance on friends' transport and concerns about her own personal safety. So she had to settle for doing the study between 11 o'clock and midnight, which was fine as a research exercise in its own right, but not what she had originally hoped to achieve and almost certainly meaning that she was interviewing a different kind of sample.

Pitch it at a level appropriate to your expertise

If this is the first time you have done a research project, don't be overambitious. Keep your objectives modest and your focus tight, and you won't go far wrong. Many beginning researchers try to cover too much ground in too short a time – and if you are guilty of that, your project report will not be as good as you would like it to be.

When you've given some thought to these practical matters, you may find that you want to make changes to your original idea – even to the question that you thought you had settled on. This is not a sign of half-baked thinking or bad planning on your part. On the contrary, it shows that you are learning that the process of 'doing research' is not linear but dynamic; it evolves, and in the course of its development, you may well have ideas that take you up blind alleys from which you have to retreat. The greatest intellectual assets for the researcher in any discipline are flexibility, an open mind and curiosity – and that is so just as much at the pre-planning stage as it is later on.

If you asked me to recommend just one book on ...
general research methodology from a psychological perspective *it would be:*

Coolican, H (2006)
Introduction to Research Methods in Psychology, 3rd edn, London, Hodder Arnold

Selecting your methodology

Having identified a research question, you face a critical decision. Once you have decided which methodological route to go down and have embarked on the process of preparing for data collection, your course will be set. It is important for you to feel confident that you have made the right choice.

There are two principal options open to you:

1. You can choose quantitative research methods, using the traditions of science

2. You can opt for qualitative research, employing a more reflective or exploratory approach.

The distinction between the two is not as clear-cut as is sometimes assumed. Career researchers may make use of both methods at different times (or even at the same time) depending on the nature of the question they are seeking to answer. In large-scale projects, investigators may use a circular sequence in which exploration is followed by measurement which is in turn followed by a qualitatively analytical phase in order to throw more light on aspects of the scientific findings.

It will, however, become clear in Parts 2 and 3 of this book that there are marked differences between the two methods – both in the objectives they pursue, and in the sequential pattern of research activity that they require and the time-scale relative to the different elements that are involved. Both methods present challenges to the researcher. To put it rather simplistically:

- quantitative research requires imagination, patience and discipline at the planning and design stages; data collection may present technical problems and requires tenacity but is often straightforward; the tasks of data analysis and write-up are largely, although not entirely, determined by the way the project was set up
- qualitative research requires careful thought at the outset; it demands mental agility, flexibility and alertness during data collection; it calls for advanced skills in data management and text-driven creativity during the analysis and write-up.

This book will provide detailed guidance for both routes.

In deciding how to answer your research question, it will be helpful to get clear in your mind which of various research objectives your question seems to be pointing towards.

Will your project be aiming to:

- *Describe, monitor or investigate* Both qualitative and quantitative research can deliver this – but they will produce different *kinds* of descriptions.
- *Explore* It depends on the nature of the exploration, but both quantitative and qualitative research can be used: quantitative methods may use a survey of some kind, while qualitative methods often rely on interviews or observation. Again, though, the nature of the exploratory material produced is significantly different in each case.
- *Interpret* Qualitative research is especially strong in this area, although advanced methods of survey analysis can be effective in a rather different way.
- *Look behind the surface* Much qualitative research aims to do just that: to reflect upon the feelings and experiences relative to the research question, to explore the nature of the relation-

ship between person and situation, and to take account of the effect of the research analyst's own background and role.

- *Evaluate* Independent, detached and replicable evaluation (as distinct from user or customer opinion, which can be based on either methodology) is almost wholly dependent on quantitative research, generally using an experimental model. Evaluation of a kind that allows for variations of perspective between the different parties involved (for example doctors and patients, management and workers) may make some use of qualitative methods.
- *Explain* Both methodologies can be used to deliver explanations and may well be employed in tandem, but a significant factor is to be found in the intellectual agility of the researcher. No method is more than a tool, requiring the skills of an expert craftsperson if it is to lead to an explanatory conclusion. Judgements about the legitimacy of the explanatory focus may, in either case, be subject to dispute – unless the conclusion is supported by corroborating evidence from a different perspective or source.
- *Prove* 'Proof', as traditionally understood, is essentially a scientific concept that depends on findings being tested to breaking point. Examples can be found in psychology, economics, marketing and advertising, but they are noticeably rare in mainstream social science or social policy, much to the chagrin of politicians and managers. The delivery of 'proof' tends to rely on experiments or quasi-experiments, but it can also draw on simple observation or a survey; the best example of this lies in the refutation of the assertion that 'all swans are white' that comes with the sighting of a single black swan.

Fourteen ways of 'doing research'

What then are the various research techniques available to you? How do they relate to the question you have identified?

I begin with the models that are most frequently employed in student research and that lead to the production of largely descriptive or exploratory reports; then come the experimental methods; and finally a small group that use mixed methods.

Remember, though, that the models are not mutually exclusive; none of them can be identified as being superior to any or all of the others. The right choice for you will depend entirely on the nature of your research question, coupled with your personal preference and the constraints imposed upon you by the course.

You can interview people using closed questions

This is probably the method of social research most familiar to laypeople. An interviewer approaches you in the pedestrian precinct or calls at your door and asks if you are willing to answer some questions. If you agree, you find that the questions tend to be highly structured, inviting tick-box answers that you may or may not feel reflect accurately the view that is yours. You may be asked to look at some pictures and answer questions about them.

The purpose of this method is often descriptive or exploratory. The researcher may want to know some facts about you and your behaviour (what kind of car you own or would like to own, what TV adverts you can remember) for a commercial company. Or it may be that you are the subject of an enquiry that will result in the preparation of a student research report very similar to that you hope to produce.

You can ask people structured questions by sending them a letter and questionnaire through the mail

With the passage of time, the value of mailed questionnaires has come to be seriously questioned. When research studies were a rarity, it was not impossible to persuade people, particularly professionals in a working context (school teachers, probation officers, car sales personnel), to respond cooperatively to a well-designed questionnaire sent through the post – especially if it was accompanied by a stamped addressed envelope. The form of questions would generally be quite structured, and the quality of the design and layout would have a major influence on whether targeted recipients would resist the temptation to bin it.

Still today, the key to a successful mailed questionnaire enquiry lies in the quality of the preparation that has gone into it, the extent to which it links in with the interests of the recipients, the courtesy of the approach (perhaps including a prior or follow-up phone call and the enclosure of a stamped addressed envelope) and the achievement of brevity and tightness of focus.

You can use email or the net to deliver questionnaires and receive replies

There is something very tempting about using one's PC as a medium for gathering data from a research sample. You create a structured questionnaire in exactly the same way as you would if you were preparing for an interview or sending a mailed question-naire to a targeted body of recipients. You then mail it electroni-cally. It can include click-button response opportunities and incorporate pictures, diagrams or sounds.

You will need access to the email or web addresses of an appro-priate population.

With luck, the method can shorten the period of data collection considerably, but, outside the framework of a closed organisation (like a church, place of work or leisure group to which the researcher belongs) where the level of interest and cooperation may be high, there is likely to be a disappointing response rate.

You can conduct semi-structured reflective interviews

In the student context, this approach might involve a sample ranging between six and twenty. The basic tool will be an interview prompt sheet containing a carefully selected list of topics. The ques-tions should not be of a kind which invite simple yes/no answers. Your aim is to stimulate reflection and exploration.

The approach is often concerned with people's feelings: for example, about being divorced, living in the flight path of a planned new airport runway, having a terminal illness or having spent time in a mental hospital. At its best, the method can lead to significant advances in our theoretical understanding of social reality; more routinely, it is particularly good at enabling the researcher to learn, *at first hand*, about people's perspectives on the subject chosen as the project focus.

You can conduct group interviews

Partly because of the widely publicised use of focus groups by political parties in their attempt to identify trends of thought and feeling among voters, the idea of group interviewing has caught the imagination of students. The ideal number of group members is six, seven or eight. Depending on the nature of the exercise, the project should aim to obtain data from at least five or six groups.

The researcher needs a topic guide and the setting should be comfortable and convenient. Care must be taken to ensure that all shades of opinion in the group are heard. The researcher's own views should never become obvious, and the flow of ideas emerging from the group must not be constrained by the researcher's own perspective.

The group sessions will be audio-recorded (video-recording is too intrusive), and the analysis requires contextual interpretation rather than any suspicion of quantitative counting.

You can observe people (or animals or birds) in action

Observation is the classic territory of the anthropologist and the zoologist, but in psychosocial science it can take many forms:

- *Participant observation*, in which the researcher lives or works with the subjects of study. Ethnographic research is a form of participant observation in which the emphasis is on the recording of details about the object of study in its cultural setting.
- *Covert observation*, a form of participant observation in which the researcher's purpose and identity are concealed. Currently, ethical requirements make it very difficult to carry out covert observation, but it has been used by newspaper and television companies to infiltrate organizations and report abuses.
- *Non-participant observation*, in which the researcher remains 'outside' the focus of study but 'looks on' and records activities, verbal and non-verbal interactions and consequential happenings just as a work-study analyst does in the factory or office. A video camera can be employed.

Although much observation analysis is qualitative, the researcher can build numerical structures into the data collection process.

You can analyse the written or spoken word

There are a number of different research methods concerned with the analysis of verbal or written material. Historical research is heavily dependent upon archival research, but the method can be employed contemporaneously. It tends to require a high level of theoretical understanding and, where that is missing, the results are often disappointing. Three such methods are:

1. *Content analysis:* the study of published or other written material such as diaries, archives, transcriptions of broadcasts or film scripts, committee minutes, financial records or newspaper articles; this is the bread-and-butter territory of the historian, but it can be difficult for the untutored student to match the standards that should be aspired to.

2. *Thematic analysis:* the study of the social meaning of tape-recorded conversations – either naturally conducted or in an encounter with a research interviewer.

3. *Linguistic analysis* or *ethnomethodology:* the study of how people use words, sentences, pauses, silences, grunts, laughter. The method focuses on the verbal and situational nature of the material rather than its explicit meaning.

You can test a hypothesis

A hypothesis is a statement, an assertion, often indicating a claimed pattern of cause and effect:

- Travelling abroad increases the risk of you catching (a named disease)
- Recycling domestic waste saves money
- Sub-zero temperatures lead to an increase in car accidents.

Or the assertion can involve making comparisons between two groups or classes:

- Women are more emotionally sensitive than men
- 20-year-olds have sex more frequently than 50-year-olds
- People who use computers get more headaches than people who don't.

The task for the researcher is to find a way of testing the chosen statement. As you will realise if you think about these examples, this may not be easy.

You can carry out an experiment by doing a randomised controlled trial (RCT)

Experiments usually begin with a testable hypothesis: for example, 'following a particular diet for a specified period is effective in achieving weight reduction'. In order to see whether the hypothesis is true or false, the experimental researcher artificially does 'something' to one group of subjects (persuades them to follow the diet), and does not do it or does something else to a control group.

Randomised controlled trials are often said to represent the gold standard of experimental research. The findings from RCTs have a higher level of validity than those from any other method of comparing the impact of an intervention.

With respect to the diet hypothesis, you need to have access to a willing population big enough to give a reasonable chance of obtaining measurable results. You randomly allocate each person into the experimental (E) group or control (C) group. Only those in the E group follow the diet plan. You do not need to control for age, gender or body shape: provided your sample is big enough, the variations will be randomly reflected in both E and C groups. The experimental group will be expected to obey your instructions, and, after an agreed period of time, their corporate weight loss (or gain) will be assessed and compared with the comparative weights in the control group.

The classic territory for RCTs has been in agriculture (comparing the relative merits of different kinds of fertiliser or animal feed), in the pharmaceutical industry (comparing the effects of medicines) and in laboratories, but they are notoriously difficult to operationalise in the real-life social world. For example, if, in another experiment, you had hypothesised that the provision of a counselling service is likely to benefit redundant employees, you would make the necessary arrangements to have an E and C group. But if the control group gets to hear about the selective provision of a 'supportive' counselling service, they or their trade union might clamour for equality of provision – thus blowing the experiment out of the water.

You can devise a quasi-experiment

Randomness makes for a 'true' experiment, but there are other ways of organising two groups of people for comparative purposes. Quasi-experiments use the experimental model as an ideal but fall short of the standard set by RCTs because they take into account the practical and ethical problems of experimentation in the real world. They are much commoner in the social sciences than 'true' experiments.

Quasi-experiments compare groups that cannot be assumed to be strictly equivalent, although it is open to researchers to take steps to increase the level of equivalence between the E and C groups: most commonly, they can match pairs by age, gender, experience or other variables relevant to the experiment. They can also take measures to pre-test and post-test in both groups to improve the level of internal validity.

In our redundancy counselling project, in order to avoid the risk of resentment and rebellion, a quasi-experiment might locate the E and C groups in different parts of the country (where C people wouldn't hear what was going on in the E group). But you would need to achieve good matches for the people involved (their age, gender and skill level), the type of work from which they'd been made redundant and the state of the local economy in terms of the availability of alternative employment. Not easy.

You can undertake some secondary analysis of data

There are two kinds of secondary analysis:

1. The first involves gaining access to data that other people have collected – perhaps through one of the data banks available or through a teacher or researcher with gathered material already on file. This may be data of any kind across the quantitative–qualitative spectrum, and, when used imaginatively, can produce quite fresh perspectives.

2. The second is based on the analysis of available statistics, either from government or commercial sources. This can be particularly effective when the reanalysis focuses on geographical variations. But the end-result can never be better than the quality of the original data permits. A particularly clever

research skill is to conduct quasi-experiments within an existing body of data and without the need for any social intervention: for example, by interrogating the records of criminal courts to identify differences in sentencing patterns – perhaps by comparing urban and rural areas or by identifying the ethnic background or age of defendants.

Such methods deny you the full experience of project design and contact with the subjects of your study. Educationally, therefore, their value may be seen as being somewhat limited.

You can do action research

The idea of action research reached its peak with the community development movement and with feminist activism in the second half of the twentieth century. Radical campaigners built research elements into their programmes, with the aim of achieving a fruitful interaction between the accumulation of evidence (usually about poverty, discrimination or oppression) and the implementation of funded projects. The argument is that, once researchers have identified areas of need, change will be more easily achievable.

The model can be a useful one, even though, by definition, it is not value-neutral in the way that classical research methods are supposed to be. Problems can arise if the researcher doesn't deliver the results that conform to or confirm the activists' desired policy.

You can write a case study

The case study approach offers an attractive way of using a variety of research methods to produce a rounded portrayal of an identified subject. It might be a working environment, a small community, a family, a marriage or other intimate relationship, an individual with a medical or psychological condition of some specified kind, a youth group, an office environment or a local political party.

You can use a triangulated approach

The metaphor of triangulation is drawn from the world of surveying. In social research, it is based on the idea of using two or three different methods to explore the same subject. The scheme tends to be popular with students, and it can be used to good effect. However, with limited time at your disposal, it may be preferable to use one method and get it spot-on rather than risk delivering second-rate material in two or more different methods.

Conclusion

In practice, most beginning social researchers will expect to use some form of interview, questionnaire, observation or document analysis. You should only venture into complex theoretical territory (using, for example, ethnomethodology) if you have been prepared for it through course teaching and reading. Depending on the nature and subject matter of your programme, you can build in to your objectives an element of hypothesis-testing or an emphasis on exploration – whether reflective, interpretive or descriptive.

When you have finished your project, you will have demonstrated your understanding of and your ability to handle efficiently all the various stages of the research process. It is the aim of this book to enable you to do just that.

3 Drawing up your personal project road map

Even though, as a good researcher, you will always be ready to respond to the unanticipated problems that will certainly beset you in the course of your study, you must nevertheless begin by painstakingly drawing up a plan for every stage of your project from start to finish. It will need to be fluid enough to be regularly updated in order to accommodate unexpected events, but it should, at any one time, represent an accurate road map that will guide you and enable you and your supervisor to see the progress you are making.

This chapter will provide you with a template on which to base your own project road map, although you will need to make appropriate adjustments to reflect the unique circumstances – methodological and substantive – attaching to your study.

Once you have settled on a research question and decided on your preferred methodology, you are in a position to draw up your road map. There are several steps that will take you to the starting line for data collection. Most overlap with each other chronologically – the first four foundation-laying steps in particular are interwoven – but it will improve the standard of your work if you are able to reach the conclusion that you have dealt successfully with each of them in turn.

Clarify your own ideas

The first step is one that all experienced researchers recognise as important and worth spending time on. It is this: you must explore the topic, not just in the literature but by means of a range of conversations – with friends and relatives, other students, your supervisor, even people at the bus stop or other casual acquaintances. What you are doing is partly tapping into other people's opinions, feelings, knowledge and wisdom, but also gradually clarifying and firming up in your *own* mind crucial aspects relevant to your starting point.

By various means, you aim to rehearse the way in which your research question can be expressed. By this means, you become clearer in your thinking and less tentative, although still open-minded, in your approach to it. The process begins to give you a degree of confidence as you embark upon the journey of 'becoming an expert' on your chosen subject. (By the time you get to the end of your project, you will know more about your findings and how you reached them than anybody else, and you will have learnt a great deal about other aspects of the same topic; to that extent, you will be a mini-expert in your own right.)

Make time for an exploratory stage

Built into the thought-clarifying process will be an organised attempt on your part to approach and secure conversations with a small number of subject 'experts'. By that, I don't mean 'academic experts', but people who are not strangers to the topic you plan to research. For example, in the unlikely event of you carrying out a research study that began with the question 'What is the nature of the relationship between the cat owner and the cat, as perceived by the owner?', an 'expert' would be a cat owner, and good exploratory planning would lead to you engaging in unstructured or lightly structured conversation with four or five cat owners in order to identify the draft questions that might be used in a questionnaire or to pinpoint the best topics to concentrate on in a semi-structured reflective inquiry.

Please note, you mustn't call this a pilot study – we shall come to that shortly. It can be called a 'pre-pilot study', but a better term is 'exploratory study'. Interestingly, as you will realise, it is a good illustration of how, even when you are committed to carrying out a structured survey, you start off with an approach that is tanta-mount to the modest use of a qualitative method: you are exploring the ground in a very open-minded, reflective way, and you want people to tell you their 'story'. This stage is a process of self-educa-tion – and it is an essential step towards good research design even if you think you know the subject well yourself (in this example, even if you are yourself a cat owner). Indeed, it is even more essen-tial to spend some time on this stage if you *are* familiar with the topic – because there is a real danger of you having preconceptions and biases that will affect not just the results but the very design of your study in the first place.

Make sure you carry out an exploratory study, write it up carefully, and indicate in your records how it influenced you as you moved towards the design stage.

Find out how people will react to your method

A quite separate element in the exploratory stage will be for you to find out how people might respond to whatever methodology you are thinking of using. For example, if it is your idea to bring together some people to form a focus group, you shouldn't just rely on the fact that the methods literature indicates its feasibility. Ask your exploratory contacts what they would think of the idea. Would they come, if asked? What might persuade them to come? Do they have views on where it might best be held? How long would they be prepared to give to the occasion? What do they think would encourage them to be either reticent or forthcoming in such a setting? How would they react to the use of an audio system to record the discussion?

For you as a beginning researcher, this kind of preliminary conversation is useful, not just to help you with your planning process; it also eases you into the project management role by teaching you about people's attitudes and feelings at first hand.

Do a literature review

From the moment you start thinking about your project, you will probably spend time exploring the literature. You will read books and articles as you settle on a research question and decide your methodological approach. Once embarked on the planning stage, though, the literature review proper can begin: reading accounts of what others have had to say on your topic or on closely related topics, and, in particular, tracking down and reading as many research reports as you can find on the subject.

The timing and nature of a literature review can vary: some

courses expect students to write as much as 10,000 words on it, and demands for 20,000 or 30,000 words are not unknown. Literature reviews of this length are designed to demonstrate that students have gained significant and substantial knowledge independently of their own research project. Other courses require students to report relevant background material in a length of text proportionate to the size of the project report as a whole (perhaps contributing one-third of the text), and that is the model normally found in published research papers. In either case, although it is important for the researcher to learn as much as possible about the subject before finalising their own research design, the reality is that the 'literature review' as such will extend throughout the period of the project, with a probable further burst of reading activity towards the end, during the writing-up phase.

By the time you come to do a research project as a part of your course, you will have had a lot of experience in the use of libraries and in reading books and articles for the purpose of writing essays. In some ways, a literature review is only a kind of essay, and, of all the research tasks you are about to embark upon, it ought to be the one that worries you least. However, there are certain guidelines that need to be spelt out.

Make it a good quality piece of writing

The literature review should make an interesting read in its own right. It should be elegantly and professionally written. Give it a good overall structure, with headed sections and subsections; aim at good paragraph construction and good sentence construction; let it flow naturally through the topics covered; and make sure that you conclude with a section that indicates your own judgement on the messages that have emerged from your reading of the literature. In particular, you ought to discuss whether there are aspects of the subject dealt with by other authors that particularly interest you and that you might want to return to when you report your own results.

What tools will you use?

The use of libraries, together with e-journals and search engines on the web are your main instruments when you set about tracking down the relevant literature. Snowballing as a technique is standard practice: that is, find one useful article or book, and it is virtually certain that scanning the references or the bibliography will lead you to others, then do it again with each of them. Browsing – whether on the library shelves or in front of a computer screen – is always a fruitful way of proceeding. (In recent years, as an external examiner, I have read a growing number of dissertations in which the literature review is based solely on the unorganised results of the student entering a handful of key words into search engines; as a starting point, that's fine to begin with, but the material so obtained still needs to be restructured so that it emerges as a good quality essay in its own right.)

1. When you are carrying out a net search – which will lead you in all manner of directions – be sure to make notes of the interesting and useful items and sites that you come across. You can use a Word file to do so, but while you're actively net-searching, you may find it more efficient to make hand-written notes and references.

2. When you come across quotable items that you might want to include in your report, copy and paste them to a file straight-away.

3. Save any good websites that you come across to your Favourites.

4. Remember that there is a lot of rubbish on the net. When you are using a search engine, make sure that what comes up is useful, true and reliable. Be discriminating and selective in your choices.

5. If you are stuck, your academic library will have information specialists who are there to guide you in your net searches. Make sure you can tell them just what it is that you are seeking, and be prepared to listen to their advice.

Swamped by too much material?

You may find yourself feeling overwhelmed. For example, if your research topic is in a subject like the 'social psychology of aggression' or 'the environmental impact of recycling', you will probably discover a vast body of writing. What this suggests is either that you are casting your literature search net too widely, or that you need to reduce the focus of your research question or topic so that you can narrow the target of your literature trawl, focusing on only a part of the broader topic.

If you asked me to recommend just one book on ...
the literature review *it would be:*

Hart, Chris (1998)
Doing a Literature Review: Releasing the Social Science Research Imagination, London, Sage

Can't find anything relevant?

The opposite problem is often greater in the student's mind than in reality: the fear that nobody has ever written anything about the chosen topic. There may conceivably be occasions when that might be found to be true, but my experience is that the fear is rarely justified. If you set about your literature search thoroughly and are prepared, if necessary, to venture away from familiar academic tracks, you will almost always find relevant writing and research. There are not many contemporary topics that somebody somewhere in the English-speaking world hasn't written about – either in a government document, a doctoral thesis, a popular magazine, an academic journal, a newspaper or a non-fiction book. Remember that if you are used to occupying one professional world – say, nursing or the criminal justice system – there will almost certainly be relevant material in the journals published for professions different from yours: so don't be too insular in your search. Use your imagination. Keep asking for advice and suggestions. Persevere.

Keep it all in good order

From the moment you begin exploring the literature, however tentatively, make sure that you have a good system for keeping a record of your sources and an accurate copy of quotations that strike you as interesting and useable in your review. You can use a card index, sheets of paper or a notebook, or you can carefully enter all your material in computer files. Even as I was writing this book, I was guilty of not following my own guidelines in this respect: one morning in the newspaper that I was reading, I came across a short article saying that a published research study had reported that 60 per cent of men in meetings spent at least some of the time when they should have been concentrating on the agenda having erotic thoughts about other people present; the equivalent figure for women was only 1 in 6. The researchers tried to put a figure on the likely cost to companies of this loss of concentration and it sounded pretty impressive. So I wanted to use it in my list of research examples in Chapter 1. But the newspaper had gone; I couldn't remember which one it was and, although I searched high and low through twelve back copies, it had vanished. In some ways, that's a silly example but, by my own bad practice, it illustrates the cardinal rule: make a detailed note of everything you read while you are reading it. You never know until you've finished which pieces of literature you are going to want to use in your final document.

Referencing

The Harvard method of referencing is the normal one used by academic authors. In the text, when you are referring to a literature source or inserting a quotation, you put in brackets the author's name, year and page number, and then in the list of references at the end of the report (not at the end of each chapter), you include all those that you've drawn on, laid out alphabetically, with the first named author's surname determining where each reference goes. The general rule is that the major title of the book or journal appears in italics; if the source is an article or paper within a volume or journal, the title of the paper is given inverted commas. The following illustration covers most eventualities.

For authored books: Author's surname, initials (year of publication in brackets) *title of the book in italics*, place of publication, publisher.
For example:
Mason, J (2002) *Qualitative Researching*, London: Sage.

For journal articles: Author's surname, initials, (year of publication in brackets), 'title of the article in inverted commas', *title of the journal in italics*, **volume number in bold**, (issue number in brackets), page numbers.
For example:
Porter, S (1993) 'Critical realist ethnography: the case of racism and professionalism in a medical setting', *Sociology*, **27**(4): 591–609.

For papers published in edited books: Author's surname, initials, (year of publication in brackets), 'title of the paper in inverted commas', in editor's surname, followed by the editor's initials, *title of the book in italics*, place of publication, publisher, page numbers where the paper can be found.
For example:
Pugh, A (1990) 'My statistics and feminism – a true story', in Stanley, L (ed.) *Feminist Praxis: Research, Theory and Epistemology in Feminist Sociology*, London: Routledge, pp. 13–22.

Give thought to five additional issues

They are all matters with clear practical implications, and after you have considered them, you may have to do some fine-tuning in regard to your research question, your planned timetable and the choice of your research method.

Are you likely to face any problems of access?

You need to be sure that you can obtain access to your research population. In any student group of, say, fifty, my experience is that at least two or three discover that they had been too optimistic in their expectations regarding ease of access. The problem is not getting any easier – especially if you want to interview the employees, customers or clients of an organisation, whether in the public or private sectors. For example:

- *Police checks:* Any kind of access to interview or observe children may mean that you have to be given a police records check – and this can be a very slow process.
- *'Information is power':* You may have assumed that, because of your 'contacts' or by virtue of your own previous (or current) work setting, your research project will be welcomed by an employing organisation. There was a time when that might have been so, but managers have come to realise that research activity of any kind can cause problems – especially if its findings emerge in the public arena. People in positions of power and responsibility do not usually want 'a snooper' watching the reality of how they operate; they have learnt that research reports usually contain, implicitly or explicitly, some criticism of their organisation, and they would prefer to live without that. Information, it is said, is power; and people in power are not going to give it away as a gift.
- *Governance:* There is growing importance being attached to research governance procedures in some settings. To some extent, this is a reflection of the last point, but, more importantly, it has arisen because managers have come to realise that research can be intrusive and time-consuming. In the eyes of the student researcher, the project may only involve a few short interviews, but the cumulative impact of an ongoing enquiry in any one setting and the steady increase in the number of student projects being carried out have raised concerns that staff are being deflected from doing the work that they are employed to do. Moreover, it is often felt that, in the light of previous experience and contrary to what the student researcher might hope or claim, the value of the research may be quite limited and, in most cases, serve only the student's own interests. Governance procedures are in place not to veto all student research but to ensure that that which is done is well planned, properly supervised and likely to be carried out to a high standard.
- *Ethics:* Right from the outset, you must take full account of ethical questions. These can relate to the topic you choose to study, the way in which you approach interviewees and other research participants and how you handle your data once you have gathered it. Most university departments require students

to submit their research proposals for approval by research ethics committees, and this can be a long drawn-out process involving revision and resubmission. In some instances, researchers find that, in addition to obtaining university approval, they are required to go through separate ethical procedures in the setting where they plan to carry out their work. In Europe, for example, there are strictly controlled ethical constraints on research that involves contact with health service staff or patients. You should always be careful to obtain details of ethical requirements at an early stage in the planning process, and prepare your research proposal in a format that will meet the ethics committee's requirements. Ethical approval can, in some instances, take several months, and that timescale needs to be budgeted for.

If you asked me to recommend just one book on ...
research ethics *it would be:*

Oliver, P (2003)
The Student's Guide to Research Ethics, Maidenhead, Open University Press

Remember that the participants in your research have rights

You must not *use* people inappropriately in pursuit of your research objectives. During the planning phase, you must clarify and resolve issues of confidentiality and anonymity. If you are required to secure clearance from either a governance or ethics committee (or both), it is likely that one of the issues raised will be the rights of those who are to be the subject of your study. Your participants should be given clear information about your project, and you must ask them for their consent before you go ahead; they should always be free to withdraw from your project at any time.

In some public sector fields, the importance of researcher–participant relations has moved centre stage, and some authorities will expect you to have consulted with would-be participants in the planning process. Of course if you have followed my road map guidance about the involvement of 'experts' on the ground, this will not be a problem. Governance and ethics committees may want to pay special attention to planned research studies that are focused on participants who are deemed to be vulnerable – children, people with learning disabilities or suffering ill-health, prisoners or any others who might feel pressurised into participating.

Are you yourself going to be at risk?

You should ask yourself whether you are laying yourself, your participants or your university open to any element of risk by doing the research as you've planned it – especially if the risk is such as to leave you feeling aggrieved that your supervisor 'allowed' you to go ahead. Many workplaces now have a 'Lone Worker' policy, designed to ensure the safety of staff visiting people in domestic settings or other locations where they may be deemed to be, in some degree, vulnerable to acts of abuse or violence.

You will be creating intellectual property. Who owns it?

There is the emergent issue of intellectual property – the idea that the products of people's brainwork have monetary value. This is rarely likely to arise in a student dissertation context, but if you were able to produce an end-product that was in some degree commercially marketable, to whom would the rights belong?

Take account of the diversity in our world

Issues surrounding gender, ethnicity, class and culture cannot be ignored. In respect of research studies that are 'exercises in research methodology' – which most student exercises are – the power of generalisation will usually be severely restricted. But it is an important part of the learning process that from the outset you should understand that any conclusions that you seek to draw must clearly relate to the nature of your research sample.

Prepare a final draft of your research instrument

Depending on the kind of project you have chosen to carry out, your research tools may be highly structured questionnaires, checklists, semi-structured interview schedules, prompt sheets, observation charts, diagrammatic sheets or pictures. You will have been preparing these during the planning stage, firming them up in your own mind and on paper, inviting other people to tell you what they think about them, and asking for ideas and criticisms.

To some students this can seem like an unusual way of proceeding. In an academic setting, there is a natural inclination, as in an examination hall, to metaphorically shield your work from the gaze of others. Of course, some commercially driven research settings might require secrecy and a competitive approach, but student research almost always benefits from being exposed to the critical attention of others. The researcher remains responsible for all the decisions made and retains editorial or authorial control over the instruments as they emerge, but it is very unwise not to listen to the comments and reactions of others.

Carry out a pilot study

When you have a good draft of your research instrument, you must pilot it – try it out on subjects as similar as possible to those whom you are going to target in the main study. The more structured your questionnaire, the more rigorous the piloting process must be. In quantitative methods, the completion of the pilot stage should leave you feeling confident that all your preparatory work has paid off and that you have the tools that will do the job for you.

Even if you are using qualitative methods or your schedule contains open-ended, semi-structured prompts, there is a strong argument for a pilot stage. Many is the time that I have supervised entry-level qualitative research students who have gone straight into the main data-gathering stage with semi-structured prompt sheets intending to secure a sample of about a dozen, but whose plan has had to be revised because they found that they were effectively using the first six encounters as the final part of a planning and/or piloting stage. As a consequence, they failed in those initial interviews to obtain material of the quality that they came to achieve in the light of their early experience.

Of course, the exploratory nature of the qualitative methods approach means that 'imperfect' first stage encounters do not get wasted. The material can still be absorbed into the findings-and-interpretation element of your project, but novice qualitative researchers will normally find it easier to deliver a professional end-product if the two phases (planning and data collection) are kept at least conceptually separate – even if they overlap in time. In qualitative research, the purpose of piloting is more to do with the overall period of data collection than the detail of any instruments used: will the planned research process give you what you need to get a result?

Whichever method you plan to use, by the time the pilot stage is complete, it is essential that you are happy that the language and phraseology you are using is language and phraseology that your targeted research subjects will understand and be able to relate to.

In the light of each pilot encounter, you can (and should) continue to amend, adjust and tighten up your research instrument or your overall approach – until you decide that you have got it as near perfect as possible. When you reach that point, you can go into your data-gathering phase not only feeling that you have prepared the project properly, but also with a sense of professional pride in your own technique. Moreover, if, like many student researchers, you are shy about approaching interviewees to begin with, you will find that thorough use of the exploratory and pilot phases will go a long way towards enabling you to rehearse your performance and feel confident in your role.

Put it all together in a timed road map

When you have no previous experience of carrying out a research study – and, it has to be said, even when you have – one of the hardest things to get right is the timescale, the working schedule that you are going to follow. It's impossible in the abstract for me to estimate how long each stage in your project is going to last; some stages will overlap with others; you may be able to discount some of them; and others may need only a short period of time. But in almost all the research proposals that I see, I get a sense of unrealistic optimism being pervasive. This is especially so where the planning and write-up stages are concerned: both need more time than is usually allowed.

The preparation time needed for quantitative research tends to be greater than that required for qualitative research. For the latter, you must be careful not to squeeze the time allowed for data analysis too tightly – even though (as we shall see in Part 3) it overlaps with the data collection phase.

You need to put realistic time estimates on all the stages of the planning process, together with the substantive stages of data collection, analysis and write-up. You can and should adapt your road map to fit your own needs and circumstances, but a good model outline will look something like this.

timed road map

Estimated date of starting	Estimated date of completion	Research stage
		1 Clarifying your ideas
		2 Exploration: your topic
		3 Exploration: your method
		4 Literature review
		5 Checking additional issues: access; participants' rights; risk; ownership of intellectual property; taking diversity into account
		6 Securing formal approval from relevant ethics and governance committees
		7 Preparing the final draft of your instrument
		8 Piloting
		9 Data collection
		10 Data analysis
		11 Discussing your results and write-up with supervisor/colleagues
		12 Writing a draft report
		13 Revision of the draft and completion of the project report

In more complex projects, you will need to draw up separate but linked road maps for each different element of data collection and analysis. You'll find that more convenient than trying to incorporate all elements into one road map – partly because they may well be interdependent.

And by the way, surely you don't need me to remind you, but:

- Always save your computer files regularly as you work
- Always keep a backup file on a portable disk.

PART 2 Quantitative research

- The blanket term 'quantitative research' conceals the fact that, within it, there are two methodologically related but very different approaches: survey research and experimental research.

- Survey research can take many forms, and the scale of it can range from the 10-year National Census targeting the entire population to projects that involve a series of brief interviews with a sample of, perhaps, 60 people.

- Both survey research and experimental research depend on careful planning, an understanding of sampling techniques, disciplined data-gathering and skilled data interpretation. Probability testing is almost always employed.

- The researcher carrying out a survey will emerge with findings that describe and interpret aspects of current psychosocial reality, while the experimental researcher will be looking for (tentative) proofs – possibly following the introduction of new practices.

4 The principles of sampling

One theme runs right through the pages of this book: the very act of doing research to a high standard is almost always more problematic than you had anticipated. Therefore, there is much to be said for keeping your research objectives and your methodology as simple as you can make them. In research, you generally achieve more by attempting less.

With the exception of the National Census, all scientific research focuses on a small segment or 'sample' of a bigger population. That is true whether the subject matter is the buying habits of men in supermarkets, the impact of fertilisers on sugar beet, or the experience that children have of bullying in school. You can only interview so many men, only try out your fertiliser in a small number of farms, only organise a few playground observation exercises. But the magic of sampling at its best is this: provided your sample is truly representative of the population and not too small, you don't *need* to do more in order to arrive at conclusions that are generally applicable.

In professional research, when a project has been completed, the investigator wants to be able to apply the conclusions to the total population from which the sample was drawn: to all men in all supermarkets, to all sugar beet in whatever part of the country, and to all children in schools of the same kind as those used in the research project.

The history of research is tied up with the theory of sampling, and understanding its importance is as vital for the novice researcher as it is for the professor. The point is this: you may or may not be able to get a good (or a 'representative') sample, but, in any research exercise, you must be rigorous and honest in judging to what extent the nature of your sample enables you to generalise from your findings.

Generally, in social research at student level, because a high-quality national sample is difficult to obtain, it is rarely possible to draw conclusions that apply unambiguously to the national population. Student projects are primarily designed to enable the researcher to learn about the techniques of research methodology and to understand better the nature of evidence in scientific or reflective analyses.

In your project, you will need to gather a sample that

1 **... is appropriate to your objectives**
   If you are organising a survey, the size of your sample will be determined by the kind of data analysis you plan to carry out and the nature of the conclusions you may want to draw. For a descriptive or an exploratory survey, a sample in the range of 60–120 is normal for student projects. If you are testing a hypothesis, you will need to gather a sample that is big enough to enable you to observe anticipated differences between variables or draw legitimate conclusions from their absence, which will require you to estimate the anticipated difference and do a power calculation to guide you in your decision about sample size. It is a common error in hypothesis-testing to underestimate the size of sample needed, so frustrating the aims of your data analysis. (Shaughnessy et al., 2000, has an excellent discussion on power calculations, pp. 289–90.)

2 **... you can recruit in the time available**
   All research is constrained by the level of resources available, and time is a key resource. Even professional researchers sometimes underestimate the time needed to complete their task. Students, with deadlines to meet and degree completion dates looming, cannot afford to make that mistake. The requirement will inevitably influence your choice of topic and the kind of sample you decide to gather.

3 **... you can recruit in the setting to which you have access**
   Critics often scoff at the number of psychology or social research projects that are based on interviews with students, and it is true that the conclusions that can be drawn from them are correspondingly limited, but student interviewees are easily accessible, are likely to be cooperative and – the key fact – they give the student researcher legitimate experience of collecting data.

4 … is as good as you can make it
Even if the geographical area that you can target is restricted, there are ways in which you can improve sampling quality. One step would be for you to gather two equally sized subsamples from separate locations – say, the inner city for one and an outer suburb or a nearby small town for the other. Not only does this expand the range of the population from which you have drawn your sample, but it enables you to carry out a statistical comparison between the findings from the two subsamples. If they don't differ, this is hugely reassuring for the conclusions you may want to draw; if they do differ in some ways, you will be expected to discuss why that might be and what it might mean for your conclusions. Either way, you will have demonstrated a sophisticated approach to sample-gathering and data analysis, and you will have shown that you took steps to 'make the sample as good as you could make it'.

Types of sample

In survey research, the term *population* refers to the category of people (or animals or objects) about whom you intend to write in your report and from which you plan to draw your sample. Your 'population' might be all the citizens of one country, but it could equally and more realistically be all students who smoke in your university, all lecturers in one department, all adult women living in a defined urban area or village, all dustbins in one particular location, all weekday buses on the number 11 route, and so on. In other words, the population in your study can be whatever you decide it should be, and this is determined primarily by the objectives implicit in your research question.

Once you have defined your population, you can embark on the sampling process. The following six options are open to you.

Convenience sample

In convenience sampling (sometimes called 'accidental sampling'), you simply take what you can get where you can most easily get it. You approach your friends or relatives; you stand in the market-

place and interview the first 80 people you meet who agree to cooperate with you; you cold-call telephone numbers; you meet up with
students in the union bar; or you email 1000 students and ask for
volunteers. In other words, you exercise no control over who falls
into your sample and consequently you have no means of knowing
to what extent the information you get or the opinions that are
expressed do or do not reflect the total 'population' – or even what
that 'population' might consist of.

One of the confusing elements in this process lies in the fact that
common usage of the term might lead you to say that you were
gathering a sample 'at random', but what you are gathering, as we
shall see, is not a *random* sample in the technical sense of the word.
True randomness enables you to have confidence in the conclusions
you can draw about the total population from which the sample is
drawn. A convenience sample does not give you any confidence at
all in that respect: you have no means of knowing to what extent
the sample is biased, that is, to what extent it varies from the
pattern you would have observed had you been able to study the
total 'population'.

Let me be frank, though. Although some subject areas (especially
those in or close to the natural sciences) lend themselves to a
random sampling approach, in many social- and psychology-
related disciplines, the student project is designed primarily as an
exercise to enable you to demonstrate your ability at all stages of
the research process: in such instances, a convenience sample is
often fine – so long as you explicitly identify it and acknowledge its
limitations. It doesn't stop you going through all the steps outlined
in this book.

Quota sample

In quota sampling, the researcher identifies key variables, the distribution of which is known for the *relevant population*; the sample is
then selected so that it reflects the same proportionate breakdown.
For example, in a survey of supermarket shelf-stackers, if it were
known that 70 per cent were female and 30 per cent were male,
then the sample gathered would aim to be made up of the same
gender proportions. Typically, quotas are arranged in respect of
gender, age, ethnic identity, place of residence, educational back-

ground and social class. In market research, interviewers are often given quotas that they are required to fill in the course of their street or door-step interviewing: for example, 50 per cent male; 20 per cent ethnic minority (perhaps specified more precisely), 30 per cent with a qualification from higher education, and so on. Some of the characteristics are visible, some are not. You may have seen, as I have, in a shopping centre a rather desperate woman with a clipboard looking for her last target interviewee of the day: for example, a female university graduate in her sixties from an ethnic minority. Quota sampling can be difficult.

Quota sampling constitutes an improvement on convenience sampling, and, if used in a student project, would greatly improve the quality of the data. But, apart from practicalities, there are a number of theoretical problems with it. It depends on whether the researcher *knows* the proportions to apply when drawing up quota requirements. What *is* the gender balance in the targeted population? Or the ethnic mix? Or the social class structure?

The more factors that are identified as warranting quota-listing, the more complex the task of data collection. At student research level, it might be reasonable to restrict it to, say, three: for example, if the study were being carried out among undergraduates, the quotas could be applied to gender, humanities/social science/science faculties and year of study. A survey that could lay claim to that level of proportionate accuracy would be judged of excellent quality.

But the fact remains that, within each quota group, the sampling process is still 'accidental'. Quota requirements ensure that the identified categories are all covered proportionately, but they don't deal with the criticism that the researcher has gathered information only from those respondents who are accessible, easily persuaded to collaborate and who, perhaps, appear to be pleasant, attractive or 'normal'.

Purposive sample

Purposive sampling invites the researcher to identify and target individuals who are believed to be 'typical' of the population being studied, or perhaps to interview all individuals within a subpopulation that is deemed to be typical of the whole. Newspaper journalists writing a piece about 'Middle England' might try to identify a town or a village that, to them, epitomises that phrase and then go there and talk with the residents.

In research terms, there is no way of knowing to what extent the sample so chosen is indeed representative of the whole, or whether the so-called 'typical' qualities are so. Scientifically, it offers no improvement on convenience sampling, and, because it fails to make explicit the qualities being employed during sample collection, it is inferior to quota sampling.

Simple random sample

The principle of simple random sampling lies at the heart of all scientific research. It is, for example, the idea that drives the use of quality control checks in any manufacturing environment – whether the products are chocolates, electric kettles or concrete panels.

The principle has two requirements:

- every member of the 'population' has an equal chance of being included in the sample
- every possible combination of individuals from within the 'population' is equally likely.

If you want to use simple random sampling, you need to have access to an accurate list of names of the population you want to study. This is your 'sampling frame'. For studies of the general population, it is by no means easy to obtain access to such a list.

In the world of student project-writing, however, some topics and their theoretical framework lend themselves to a focus on a small part of the university population close at hand, and this in turn allows you to draw generalised conclusions from a properly selected probability sample. For example, you could question a random sample of first-year geography students about their use of recycling procedures, and then draw conclusions about environmentally friendly practices in that year group as a whole. You could go one step further by comparing the results obtained from random samples of first- and third-year students.

How would you set about it? You would probably find it quite easy to access a list of the names of the students and, hey presto, you have a sampling frame.

Perhaps there are 200 undergraduates on your list, from which you are planning to carry out interviews with 50. First, you should give each student in your population a number from 001 to 200. Random sampling does not mean that you take every fourth name (or whatever interval frequency would be appropriate), as this would not accord with the two principle requirements noted above.

There are two alternative ways of proceeding. First, you can use a random numbers table (entering it at random – shut your eyes and bring a sharp point down on to the page!), which will look like this, but much bigger (extracted from Shaughnessy et al., 2000, p. 460):

547	855	909	161	078
188	635	534	096	148
235	034	274	962	669
445	186	637	269	552

You're planning to gather a sample of 50 out of your sampling frame of 200. Ignoring the numbers from 201 upwards, carefully list the ones that fall in the range 001–200. In this case: 161, 078, 188, 096, 148, 034 and 186. Ignore numbers that repeat earlier selections – this will almost certainly occur. Carry on until you have 50 numbers (ideally also listing an additional 10 to use as replacements in case you are faced with interviewee refusals).

Alternatively, you can access a set of random numbers from MS Excel. Open a new Workbook. Then, in the formula bar (fx) at the head of the screen, enter the formula =RAND()*200. Hit *Enter*, and a random number will appear. Ignore the decimal places and treat it as a whole number. That is your first selected name. Write it down. Then hit the function key F9. There is your next name. Carry on hitting the function key F9 until you have your full sample of 50 – ignoring any duplicated numbers.

Whichever method you have employed, these 50 numbers, converted into names from your sampling frame, represent your random sample of first-year geography undergraduates in a given university, which (if you manage to get an acceptable response rate) will enable you to make statements that begin: 'First-year geography students at XY University say that/believe that/think that ...'. Whether the results reflect the views of geography students everywhere or whether the results would remain consistent over a long period of time is not something you can assert. They are specific to time and place, but you can be reasonably certain that your sample of 50 will give you results very close to those which you would have got if you'd interviewed all 200.

Stratified random sample

Stratified random sampling combines the purity of simple random sampling with the researcher's awareness of the existence of different subgroups within the population and the fact that their beliefs, characteristics or attitudes might differ significantly from each other. Suppose, in another study, you decide to survey a random sample of 200 students from a law school that has a student population of 1000. In such a case, it might make sense to discover at the outset what the gender balance is in the school and gather simple random samples first of the male students and then of the females. You need to ensure that the numbers of men and women you gather are in the same proportions as their number in the law school as a whole.

More ambitiously, there might be a small but important group of mature students in the school. In order to ensure that their opinions, behaviour or experiences are properly reflected in your findings, it might be wise to gather a disproportionate number of them (let's say, for the sake of illustration, 30 rather than the 10 that might be proportionately correct in a sample of 200); this will enable you to overcome the risk of small number bias. In the overall analysis, you would be able to focus specifically on the views of the 30 mature students, but, for full-sample descriptive findings, the figures relating to the stratified subsample of mature students would be reabsorbed into the main sample, having been divided by three. This is a fairly straightforward procedure in frequency distributions, but is less so in cross-tab calculations. It is not, perhaps, an exercise that should be attempted by the faint-hearted too early in their research careers – certainly not without access to good supervisory guidance.

Cluster sampling

Realistically, even in survey work done by expensively resourced research agencies or academic departments, true national random sampling is impossible. Projects have to settle for a compromise and cluster sampling is the usual route forward. The researcher starts the random sampling process not with the names of people to be interviewed or approached but with the names of geographical locations (towns, for example), the branch names of companies, classes in a school, or streets in a city. These can be selected using a random sampling process, after which lists of individuals compiled from within the targeted clusters are chosen.

If you asked me to recommend just one book on …
the principles of survey sampling *it would be:*

Barnett, Vic (2002)
Sample Survey: Principles and Methods, 3rd edn, London, Hodder Arnold

Probability samples

Random samples and cluster samples gathered using randomness principles (the last three discussed above) are known as probability samples because, using established statistical procedures, you can estimate the likelihood that your findings for the sample differ from the population from which the sample was drawn. This will lead you to conclusions that read like this:

• There is less than one chance in a hundred that the difference you've identified between your sample groups (men and women, for example) in their expressed or observed preference for types of chocolate differs from that you would find in the whole population from which you drew your samples. In other words, if you carried out the study again and again, at least 99 times out of 100 you would expect to get the same result. This conclusion is usually written as p <.01.
• There is less than one chance in a thousand that the use of a particular pharmaceutical product will prove to be inferior in

its impact on a given medical condition, when compared with a placebo (or no treatment). The conclusion would be signified by the message: p <.001. This is certainly not saying that the product will cure 99.9 per cent of people. Far from it. The difference between the experimental pill and the placebo might only be the difference between a 30 per cent cure and a 10 per cent natural recovery rate. The probability rating only indicates that a 'statistically significant' difference has been demonstrated in the study.

Non-probability samples

Convenience, quota and purposive samples (the first three discussed above) are non-probability samples because the way in which they have been put together gives you no assurance that the results obtained can be related, in terms of probability levels, to the population from which they were drawn. Indeed, as we have seen, you can't really know what that population is. All you can be certain of is that they shared a common characteristic of being conveniently available to you.

This means that the results you obtain must be treated with great caution. However, because student projects are primarily exercises in research practice, I would never discourage or prevent a student from carrying out statistical tests on the data collected from non-probability samples, even though many statisticians frown on the practice.

The confidence that can be claimed for the generalisability of the conclusions is limited, but it is still reasonable to expect that variables may be tested for their relationship with other variables. As in woodwork, just because you can't produce a perfectly fashioned piece of barley-twist, there is no reason why you shouldn't be expected to try your hand at a rough-hewn mug-tree. Learning comes through doing. And it comes incrementally.

Market research firms and political opinion poll companies have to achieve high-quality probability samples, but students in many social science fields can rarely be expected to aspire to such levels of purity. It would be a shame if that fact precluded them from getting as close to a technically accomplished end-product as the reality of their situation allowed.

in defence of the convenience sample

If, as is often the case, you've no choice but to base your survey on a non-probability or convenience sample, then your report should make clear:

- what the limitations of this procedure are
- why the procedure was unavoidable
- how your research nevertheless gave you experience of the full quantitative research process and enabled you to deliver findings that, if supported by studies carried out in different locations, could be found to reflect the views or experiences of a wider population.

Representativeness and bias

Random selection does not, on any one occasion, guarantee representativeness. The standard classroom illustration of this involves the tossing of a coin or the dealing of a hand of cards – and you can do it yourself at home to demonstrate it. There are times when heads (or tails) will land face up 8 times out of 10; and, as any bridge player will tell you, you can have a hand of cards in which 7 or 8 are from one suit. But the importance of random selection is that when you add exercises of coin-tossing or card-dealing together, they will even out: that is, the sum total of 20 hands dealt, divided by 20, should come to 3 or 4 hearts, 3 or 4 spades, 3 or 4 clubs and 3 or 4 diamonds. And similarly, in your research study, if you set about gathering a sample of substantial size, the accidental presence in it of oddball individuals or groups will get lost within the totality of the full number.

The great enemy of representativeness in sample-gathering is *bias* – and any system other than random sampling is prone to it. Examples of bias might be:

- Interviewing only those who smilingly agree to be interviewed
- Talking only to friends and relatives

- Receiving postal replies only from those who have the time to respond
- Receiving email replies only from those who use email
- Cold-calling telephone subscribers
- Interviewing only men or women you'd like to go out with
- Not gaining access to people who are housebound, watch daytime TV, work nightshifts or inhabit rural areas
- Accessing only students who drink in the bar
- Being fearful of approaching older people, scruffy people, posh people or any other identifiable group
- Failing to secure written questionnaires from people who are illiterate or have only a foreign language.

Bias can be cumulative. Although a large random sample virtually guarantees you a high degree of representativeness, merely increasing the size of a non-probability sample does nothing to solve the problem of bias.

the basic rules of sampling in a learning context

1. Always use the right technical term to describe the sample you have gathered.
2. If it has elements of more than one kind of sample, be sure to identify them clearly.
3. Try to move your sampling method – however modestly – in the direction of randomness or representativeness, so far as that is achievable and realistic.

Let's think about an imaginary example

Your project might have as its objective a comparison of the opinions, attitudes or feelings of two groups of people towards a specified topic. Let's say that you want to compare the attitudes of Christians with the attitudes of Moslems towards any one topic: it could be abortion/domestic violence/gender role/career ambition/television soap operas. Even a professional polling agency would struggle to achieve national random samples if commissioned to carry out such an enquiry and the cost of doing so would often be prohibitive. So what do you do, bearing in mind limitations of time, lack of money, and other pressures in your life?

One approach would be for you to go and stand outside a church and a mosque respectively on a number of occasions before and after religious events. You could approach people with good reason to assume that you were targeting Christians and Moslems. You would acknowledge that they were a particular kind of Christian and a particular kind of Moslem, depending on the site chosen. You could broaden the range substantially by working with two churches and two mosques.

Identifying quotas

You would, however, still find it impossible to achieve a random sample, and you would be wise to describe the targeted population as one that offers you the opportunity of gathering a convenience sample. But you can hugely improve the quality of your work by building in quota elements – partly by standing on four sites rather than two, but also with regard to age and gender. Say that you have a very short and highly focused questionnaire and you believe you have the time and patience to reach 100 Christian and 100 Moslem interviewees, then you could achieve an age spread by breaking your samples down into four subgroups divided by age, aiming to gather responses from 25 people in each subgroup.

In traditional methodological terms, this is quite a crude way of proceeding, because the more 'correct' way would be to relate the numbers of people in each subgroup to your prior knowledge of the age structure of church and mosque attendees. You would, however, be unlikely to be able to deliver such sampling sophistication without a great deal of prior effort, and you would need to acknowledge as much.

Age comparisons

On the other hand, there is a subtle and quite clever reason why your chosen approach of using quotas might be deemed to be *more* sophisticated; that is because the age structure of the two targeted populations may be very different. Perhaps (I don't know, of course) the Christian congregation is predominantly over 50, while the

Mosque attracts a lot of people under the age of 40. If your comparison had sought to reflect the age structure of the two settings accurately, you would have been faced with one of the constant
problems of interpretation that confront survey analysts: would any
differences that you had successfully pinpointed have been due to
religion (as you'd intended to demonstrate) or might it be that the
factor of 'age' had muddied the waters of interpretation in an
aggravating fashion? You could have been left with the feeling that
you had ended up with a spurious finding that was at least as
much to do with generational attitudes as with religion.

You still have to acknowledge that what you have gathered are
two convenience samples and therefore you need to be cautious in
the conclusions you draw. But by introducing quotas for age (and
therefore being able to compare differences of response by age as
well as religion), the interest of your findings will be hugely
increased and the power of your conclusions will be greater than it
otherwise would have been. With quotas, you are in a position to
compare the attitudes of young Moslems and young Christians and
similarly in the three older age groups.

Gender

If your time and energy were unlimited, how about dealing with
the obvious point that gender is likely to be an important dimension in the expression of attitudes? You would need to increase (by
at least double) your sample sizes, and then divide each subgroup
into two roughly equally gender halves.

Other factors

There are many other potential difficulties with our exemplified
research idea. Will all the people you approach be English-
language speakers? Will the men or the women be equally willing
to talk to you (bearing in mind that you are a man or woman yourself)? What about confidentiality? Will a spouse or a friend or the
clergyman/imam want to listen in to your conversation? What
difference would it make if you yourself were a Moslem? Or a practising Christian?

Exploration

This is a good example of how a quantitative research study using survey techniques is no less exploratory in its nature and its conclusions than would be the case if you were using qualitative methods. Because it is based on convenience samples, you could be left wondering whether the same sort of findings would emerge if the exercise were repeated in different towns, with different churches and so on. Of course, if the study were replicated by another student elsewhere and the same (or similar) findings emerged, this would greatly increase the level of confidence you would have in your findings. If the findings were different, you would immediately want to ask the perennial research question 'Why?'

It is when faced with these technical but intellectually challenging problems that some students begin to get a sense of the excitement that professional researchers feel when designing a project that aims to answer what, initially, were apparently simple questions. Other students feel overwhelmed by the sequence of hurdles they find they have to cross, thinking 'No way, I'll set up two focus groups: eight self-avowed Christians and eight Moslems. That sounds a bit easier.' In Part 3, we shall see whether the qualitative research option is as simple as that.

When you come to write your report ...

You must describe accurately the population from which your sample has been drawn

Is it from one university, from one faculty or school in one university, from one suburban shopping precinct, from among your friends and neighbours, from randomly selected names in a telephone directory, from MPs, from local government officials locally or nationally, from residents of a hostel, or what? For the entry-level researcher, the shortcomings of your population are less important than the accuracy of your description of it and an acknowledgement of its limitations.

You must advise the reader what can be concluded from your findings

If you have used a probability sample, the level of confidence in your findings will be substantial, but, with a convenience sample, you need to invite caution and emphasise that the project was primarily a learning exercise.

a note about experiments

If you are able or are required to carry out an experiment, you will find that the sampling principles concerning survey research outlined in this part of the book are largely applicable to an experimental context (Robson, 1993, Chapter 4, provides excellent coverage of experimental research). The greater burden lies in the task of organising the project in respect of the two groups – the experimental (E) group and the control (C) group – and ensuring a complete absence of contamination between them.

- You must have a probability sample – one that ensures equivalence between the two groups. Without that, there is little point in proceeding.

- A risk that must be guarded against is an 'experimenter effect' – the introduction of bias through the conscious or unconscious exertion of influence by any person involved in administering the 'treatment'. In order to counteract this, the administration of the treatment can be subcontracted to parties who have no knowledge that an experiment is taking place and are unaware of the difference between the two groups; in a pharmaceutical setting, the control group will often receive a placebo in place of the product being investigated. The process is known as 'double-blind' because neither the frontline research operator nor the subject of the research is aware of the details of the experiment.

- Experiments present particular problems for ethics committees, and, because of this, many types of experiment are probably best left till later in your research career.

a note about experiments *continued*

A fascinating glimpse into the hazards of even a very high-profile and commercially significant experiment has been given widespread prominence through its discussion in Malcolm Gladwell's book *Blink* (2005, pp. 155–9).

Gladwell describes how Pepsi embarked on a major marketing campaign by running an experiment in which cola drinkers agreed to participate in the 'Pepsi Challenge'. They took a sip from two different glasses of cola and were asked to choose the one they liked best. Most chose Pepsi.

Coca-Cola managers were horrified and suspected foul play. So they ran the test themselves – but they got the same outcome: the volunteers chose Pepsi.

This one experiment led the Coca-Cola company to review its marketing strategy and to launch a new type of Coca-Cola – with a new taste. The initiative was a commercial disaster.

When the whole sequence of events was reviewed, it was discovered that it was the design of the experiment that had been crucial to the original results. Participants were given *sips* of the drink as a result of which they were getting a front-of-mouth taste experience. This led them to prefer the sweeter, lighter taste of Pepsi; Coke, they said, had too much 'bite'.

But when the experiment was varied to allow the participants to consume whole cans of the drink, the expressed preference did not persist. The sweet taste became less attractive.

It is a useful cautionary tale.

CHAPTER 5

Carrying out your survey

There is a widespread assumption that 'doing a survey' is child's play. In primary schools everywhere children are invited to do 'projects' by writing down some questions and taking them home to ask their friends and relations: 'Granddad, where were you born?' 'Auntie Vera, do you like cabbage?' In the hands of a creative teacher, the facts so generated can be used in all sorts of imaginative ways. (Teachers, though, have to be careful to ensure that they can't be accused of prying into private domestic lives, nor of pinpointing socially divisive accounts of children's backgrounds.)

Among adults, doing a survey is a surprisingly common activity – in the work setting, in leisure time clubs, in churches, in charities and pressure groups. The results are reported in committees, used in campaigns and reproduced in the media.

In a closely related area, the design of forms involves asking survey-type questions. Government departments, commercial companies, sports clubs and other organisations create forms by the million. Very few form designers have had any tuition in the task.

So, if anybody can do it, what is there to learn? And why does it matter?

Let's take the second question first. Quality matters because:

- Surveys are almost always carried out for a specific purpose.
- The serving of that purpose makes an implicit assumption that the material produced by a survey will be an accurate reflection of the reality it describes. In other words, it assumes its validity.
- Moreover, surveys often have either a political or a policy-related objective – for example, in relation to urban planning or crime control – or they purport to be delivering findings that contribute to a body of existing knowledge or theoretical understanding. Surveys, however badly designed, may affect decision-making and change practice or they may cumulatively alter the way we view the world. Even a mini-survey

carried out by an individual and not reported to anybody else has practical or educational significance for that individual, and if the findings are flawed, the author of them will be the poorer as a consequence.

Surveys matter, then, because they tend to have a purpose beyond themselves. They have *meaning*. The task of the professional survey designer is to ensure that, as far as possible, the meaning of a survey can be relied upon by those who read the results.

So, back to the first question: What is there to learn in order to achieve high standards of survey design? The principles of sampling are important to any assessment of the value of a completed survey, but, in addition, I can offer you 20 quality questions to which your answer should be 'yes'. If you can put a tick against all of them, not only will you be able to claim professional expertise as a survey designer yourself, but you will be in a position to analyse critically and identify the shortcomings in other people's surveys in order to judge whether the conclusions drawn and the recommendations made are justified.

Twenty quality questions for carrying out a successful survey

1. *Are all your questions essential?*
   The size of any survey is determined partly by the nature of the study (How broad is it?), the researcher's personal objectives (Is it for a doctorate?) and the kind of end-result the commissioning body might be looking for (Do they want an answer to a simple question or a descriptive account of a complex subject?). The exclusion of inessential questions is a mark of efficient survey design, but, sadly, it is only with lengthy experience that researchers come to realise it; novice researchers and form designers tend to find it easier to add more and more questions 'that might be interesting' than to edit any out.

2. *Is the structure of each question elegant and efficient?*
   Each question is a work of art – good, bad or incomprehensible. Every one should be drafted and redrafted, tested and amended, sharpened and given the highest quality level of

elegance that you are capable of achieving. A rushed and cursory construction of questions is one of the most common faults of amateur survey designers – and especially of people (or committees) who design forms.

3. *Are there ambiguous words in any of the questions?*
Pre-piloting and piloting are crucial – because you yourself may not notice ambiguities. It can be helpful, in the pre-pilot stage, to subject your questions (or some of them) to group discussion among colleagues – get them to role play a respondent. Sometimes they can be too nit-picking and awkward, but honest comments are always invaluable.

4. *Are you certain that the words you have used in your questions will have the same meaning for your respondents as they have for you?*
Words are a product of class, culture, educational background and even of gender and chronological age. You'll be surprised – as I have been – that words whose meaning you have taken for granted can convey something entirely different to your interviewees. You also need to be sure that you are using words that are going to be comfortably within the normal range of usage so far as your respondents are concerned.

5. *Are there probable ambiguities in any of the answers you might receive?*
This is more to do with question construction than with words, and it is particularly problematic in respect of prestructured responses. Have you scrupulously avoided all double-barrelled questions? For example, 'In the past year, have you taken sick leave from work or been admitted to hospital?' You must break that down into two questions, enabling your respondent to say 'yes' or 'no' to each of them. If you are offering a line of tick-boxes, do you want one tick or as many as are applicable? You need to think very carefully about this one, and be sure that your respondents understand what you want.

6. *Is your questionnaire free of leading questions or loaded words?*
This is one of the hardest areas of all to get right, partly because it means that the wording used in questionnaires has to be different from ordinary usage (for example, research questions normally need to be morally neutral) and partly

because we don't always realise when the words and phrases used are loaded or when the question we ask is leading. A good example of a loaded questionnaire would be one sent out by a planning department to 20,000 people listing optional routes for a new bypass and asking for people's preferences, but not offering respondents the option of saying that they would prefer it not to be built at all. (Maybe such 'loading' would be politically deliberate rather than a design oversight.)

7. *Are you making any false assumptions about whether the respondents will have the appropriate knowledge to enable them to answer the questions?*
Although most questionnaires offer 'Don't know' as a response option, many people don't like to admit their ignorance. So if you are doing a study that seeks feedback in areas of technical expertise, for example into people's experience of using the latest entertainment technology, then you must allow for those – of all ages – who haven't a clue what you're talking about. And the questionnaire should be designed in such a way that you don't make them feel silly as a result.

8. *Similarly, are there any questions that require respondents to express an opinion, when, in truth, they may never have thought about it and therefore have no opinions at all, not even neutral ones?*
There are all sorts of topics that the researcher is at risk of assuming that everybody has views on – in the realm of politics, deviant behaviour, sport, television, cinema, and so on. It can come as quite a shock to intellectually curious people (which students should be) to discover that many citizens quietly get on with their own lives and are oblivious to aspects of everyday existence to which you might assume everybody was alert. The good researcher makes no presuppositions of that kind.

9. *Are all your instructions to the respondents clear and unambiguous?*
There is a tricky balance to achieve here. On the one hand, you don't want to provide lengthy instructions that will test the patience of the respondent to breaking point, but you do need to be sure that what you are asking the respondent to do is clearly understood and is acted on in precisely the same way in every case.

10. *If it is a written questionnaire, is the layout such that the respondents have room to write what they want to write?*
One of the most aggravating things about badly designed questionnaires or forms is for you to be faced with the need to squeeze your answer into a small box using minuscule writing or – even worse – to be deterred from writing what you feel you want to say because there isn't enough space to allow you to do justice to the answer. The same fault can sometimes occur in the schedule being used by an interviewer.

11. *Are you making excessive demands on the time or patience of your respondents?*
Some interviewees may be more than happy to talk to you – old men on park benches, bored passengers sitting on a long-distance train, delayed passengers in airport lounges; but others will have better things to do – dashing to get home to cook tea, rushing for a bus, worrying about the time needed to write an overdue essay. You shouldn't presume too much on the goodwill of your respondents. The ideal has happened to some of my students when interviewees have said with astonishment, 'Is that all? I was really enjoying the questions.'

12. *Where you are seeking opinions or judgements, is the format of your question and proffered answers appropriate to all likely responses?*
When designing your questionnaire, you must explore potential responses at some length with other people. You may think you know the likely range, but you don't. Only with exploratory work can you begin to get close to the way people feel when faced with the questions you want to ask. Often there may be one or two questions where it will be better to allow the respondent to express their views in their own words.

13. *If you are asking respondents to locate their opinions along a scale, is the method you have chosen the best possible?*
There are a wide variety of ways in which you can ask people to express an opinion along a continuum or scale (usually called a Likert scale). It can have any number of points from

three to ten (or more, although I wouldn't recommend it). Do you just use numbers or spots along a line? Do you use words ('very much so', 'moderately', 'hardly at all', 'not at all')? Do you offer a scale using odd numbers (3, 5, 7) so that you have a midpoint which is neutral? Or do you have a scale with 4 or 6 optional answers, so that all your respondents are forced into suggesting that, however moderately, their inclination is in one direction or the other? There is no standard right or wrong way of resolving these questions, but the design decisions you take in the planning stage could have a significant effect on the results you obtain.

14. *Where you are seeking 'facts', is the format of your question and proffered answers appropriate to all likely circumstances?*
The key to this lies in a generous amount of time devoted to exploratory work and to an effective review of the literature, where you will find how other researchers have dealt with similar topics.

15. *Is there an appropriate balance between prestructured (tick-box) questions and open-answer questions?*
Generally, in mail questionnaires, the number of times you ask for written responses that extend beyond the range of the prestructured answers provided should be few. You will have gathered exploratory material before you begin the formal survey, and it is a basic expectation of survey work that, for better or worse, you are committed to the structure of your questions from the outset. In this, the method differs radically from qualitative research.

16. *If your questionnaire involves any consideration of sensitive or embarrassing areas, have you designed it in such a way as to minimise or overcome possible negative reactions in the respondent?*
Questions concerning criminal activity, interpersonal relationships, money, sex, bereavement and other topics can be tricky. You have to remember that your underlying aim is to get your interviewee to give you valid and reliable responses – and the way you approach topics like these can have a big impact on whether you succeed or not.

17. *Is the flow of your questionnaire as good as it can be?*
Your questionnaire should have a natural shape to it. It shouldn't feel like a roller-coaster ride touching on anything and everything in random order. Research designers disagree about whether you should get the basic factual questions (age, sex, occupation, place of residence, employment, or whatever) out of the way first, or whether you should leave them till last.

18. *If you are using supplementary materials (like show cards containing lists or pictures), are they well produced and manageable in a way that allows you to handle them in an efficient manner?*
Doing an interview is very much a professional performance, and you will also be seen as representing the university or organisation to which you are attached. You should leave your interviewee with the feeling, not that they've just been cynically used by an incompetent student only interested in furthering his or her own agenda, but that they've participated in a worthwhile exercise, well planned and professionally executed.

19. *Is it apparent that you are courteously appreciative of the time that your respondents have given you?*
Make it explicit and mean it. Build it in to your written script so that you don't forget. 'Thank you very much for your time and for sharing your thoughts and ideas with me.'

20. *Is your survey the end-product of two crucial preliminary stages: a period of exploration and pre-piloting; and a full-scale pilot study, in which your final questionnaire was tested and, if necessary, amended?*
If so, then it is probable that all the lessons spelt out in this section will have been dealt with in a natural manner. If not, you are likely to end up with a piece of work of poorer quality than it should or could have been.

An exercise

Here is a questionnaire used in a small-scale survey carried out by a woman undergraduate, Jo Kensit. The questionnaire was self-completed by 50 men and 50 women, each of whom was living in a heterosexual partner relationship. The researcher used a convenience sample of mixed ages. The researcher had one-third of her working time in a period of 13 weeks to carry out the project from initial planning to completion.

an investigation into gender differences in the division of labour within married/cohabiting couples

1. Are you **male** or **female**? (please circle one)

2. Would you indicate how often **you** do the following tasks (please circle one answer for each task):

   Washing-up
   never/sometimes/half of the time/mostly/always
   Vacuuming
   never/sometimes/half of the time/mostly/always
   Shopping for bread/milk
   never/sometimes/half of the time/mostly/always
   Changing the bedding
   never/sometimes/half of the time/mostly/always
   Putting the rubbish out
   never/sometimes/half of the time/mostly/always

3. Could you estimate the **total** percentage of domestic tasks that you do (please circle one answer):

   | 0–10% | 11–20% | 21–30% | 31–40% | 41–50% |
   | 51–60% | 61–70% | 71–80% | 81–90% | 91–100% |

   Thank you for your participation

The student makes a number of points in her report. You are invited to consider them:

- Following advice from the supervisor, a more elaborate version taking other variables into consideration was replaced by a simple questionnaire focusing on five specific tasks that would probably be performed in the majority of households. *What are the arguments for and against that decision?*

- It soon became apparent that it might prove difficult and time-consuming to find and question a suitable number of married/cohabiting couples. It was decided that it would be appropriate to present the questionnaire to an equal number of males and females that were married or cohabiting in a heterosexual relationship, but not necessarily with each other. *Is this an elegant solution or a cop-out?*
- I was advised to ignore factors such as age and employment status, as although they may have some relevance to the subject being investigated, their inclusion might make completion of the project difficult due to the time constraints. *What do you think about this?*
- The original version was tested on eight people, four males and four females. There appeared to be no misunderstandings of what was being asked of them, and the only 'problems' that arose were that participants wanted to provide an explanation as to why they did or did not do certain tasks. *Would you have taken action in response to this?*
- The questionnaire was discussed with a seminar group. Following this, it was adapted slightly, with 'putting the rubbish out' replacing 'changing a light bulb', due to some households having 'long-life light bulbs' that only require changing every 10 years. 'Shopping' became 'shopping for bread/milk', which made the task more specific and was felt to be an essential task, more likely to be performed in all households on a regular basis. *Would you have suggested changing anything else?*
- Having agreed that a sample size of 100 participants would be appropriate, every effort was made to select participants covering a wide age range and with different employment status. The questionnaire was distributed amongst a selection of mature students, friends, family and work colleagues at a school and a warehouse. *What implications do you draw from the nature of the sample?*
- Overall, the simplicity of the questionnaire proved invaluable, and the data collection process was completed within a short space of time. *Do you think it offers a good model for undergraduate research learning?*
- Although the decision had been made that participants need

not be males and females from the same relationship, a large proportion of participants were, as many people took two questionnaires home with them, one for themselves and one for their partner to complete. As the survey was in the form of self-completion questionnaires, I am unaware of whether some couples completed the questionnaires together, ensuring that their results corresponded. If couples did confer, the accuracy of the results would be affected, and if further research were to be carried out, it would be worth bearing this in mind. *Could/should this have been prevented? Or doesn't it matter?*

You have doubtless torn to shreds the methodology in the illustration. That is the way of students when looking at other people's work. My judgement, I should say, is that, if you accept that it was impossible to gather a probability sample in the time allowed, the survey itself was of very high quality – neat, focused and elegant, especially with regard to the imaginative realisation that the study did not need to achieve a sample of 50 *partners* to reach meaningful conclusions about the respective domestic roles of men and women in a relationship. Allowing couples to complete separate response sheets out of sight of the researcher was a mistake; it's impossible to know whether it affected some responses but it is certainly possible. A summary of the results obtained by the student is at the end of this chapter.

now it's your turn

Try and design a similarly structured mini-survey with no more than five questions either:

1. on a topic relevant to your own subject, or
2. with the aim of providing answers to any *one* of the following ten questions:
   - By what means do children travel to a primary school?
   - Why do girls go out with 'bad boys'?
   - What proportion of a sample of women students is currently 'dieting', and what form does it take?
   - In a sample of working women, what exercise do they take?
   - What made a sample of vegetarians become vegetarians?
   - What factors deter drivers from speeding?
   - Why do people past the retiring age carry on working?

- To what extent has a given sample of people experienced suicidal feelings?
- What is the attitude of a sample of female students to future childbearing choices?
- Do males and females (in a student population) differ in their choice of chocolate to buy?

For the purpose of this exercise, stick to a structured survey approach; avoid switching to a qualitative research method. Imagine that you have just 13 weeks to do the project, and that other course units continue to demand your attention at the same time.

Even if you only do the exercise in your mind, you should nevertheless think about the following questions:

- How would you go about gathering a sample? What kind of a sample would be achievable? What problems would you face?
- What reliance could you place on the answers you get?
- Can you think of a key question that would give you just one interesting finding?
- Can you design it in such a way that you are able to compare the answers given by two different categories of people (male/female, young/old, and so on)?

Was it easy? Or was it hard? Was it satisfying? Or frustrating? Did it feel creative? Or did it confirm you in the view that 'doing a survey' is child's play?

Jo Kensit's project results

Bearing in mind that the student had gathered a convenience sample, the results were as shown below. The table shows how many said they did the various duties *mostly* or *always*.

DUTY	MEN	WOMEN
Washing up	16%	68%
Vacuuming	6%	86%
Shopping for bread/milk	4%	68%

Jo Kensit's project results *continued*

Changing the bedding	2%	92%
Putting the rubbish out	42%	36%

- Both the men and the women say that the women are still doing the lion's (or the lioness's) share of the work.
- Only when it comes to putting out the bins and the rubbish bags do the men form the majority.

You could replicate the exercise and see how the results differ.

If you asked me to recommend just one book on ...
survey methods *it would be:*

Vaus, David de (2002)
Surveys in Social Research, 5th edn, London, Routledge

6 Questionnaires

Q: What's the difference between a survey and a questionnaire?

A: A questionnaire is one of the tools used to carry out a survey. The other two principal methods are:
1. face-to-face contact using interview schedules
2. the observation of people and events in real time.

Questionnaires are driven by the researcher's own agenda

We are all familiar with questionnaires in our lives. Often they are disguised as forms: job application forms, tax forms, customer satisfaction forms. Sometimes they drop through the letter box from the council planning department asking our opinion on a new road or housing development. Or an interviewer from a market research company stops us in the street to ask what we think about a particular product.

Questionnaires are intended to facilitate communication, usually brief, but always driven by the researcher's own agenda. You are asked a question, and you reply to it conversationally, in writing, by ticking a box, or in a website by clicking your mouse to make an electronic response. There is something disarmingly concrete about the process and the response you make will often be treated as absolute. That response will itself be absorbed into the tens or hundreds or thousands of responses from the rest of the sample that provide the raw material for the researcher to use in reaching conclusions.

Questionnaires had their origins more than a century ago when a generation of social policy activists recognised that campaigns to counteract poverty would be helped by the accumulation of reliable evidence. A major breakthrough came when it was realised that the statistical theory of sampling meant that you could draw conclusions about a total population by only asking questions of a small proportion. In the US in the middle of the twentieth century, the pioneering study of *The American Soldier* (Stouffer et al., 1949) demonstrated the way in which the use of high-level skills in the design and analysis of questionnaires improves the quality of the results.

In the decades since then, questionnaires have continued to be employed in the social, psychological and environmental sciences, as well as in professional settings such as teacher training, nursing, urban planning and the leisure industry. Sadly, though, applied researchers often use the questionnaire method in a naive way and without any apparent awareness of the critical attention it has been subjected to in the social and psychological sciences. Indeed, it sometimes seems that there is an assumption made that no skills are needed – just common sense.

That this is not so is recognised by experts in advertising, marketing and opinion poll testing. In spheres where the maximisation of profits, the assumption of political power or the achievement of a reputation for communication skills depend on getting accurate results, great care and highly sophisticated techniques are employed. Elsewhere, standards are not always so high. The easy acceptance of poor quality social surveys is encouraged by the existence of casual exercises that are reported in the newspapers or on the web but are designed more for coffee break laughs than for serious attention: although often amusing, there is a risk that surveys such as these distract attention from the need for high-quality work in questionnaire construction.

The researcher has a professional obligation to maintain high standards

One aggravating feature of questionnaire-based research is that an assertive conclusion, quoted far and wide, may just as likely be based on a thoroughly flawed, incompetent or superficial piece of work as on a random sample survey using meticulously collected data and subjected to skilled analysis. The fact that, when results are published, the methodology employed is likely to be invisible to most ordinary readers places a professional obligation on good researchers, as a matter of principle, to maintain the highest standards in all stages of their work.

Three statements will help us to consider this chapter's lessons:

1. Your questionnaire will be heavily influenced by the *subject of your research*: the words you use will reflect it; the flow and the structure will be of a kind that will feel comfortable to colleagues or customers within your field; and the type of respondents you target for your sample will be determined by it.
2. Your questionnaire will be *unique to you*. If 50 people are told to carry out a survey on an identical topic, none of the 50 questionnaires will be the same. Some will vary from the norm in quite remarkable and perhaps imaginative ways.
3. The business of questionnaire construction has, nevertheless, many common features. There are *rules and guidelines* about the ingredients that you would be foolish to ignore, and this chapter will summarise the key factors that you need to take into account as you set about the task.

In many ways, designing a questionnaire is rather like planning to write a long essay. From the beginning, you need to think holistically. You can't just go for 'stream of consciousness' stuff. Although there are technical skills to learn, the most important thing is for you to be prepared to spend a lot of time thinking through each stage of the process. Some big projects will embrace more than one stage, with as yet unplanned second or third stages of work depending on the outcome of the first stage. They may even be 'cohort studies', in which the same people are questioned at intervals of one, five or ten years. This chapter deals with 'one-stage' or 'first stage' projects.

If you want your project to be successful, you must resist the temptation to hurry the preparatory stages and dash out into the field in order to 'get on with it now'. In survey research, with a structured questionnaire at the heart of it, such impatience is a sign of professional incompetence.

Step 1: What is your question or topic?

As I argued in Chapter 1, you need always to clarify the nature of your task. What is your question? What ground are you planning to cover? This can be a difficult step for several reasons:

- Your mind may simply not seem to work that way – you'd rather just 'go with the flow' and see what materialises. If you are serious about doing a high-quality survey, I'm afraid you will just have to change your style.

- You may have chosen a question or topic that anyone with more experience will tell you lacks clear focus. Feedback from an experienced supervisor will alert you to that fact and help you tighten it up. Many students resist such guidance – they think they 'know best' – but a willingness to take advice at this stage will lead to a better performance overall.

- Even if your topic is well focused, it may be overambitious: perhaps suitable for a three-year multistage project, with a team of research assistants; or just needing three more weeks or months than you will have at your disposal before the deadline date. You should talk it through with someone in order to identify a single aspect of the broader question or topic that will lend itself to a project achievable in the time available. Or maybe you go for a slight reduction in sample size or a change of tack in order to obtain easier access.

- A not uncommon problem arises because organisations (in the commercial or public sector) may ask a student to do a research project on their behalf. You may even be offered modest sponsorship. This is very flattering and, at first sight, tempting. But beware. The kinds of managers who make these suggestions often have even less idea than you of what is feasible in a student project, and if you fail to meet their expectations (because they were unrealistic in the first place), you will feel disappointed and they will feel let down by you. Do it if it's realistic, but steer well clear if they ask you to 'evaluate' something; the most you can usually achieve through a student survey is to 'monitor' some activity and provide some customer or user feedback.

Often the best way forward is for your course teacher to suggest a list of possible options or for you to look at what previous students on your course have done. You need to stimulate your brain – put your thinking cap on – talk it through with friends and colleagues. But don't rush into anything until you can say yes to these five questions:

1. Is it an interesting question/topic?
2. Does it lend itself to a tight focus?
3. Is it achievable in the time available?
4. Will the target population be within reach?
5. Has your supervisor approved it?

Getting the question or topic right is a critical first step in your work. Getting it wrong will mess up the whole experience, give you a low grade and leave you feeling frustrated and unhappy.

Step 2: Draw up a timetable

Try and think through every detailed step of your research programme in advance so that you know what you are meant to be doing and when you expect to be doing it. You can do this on a big wall chart, on-screen in a file, or in your notebook. Timetabling is an essential part of this phase. The timing details depend on how many months or years you are allowed and on your eventual submission deadline, but it should look something like this.

The four stages of research	Target date for completion of each stage
1. THE PLANNING STAGE • Identify a question/topic • Plan the process (this is what you are doing now) • If your project is substantial, draw up a short outline of your questionnaire's various parts • Rough out a first draft questionnaire, following exploration in the literature and conversations with subject 'experts' • Try it out on one or two friends or relations: what do they think of it? • Tighten it up and produce a revised first draft questionnaire • Try it out on between two and six of the kinds of people you'll be interviewing or sending it to. Ask them not just to complete it but to give you a running commentary on their reactions to its	

various parts as they are doing it. Do they understand all the words?
- Produce a second draft questionnaire
- Pilot it and amend it if necessary
- Possibly pilot it again (if there is time and if you
made many changes) before you emerge with your
confirmed questionnaire. Run with it

2. THE DATA COLLECTION STAGE
- Set a date for the completion of the sample-
gathering process
- During the data collection stage, you should aim to
produce a 'dummy' report, based on the contents of
your questionnaire but without results – it should
also include your draft literature review and some
preliminary discussion about your topic/question

3. THE DATA ANALYSIS STAGE
- Code the questionnaires. This can be done during
the data collection stage if you have time
- Input to SPSS (although, if numbers are not too
great, it is possible to analyse parts of your data
by hand)
- Allow time for thought, discussion (with colleagues
and your supervisor) and statistical guidance
- Think about the meaning of what has emerged

4. THE WRITE-UP STAGE
- Write-up:
  draft 1 – this can be a really rough draft, but it
  makes draft 2 much easier to tackle
  draft 2 – this is the most crucial of the four drafts
  draft 3 – tidy up draft 2 and fill in the gaps
  draft 4 – turn it into a finished product with good
  referencing, decent layout and readable
  conclusions
- Copying and binding, as required
- Submission by the deadline date

Having a timetable like this will give you a realistic idea of how much time you have to allow for the data collection process. It will help you to see whether your sample size is realistic and the data-gathering process achievable. It will ensure that you leave sufficient time for data analysis and write-up and avoid the last-minute rush that so often bedevils students' work, leading to disappointing final reports.

Of course, your project *won't* all go according to plan. No research project ever does. But you will be better able to cope with the inevitable snags and hiccups if you have a clear idea of what should be happening and when.

Step 3: Design and create your own questionnaire

A major part of the planning phase requires you to spend time composing/designing/checking/revising your questionnaire. The stages in this task are:

- A literature review that will include detailed examination, not only of the end-products of related research studies, but, if possible, a look at the research instruments used. You may want to replicate some of the material – with appropriate acknowledgement, of course.
- Exploratory discussions with relevant 'experts'.
- Informal discussions with friends, lovers and colleagues – bouncing ideas off each other and inviting critical comment (being careful not to fall out in the process; some friends can be astonishingly rude and insensitive about your own best efforts).
- If your project is of any size, begin to draw up a structured outline of your questionnaire's parts. Think about the various aspects and sub-aspects of your topic or question. Break it up into, perhaps, three or four sections. Be ready to edit some questions out, to question the feasibility of pursuing others, and to obey the basic rule: try to keep your questionnaire as short and as neatly designed as possible. A fundamental error of most beginning researchers (I was certainly guilty of it) is to 'put everything in'. The result is not only that you antagonise the respondents but you run the risk of being faced with a mass of indigestible data and losing sight of your primary

focus. Of course, with modern electronic methods of analysis, it's easy to 'compare everything with everything else' and carry out complex statistical tests that you don't understand but which you hope may give you a result that somebody else tells you is worth using. But that is not good hands-on research. If you keep reminding yourself of my basic instruction – ask a good question and find good answers to it – you will soon learn how much more satisfying it is to design a questionnaire that is geared up to that end. There are always other things that 'it would be interesting to explore' and it is tempting to hedge your bets in this way. But resist it – and your final report will be a better quality and more readable as a result.

- Next, start to work out and write up all the various component parts of your questionnaire. Don't rush it. Get some variety of style in there. Make sure the flow of ideas serves your purpose. Think consciously about the difference between questions asking about facts ('When did you last have sex?') and questions inviting the expression of opinion ('In what ways are you happy with/unhappy with your current partner?'). (Incidentally, these are both extremely tricky questions, not just because of the sensitivity of the subject matter. They encompass problems of definition, reliability and validity and would need to be accompanied by a number of related questions if the findings were to have any value.)
- There are four rules about the order in which you should place questions:
  - It isn't a good idea to start with basic bald questions such as age, occupation, and so on; leave them to the end
  - Start with friendly and unthreatening questions that are relevant to the subject matter of the survey
  - Only when rapport has been established should more complex or potentially embarrassing questions be broached
  - Be careful not to include, at an early stage, any discussion that will result in either you or the respondent expressing views that will compromise the openness you might be seeking towards the end of the interview.
- During this part of your questionnaire design task, you will be experimenting – endlessly, it may seem – with what options to offer your respondents by way of replies:

- Do you use tick boxes? What shape are they? Are they placed in the best position in relation to each question? Are the instructions clear? Are the options mutually exclusive and straightforward (as they should be) or are they overlapping or ambiguous?
- Do you invite the respondents to 'Please circle'? Have you given them enough space? Do the answers you offer truly reflect what your respondents would like to say in answer to the question – or are you forcing them into expressing artificial opinions or 'squeezing' the facts into a false framework?
- Do you invite them to 'Choose just one' and is the instruction clear?
- Or do you allow them to 'Indicate all that apply' and have you thought how you will analyse those responses?
- Do some questions ask respondents to 'Cross out those that are not applicable'? Do you offer them a blank space in case they feel that what they have left uncrossed out doesn't do justice to what they would prefer to have said?
- Are you asking them to indicate along a scale where their opinion is located? If so, does the scale look like this – in many ways, the clearest option:

Very much so   *Not at all*

or this:

Very much so   *Not at all*

In this one, are the respondents meant to tick between the vertical points or on the verticals? I can promise you you'll get both.

or this:

Very much so   *Not at all*

     5   4   3   2   1   0

or this:

Very much so

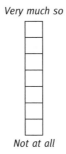

Not at all

- As I explained in Chapter 5, you need to decide how many points there should be to the scale. Odd numbers allow an 'undecided' or 'average' midpoint. Even numbers force the respondents towards expressing a positive or negative view, and enable you to conflate and analyse the results by splitting responses at the midpoint. Your decision should be determined by the logic of what the answers mean. A neutral midpoint may be essential to reflect reality.

- In scale construction, you have to be careful not only to ensure that all the words in your question and in the offered answers are 'right', but also that the instructions you give are appropriate, because they have the power to change the responses you receive and therefore the results you obtain. Here is an example.

rating the performance of job candidates

Candidates for a senior management post were asked to give a pre-interview presentation to an audience of 20, each of whom was then required to rate the candidates on a scale in respect of nine items such as these two:

'The candidate demonstrated good communication skills'
'The candidate demonstrated an ability to motivate others'.

The scale on offer was from 1 to 5, but further clarification was provided: '5 represents a statement with which you strongly agree, 3 you neither agree nor disagree and 1 a statement with which you strongly disagree.'

This instruction invites a completely different (and much less useful) pattern of responses compared with one which had simply

rating the performance of job candidates continued

said: 'Rate each candidate according to their performance along a scale from 1 to 5.'

The clarifying sentence meant that candidates prompting a range of positive feelings in the rater could only be scored 4 or 5 – allowing for very little gradation. If the simpler scoring scale had been employed, a wider range of options could have been used. Only a score of 1 (or even better, perhaps, allowing a zero) would have meant a truly negative judgement, whereas the range from 2 to 5 would have reflected more sensitive degrees of quality.

The instructions given in respect of scaling can make a significant difference to the outcome. And this applies, not just to scales, but at every point in a questionnaire.

- Are you keeping to a minimum the number of unstructured answers that you invite? If you include a lot and you have a substantial sample, they will present significant problems for analysis. Often such material doesn't get used because of the mass of data with which the researcher is presented. If you find yourself wanting to use them extensively, the suspicion must be either that you might be better off using a qualitative research approach or that you have more exploratory groundwork to do before you are ready to prepare a structured questionnaire suitable for your purpose. You can, of course, invite 'additional comments', and in mail questionnaires they are regarded as an act of courtesy to the respondent.

- Are you making appropriate use of methodological material from your own subject area that other people have previously designed and used – inventories, questions, picture questions and so on? For some (especially inventories that produce attitudinal or personality scores), you will find that copyright restrictions are restrictive and may be costly. In other instances, provided you are scrupulous about giving due acknowledgement in your report, there is a great deal to be said for taking advantage of the accumulated reservoir of methodological options – not least because it allows you to compare your results with those previously obtained and reported in published papers.

- The decisions you make about question format can have a major effect on the results you obtain. That in itself should give you cause to recognise some of the hazards of survey research, but, more significantly, it highlights the crucial importance of spending a long time on the planning stage so that you can be confident you have taken the design of your questions (both separately and as a whole) to the point where you are satisfied that the answers will truly reflect the circumstances, opinions or described experiences of your respondents.

- A vital element in this phase of questionnaire construction is the active involvement that you seek of other people – reactions from colleagues and, in particular, feedback from people similar to those whom you will be investigating. You can ask them about any part of the embryonic but emerging questionnaire, or you can do a pre-pilot with the whole thing.

- When you have a version that feels close to 'perfect', pilot it – ideally on six people similar to your target group. Amend and update it as you go through this group, finally reaching the point where you can say to yourself, 'Yes, that's as good as it's going to get'.

- Then away you go. Once you reach this point, in survey research, whatever flaws you find that you wish you'd spotted earlier (and you will), you really have to live with. It happens to us all. But if you've done all the stages just outlined thoroughly, it shouldn't happen too badly.

- The funny thing is that in survey research, the sense of achievement when you emerge with your finished questionnaire can feel more satisfying than the final completion of a written report (which is often quite anticlimactic). A good questionnaire is a piece of true craftsmanship; you've put a lot of work into it, and you want to 'fly with it'. Good luck! As your research career matures, so you will discover more and more tricks of the trade in survey design, and when you face a particular problem, you will continue to get a real kick from being able to come up with an elegant solution, often helped by 'thinking aloud' in discussions with colleagues.

twelve more things for you to think about

1. What words mean

In casual conversation with your family or friends, you tend to assume that the meaning of words can be taken for granted, but in designing your questionnaire that isn't so. You need to be constantly alert to the importance of clarifying and defining concepts.

- What do specific words mean to the people who will be completing your questionnaire? Even apparently simple words like success, pain, family or satisfaction can be surprisingly problematic.
- Do respondents have the same understanding of words as you do? Not only may class and culture affect this; age can present special problems: the scope for verbal misunderstandings between people in their twenties and people in their sixties is very real.
- Do all respondents understand your words in the same way as each other?
- How is the meaning of the data you will gather affected by cultural, class or regional background – yours or the respondents?
- What other sources of bias might you need to be alert to in the words and sentences you are using? Leading questions? Yes-seeking or no-seeking questions? Is there any bias implicit in what you have left out?

The problem with all these questions is that, even if you are unusually sensitive and knowledgeable, you are unlikely to be able to answer them satisfactorily without checking up on your material at the pre-pilot stage and trying out your draft questionnaire on people from a different background from yours.

2. Questions about frequency

The use of the phrase 'How often … ?' is particularly problematic in survey research and the answers are often unreliable. Much the best way of measuring frequency in a medium-sized or large sample is to ask 'When did you last … ?' If you think about it in

twelve more things for you to think about *continued*

relation to concrete possibilities (... read a book; ... kiss your partner; ... go swimming; ... vote in an election; ... steal something from a shop), you will see that what the researcher emerges with is a measure of frequency (in other words, 'How often ... .?') in respect of the total sample.

Students will sometimes say in criticism of this advice, 'Well, I actually went swimming yesterday, but normally I only go about once a year. So isn't my response misleading?' Yes, it is as far as the individual is concerned, but *in the sample as a whole* such 'accidental' facts will cancel each other out. Somebody else might normally go swimming twice a week, but has missed out altogether in the last month because of an ear infection. If your sample is 100, and you draw up a table that shows the last occasion when each individual went swimming, you will emerge with an average figure that gives a more reliable measure of frequency in the sample as a whole than you would get if you'd asked 'How often?'

3. Respondent memory

Some people have good memories; others don't. Some people can clearly remember events in the recent past; others can reminisce about their childhood but forget what they had for lunch yesterday. Some people just pretend they can remember because they feel that any kind of questioning is a sort of test they don't want to be seen to fail.

The researcher needs to be alert to the problem and may need to design the study in such a way that it takes account of fallible memory patterns. Above all, you should avoid pressurising the respondent to 'make it up' in order to save face.

4. Double questions

One of the commonest errors made by beginning researchers is to ask 'double questions' – usually characterised by the presence of an *or* in the middle:

• When did you last travel by bus or train?
• Do you like eating cream cakes or chocolate biscuits?

twelve more things for you to think about *continued*

Of course, if it's a trawling question to be followed up by further questions of clarification, that's OK; but often the researcher is left with a statistic that is less precise than it should be – because it contains within it an unidentifiable mixture of circumstances.

5. Variations in question structure

Apart from simply asking respondents to answer a question or choose a point on a rating scale, researchers have developed a wide range of methods for tapping into people's opinions or judgements:

- You can invite respondents to place a list of given items (for example, their favourite holiday destination) in rank order of choice, preference, importance or appearance.
- You can ask respondents to agree or disagree with a list of statements or written opinions that you provide. For example:

> **I think all lecturers mark my work conscientiously**
> Strongly agree/agree/ neutral/disagree/strongly disagree

- You can use the semantic differential method in which you give respondents pairs of words with opposite meanings and ask them to indicate the point along a continuum that comes closest to their views in respect of a stated subject or idea. For example:

> **University teachers:** hard working . . . . lazy
> **University students:** hard working . . . . lazy

Whatever structure you use, make sure that you keep it simple. If you are pursuing complicated data, then be generous in your use of space, and break your questions up into discrete elements. You can always bring them together in your analysis, but for data-gathering, the primary aim is to make it user-friendly for your respondents.

6. Honesty

You can never be certain that people who answer your questions are telling the truth. What people say about their behaviour or

twelve more things for you to think about *continued*

beliefs and what they do or secretly think may be far from identical. You can ask people to tell you what they do ('How much
alcohol do you drink?'), or what their attitudes are ('Do you have
racist thoughts?'); some may be honest, others may not. The
responses you get may even depend on what sort of a person
they think *you* are. In the two examples given of drinking and
racism, the potential for deception and denial is manifest.

When I registered with a new medical practice, the nurse, filling
out her form, asked 'How many units of alcohol a week do you
drink?' 'Twenty-one', I answered instantly, without batting an
eyelid, knowing this is the recommended maximum for a healthy
lifestyle in men. She raised her left eyebrow a fraction.

Because of the problem, researchers have been led to the view
that, in addition to surveys, you may also need to carry out
observational studies – so that you can study not just what
people *say* they do or think, but what they actually do in practice. Of course, this is a much harder task and, in many instances,
is not feasible. (How would you set about finding out how many
alcohol units I or anybody else actually drink each week?)

Provided you are cautious about the extent to which you place
reliance on just one set of findings; provided you design your
survey in such a way that it makes it possible for respondents to
give you sensitive information without worrying about the consequences; and provided you give massive reassurances about the
confidentiality and the non-judgemental nature of your project,
then the value of the survey method (given its efficiency and
feasibility) is not in doubt.

7. The stability of opinions

A lot of survey research is about people's opinions: What do you
think about different kinds of vacuum cleaner? Do you think you
are better off under this government? Are you happy at work? But,
as the literature in social psychology has clearly demonstrated,
attitudes and opinions are not stable. As the saying has it, 'You
can go off people, you know'. Survey research can't counteract

twelve more things for you to think about *continued*

this phenomenon; it can't cancel it out. If someone is asked to express an opinion, that opinion is specific to the moment and so too are the totality and range of opinions gathered in any survey. That is not to say they are totally fluid, but it does mean that the results of opinion polls or attitude-testing inventories have to be carefully dated.

8. Hypothetical questions and scenarios

Some types of research ask the respondents to imagine how they might behave in a given situation. 'What would you do if you were caught up in a terror attack in the city?' 'How would you react to the death of your five-year-old child?' 'What would you do with the money if you won the lottery?' The shortcomings of such an approach are obvious: none of us know for certain how we would react to any given situation in the future. The technique is probably best avoided.

Another – sometimes effective – variation is to provide the respondent with a briefly detailed scenario:

'You discover that your roommate has been given dishonest access to next week's exam paper. What are your feelings about this? What action will you take?'

Scenarios have proved useful in studies of working people – police officers, nurses, school teachers – because 'common occurrences' can be described with a reasonable expectation that the respondents will be able to identify with the events portrayed and describe their likely reactions in some detail.

The scenario approach has also been used successfully in surveys that seek to identify racist attitudes, in which the violent character and the victim are alternately identified as being either black or white, resulting in significantly different outcomes, depending on the ethnic identity of the interviewee. This is an example of creative design in research: the fact that you are asking for a hypothetical response is irrelevant. If you get differences of response, you are successfully identifying discriminatory attitudes, although they may or may not reflect actual behaviour.

twelve more things for you to think about *continued*

9. Funnelling and filtering

You don't need to know many technical terms in question-naire design, but it's as well to be aware of:

- *funnelling*, where you start by asking a broad question but follow that with a sequence of more specific queries on the same topic
- *filtering*, where you exclude respondents from having to answer particular questions if they are not relevant to them.

10. Respondents who present challenges

Some respondents may present the researcher with particular challenges. People who are illiterate can neither read a ques-tionnaire nor the prompt cards you are using; people with learning disabilities may have difficulty not only with reading but with concentration, understanding or conceptual thinking; and people with little or no knowledge of the researcher's own language – recently arrived immigrants, for example – would need a translation. One solution is to use pictures.

11. Visual appearance and layout

Your questionnaire should look attractive and professional – perhaps copied onto coloured paper and certainly making generous use of space. It should, however, not be too complex in its structure, and the reader/respondent should be able to work through it without feeling that it is worse than filling in a tax or benefits form.

12. Finally

It rather depends on the context and circumstances of your project, but you may need to consider some of the following to ensure that you have covered all eventualities:

1. Give your questionnaire an appropriate title and a front cover.
2. Provide an explanation and maybe an information sheet for your respondents.
3. In some settings, you may need to seek their signed consent.

twelve more things for you to think about *continued*

4. If you are using a postal survey, make sure you give the respondents your address and/or provide them with a stamped addressed envelope.
5. Always provide a phone number or email address for them to contact you if they wish.
6. Assure them of confidentiality and respect it.
7. If the questionnaire is anonymous, you should include an identification number on it so that you can keep track of returns (although you will find that some people might tear it off to preserve their anonymity).

If you asked me to recommend just one book on ...
questionnaire design *it would be:*

Oppenheim, A N (1992)
Questionnaire Design, Interviewing and Attitude Measurement,
2nd edn, London, Continuum International Publishing Group

CHAPTER 7 The art and science of survey interviewing

In professional academic research, interviewing is often done by a graduate assistant; in major surveys, such as those carried out by the government or market research organisations, people – usually women – will be employed specifically as interviewers; but in student-led projects, the researcher *is* the interviewer.

The initial encounter

1. However nervous you may feel, you should remember that you are acting out a professional role. You are 'performing', and you should approach your performance in a professional manner. You will, in any case, soon get used to it. As in most such situations, the first half-dozen are the worst.
2. Interviewees should never be made to feel under any pressure to participate. Their involvement in your work must always be voluntary. On the other hand, if you are nervous, they will pick up on those vibes and may be less likely to agree to talk.
3. You should always introduce yourself, explain where you are from and on whose behalf you are making the approach. Next, you must explain the nature of the survey, how the interviewee came to be selected and how long the interview will take. Then: 'Would you be willing ... ?'
4. In some settings, governance or ethics conditions may require you to hand interviewees an information sheet about the project and ask for their signed consent.
5. You should always carry some form of identification.
6. You must take care not to put yourself at risk if you are interviewing people in private or unprotected settings.
7. If you are gathering a random or quota sample, you will need to check that you are about to interview the right person.

Although there are right and wrong ways of doing it, each interviewer's style is personal to them. Experienced interviewers take pride in the development of their art and employ it throughout the interview process. The best way of learning good interview techniques is to accompany an experienced professional and watch and listen closely.

Interviews should give respondents freedom to use their own words

One aspect of interviewing has become much misunderstood – largely, I suspect, because of the poor quality of some commercially inspired doorstep encounters. It is, of course, possible for a face-to-face interview to replicate the process employed by researchers who send or hand over a questionnaire to respondents with the request that they tick boxes. There may be some elements of this in any interview, but for the whole of it to follow such a pattern is inefficient and wasteful of your time. It fails to take advantage of the superior quality of material that a good face-to-face interview can deliver.

The aim of any research interview is to create a climate in which the respondent can talk freely and be able to offer the full range of responses that apply. Interviewees should feel happy with the accuracy, validity and completeness of the answers they have given. It is the duty of survey researchers to spend enough time planning, preparing and piloting their interview schedule to enable it to accommodate anything that potential respondents might offer. The structure of research interviewing should be compatible with the complexity of psychosocial reality, and should allow the obtained material to be written up in such a way that it does justice to the richness of the data provided during the interview programme.

Some interview questions (and even complete surveys) may be simple and straightforward but many are not. Doorstep interviewers who come across householders who never watch television, men who have no interest in cars or women who hate buying clothes often display quite unprofessional reactions, because such people tend to make routine questions and answers more difficult to deal with. Good interview design ensures that such eventualities present no problems.

The principles of good practice

Your interview style may differ according to whom you are interviewing. Your approach to a teenager in a youth club, an elderly person at home or a senior manager in their workplace will be likely to involve some variations of verbal and non-verbal behaviour, although the principles of good practice are always the same:

1. Make the interviewee feel comfortable. Always arrange the location so that your respondent can achieve a high degree of rapport with you, can answer your questions thoughtfully and in confidence and will give you the detailed responses that your study requires. Background noise from a television, a constantly ringing phone, street traffic, lots of people moving around, chilly weather, friends or relatives listening in are all things to avoid.

2. How you handle the paperwork is important. The research schedules shouldn't be too prominent, but, when you are ready to begin, you should have them easily available without having to fumble around in your bag or briefcase. If you are using prompt cards, you should aim to produce these easily as and when they are needed in the course of the interview. Manual dexterity is a surprisingly important badge of professionalism.

3. Conduct the interview at a steady pace – but allow the speed to be dictated by the style of the interviewee. Don't rush, but keep moving through the questions. Make sure that the interviewee is free to offer you additional material that might be pertinent to your enquiry.

4. The high art of interviewing should make it possible for the encounter to feel like a natural conversation, although you will be the instigator of the topics for discussion and the determinant of the direction it takes. This model has implications for the design of the interview schedule and means that you shouldn't run with it until you are satisfied that it follows an interesting, logical and natural 'conversational' pattern.

5. If you are using a tape recorder, it is essential that you arrange your interview setting so that your equipment can be set up efficiently and quickly. Don't forget to take with you all the necessary recording equipment including a stand-alone mike

and audio tapes. The availability of good quality battery-operated machines means that you shouldn't have to worry about taking extension leads or adaptors, or apologise for using the interviewee's electricity. You must always ask interviewees if they are happy to agree to be audio-recorded, and, in doing so, you must reinforce your assurances about confidentiality by telling them what will happen to the tapes. Make sure you click the 'record' button, or, as happened to an experienced colleague of mine this week, you'll end up with a blank tape.

6. When the substance of the interview is complete, you may need to check some basic details: questions about age, occupation and domestic status are best not asked at the beginning (unless you need to do so for quota sampling purposes).

7. Always remember to thank your interviewee courteously, not only for sparing you their time, but also for sharing their personal thoughts with you. Depending on the subject matter you have covered, never underestimate the extent to which your interviewee might be left feeling exposed and vulnerable if they have discussed matters they might not normally mention in the ordinary course of a conversation. You may need to repeat the assurances you have already given about confidentiality and, of course, to respect those assurances in practice. Never be tempted to gossip about things your interviewees have shared with you in confidence.

8. After you have left the setting, find a quiet corner so that you can make additional notes about the interview, while being careful to recognise the primacy of the words of the interviewee, even if they didn't all seem to make sense, and especially if they contradicted your own expectations or assumptions.

The design of interview schedules

Interview schedules and self-completion questionnaires are – or should be – different in their construction. Whereas with mailed questionnaires, both questions and available answers are usually prestructured, a good interviewer will use pre-planned questions to prompt relatively unstructured replies; the responses will either be written down verbatim (or audio-recorded) or will be accurately interpreted so that, in your response sheet, they fit the coded categories you have created during the preparatory and planning stage. A good interviewer will sometimes need to check back with the interviewee to ensure that the coding employed accurately reflects what was said and what the interviewee meant by it.

In your own project, you should aim to keep both your questions and your project as a whole as straightforward as possible. Most beginning researchers start out with schedules that try to cover too much ground. Rigorously pursued exploratory and pilot stages will demonstrate to you the importance of specificity of focus and concentrating on a limited range of topics.

When the people you are interviewing are talking with a stranger about possibly sensitive or worrying topics, it is easy for them to lose concentration or go off at a tangent. It is your job to keep them on track. Good interviewing aims at the careful extraction of ideas, experiences, feelings and beliefs from the maelstrom that makes up people's normal existence.

Interviews can be about anything and everything, depending on the context of the project and the objectives of the researcher. It doesn't matter. The principles of good interviewing are completely generic, and professional interviewers – equipped with a well-prepared questionnaire – can focus their work on any topic under the sun.

The interviews may be the whole of a project, or only a part of it. For example, side by side with the survey, the researcher may be carrying out a programme of observations of behaviour. Or, in medical research, the main study may involve a clinical trial of a pharmaceutical product, while an important part of the feedback requires details to be given by patients about their perception of the treatment and its consequences or the presence of pain or discomfort in its wake.

Examples drawn from six classes of interview data

Six classes of data can be gathered through interviews. Here they are, together with five examples of each. As you can see, the boundaries between the categories are not always clear or absolute:

1. Facts about the 'here and now'

How old are you?

When you go to the theatre, how much money do you normally spend at the bar?

What brand of shirt are you wearing?

(Through observation) What time after dawn does the first bird come to your bird table, and what kind of a bird is it?

What are your shop's takings at the end of today?

2. What the interviewee knows

Do you know exactly how much you pay for gas, electricity and water every year?

Do you know anybody who eats deep-fried Mars Bars?

Do you know the name of the president of France?

How many fingers am I pressing on your back?

Do you know what the speed limit is on this stretch of road?

3. Facts about past events

How many times did you go on holiday last year, and where did you go?

Have you ever eaten a deep-fried Mars Bar?

How did you come to be a lap dancer?

When did you last exceed the speed limit whilst driving?

When did you buy your car?

4. Feelings

What aspects of your current degree course make you feel (a) happy, (b) disappointed and (c) angry?

Are you frightened of rats?

When you were a child, did you have an emotionally warm relationship with your father?

What was it like to spend Christmas alone?

When you are driving, what kinds of things might make you angry?

5. Attitudes or opinions

In your opinion, is the teaching on your degree course generally poor, of mixed quality, or generally good?

Are you for or against the plan to open a residential home for recovering drug addicts in your street?

What action would you take (as a shopkeeper) if you caught a customer stealing your goods? (This is a hypothetical question and, as such, it is effectively tapping into respondents' attitudes, although it might also be inviting them to draw on previous experience in the response they give. The answers to hypothetical questions about the future are notoriously difficult to interpret.)

At the next general election, which party will you vote for?

Would you say that politicians in general are (a) honest, (b) hard-working and (c) clever?

6. **Beliefs**

Do you believe in life after death?

Do you think that, for you, next year will be better than, worse than, or about the same as this year has been?

Do you expect shares in BP to rise or fall in the next six months?

Do you agree or disagree with the statement: 'We all get what we deserve in life'?

Do you think that, on the whole, the advice that doctors give should be followed by the patient?

exercise

In respect of each of these six categories, and with reference to the exemplified questions, consider the likely accuracy of the answers you might be given. Also, in each category, what does the idea of 'accuracy' mean?

Preparing your interview schedule

Even if you will be the only person doing the interviewing, you should nevertheless use design principles of a high standard and include clarifying instructions for the interviewer according to best practice. This will ensure that you are reminded to follow consistent procedures in each interview.

You will begin with the short script of your introduction and preamble:

Excuse me, I'm a (third year) research student at the University of ... and I'm carrying out a survey of how shopkeepers or store managers deal with theft by customers. Would it be possible to arrange a time when you might be willing to talk to me about your experience? I won't identify any shops or individuals by name, but the results will provide a broad account of retail theft in this area.

There is no absolute rule about how to embark on the 'structured conversation' that will be your interview. It may depend on the topic, your preferred style, or your estimate of the attitudes of the respondents. Some may wish to get on with it quickly because they are busy; others may need reassurance; others, with time on their hands, may be happy to engage in conversation for far longer than you yourself have time for. Just as in writing an essay, you will need to experiment with a range of options before you feel happy with the lead-in. Let's try this one.

1. I presume you have experience of customers trying to steal from your shop. How often would you say that it happens?

	Every day
	At least once a week
	At least once a month
	Less often than that

2. When was the last time you caught anybody stealing or trying to steal from you?

3. Can you tell me about that occasion? Prompt: What sort of a person was it? How did you discover it? What happened? What action did you take? How did you feel about it? (*Follow it through as far as it can be taken.*)

4. Has any thief been prosecuted as a result of your actions in your shop?

5. (If so) Do you know what happened in court?

6. What feelings did you have about the experience?

7. Have you ever experienced threats from anybody as a result of actions you have taken or might have taken over shop theft? **Prompt:** (*Focus on the most recent threat.*) What happened?

How did it make you feel? What, if any, action did you take? *(Follow it through as far as it can be taken.)*

8. In your opinion, is shop theft less or more of a problem than it used to be in this area?

You can see that, after the relatively straightforward question 1, I have left you to think about how you might design coded responses to these questions. It's not a study I have carried out, nor have I planned, prepared or piloted it so, to a large extent, the possible answers and the layout of your schedule can only be guessed at. The questions themselves might need further revision, but it's a reasonable example of an early draft questionnaire in the making.

In designing your interview schedule, you need to follow these guidelines:

1. Be prepared to use your creative skills to the full.
2. Having settled on the research question that is driving your project, you should map out the topics you plan to cover in your interview.
3. Try to work them into a logical and smooth-flowing sequence.
4. You will almost certainly be trying to cover too much ground. Reduce it.
5. *This is very important:* Although you will be doing (or will already have done) a literature survey in respect of the topic, you should look at two bodies of literature to get ideas about questions to ask and how to ask them:
   - The first is the body of literature specific to your topic. You may well find material you wish to replicate in the form that another researcher has already used. Make sure that you acknowledge the source of any 'borrowed' material of this kind.
   - The second is less obvious, but, in my experience, just as useful. Get into the habit of looking at *any* questionnaires that *any* researchers have used in respect of *any* topic. It is impossible for you to be guided precisely in research design by what others have done, but, if you look at them with an open and enquiring mind, you will get lots of usable ideas about the formatting of questions or coded answers.

Once you have reached the point of having a draft schedule, having used some of the pre-piloting and exploratory techniques outlined in Chapter 3, you will move towards full piloting. This is particularly important for your coding scheme, and you may need rather more trial interviews than you had anticipated in order to ensure you can handle all the responses your questions will evoke.

Finally

Here, in brief, are some terms you may come across and need to know about.

Prompts

Prompts (which you should build into your own interview schedule) indicate nudges you give to the interviewee in order to ensure you are getting complete information. Sometimes they take the form of structured or closed questions, but *running prompts* may require you to say, 'Yes, and anything else?' 'Is that everybody?'

Probes

There are two kinds of probes:

- *Clarifying* probes are used to deal with any ambiguity or vagueness in what the interviewee has said
- *Exploratory* probes are employed when the interviewer needs to be certain that the interviewee has answered fully.

Prompt cards

Prompt cards are widely used in interviewing. They enable you to ask sensitive questions about money in which the respondent can indicate a band into which the relevant figure falls; or you can offer a long list of options (for example, makes and models of cars) from which the respondent is invited to pinpoint one or more; or you can display pictures if it seems appropriate to do so. Prompt cards should be neatly printed on good quality card, using a large font size (at least 18pt); for your benefit, each card should be clearly

numbered in order of usage and you should have them well organised and easily accessible before each interview.

Analogue scales

Analogue scales (which can have any number of points) are used
to allow respondents to indicate degrees of something. They should
be displayed, together with the stated question, on a prompt card,
so that the interviewee gets a visual sense of the range.

Their use in assessments of pain is very common: for example,
on a scale of 0–10 in which 0 indicates 'no pain', how would you
rate the painfulness of your toothache, arthritis or giving birth to
your child?

0   1   2   3   4   5   6   7   8   9   10

exercise

Consider:
- The problem of obtaining reliable indicators of pain
- The extent to which an analogue scale solves the problem
- What other methods might be appropriate?
- Would they get better results than an analogue scale
  approach?

Inventories

There are thousands of personality, lifestyle and health-related
inventories that have been developed and validated by research
psychologists for use in a range of contexts. Some of them are available for general use; some are strictly copyrighted and can only be
used on payment of a fee. They are commonly used by psychology
students at all stages of their education. One very straightforward
and frequently used example is Goldberg's General Health Questionnaire (Goldberg, 1978), which asks 28 questions beginning with
the phrase, 'Have you recently ...' For example:

... felt constantly under strain?

Not at all　No more than usual　Rather more than usual　Much more than usual

... felt, on the whole, you were doing things well?

Better than usual　About the same　Less well than usual　Much less well

Although inventories can be used with mailed questionnaires, it is more usual for them to be administered within the framework of an interview: 'Would you mind answering these questions for me, please?'

The great advantage of using inventories like this (apart from the fact that you are saved the trouble of designing them) is that published norms are often available so that you can compare your own results with those obtained in other studies.

Coding for the analysis

When you have completed your programme of interviews, you will normally expect to use SPSS for data analysis, and it makes sense, when you have completed the pilot stage and are ready to go with a finished interview schedule, for you to build in relevant coding systems that will facilitate speedy data inputting when the time comes. You can even, if you are confident, pre-code SPSS entries during the interview without disturbing the natural flow of your 'conversation'. This allows you to enter your data into SPSS with minimal effort even while you are still continuing to arrange and conduct research interviews.

If you asked me to recommend just one book on ...
research interviewing *it would be:*

Keats, Daphne (2000)
Interviewing: A Practical Guide for Students and Professionals,
London, Sage

8 Analysing your survey data

The task of data analysis should be to the forefront of your mind from the moment you start to plan your research project. The design of your questionnaire or interview schedule must take account of the challenges you will face when you get to the stage of working out what it all means.

In particular, you need to be sure that you are gathering appropriate data on your key variables – the variables you will use when exploring results between different groups.

People get in a terrible muddle trying to distinguish between dependent and independent variables. I can't improve on Nicholas Walliman's (2001, p. 121) definition, which is about as clear and succinct as you can get: 'In causal statements, which describe what is sometimes called a "cause and effect" relationship, the concept or variable that is the cause is referred to as the "independent variable" (because it varies independently), and the variable that is affected is referred to as the "dependent variable" (because it is dependent on the independent variable). An example is "smoking a lot makes one ill", where "smoking a lot" is the independent variable and "ill" is the dependent variable.' Experiments are planned in such a way as to vary the independent variable in order to observe the effects, but the distinction applies equally to survey research and even to causal statements made by qualitative researchers.

Often, the key variables may include:

1. **Gender**
   In many studies, it would be surprising if you didn't want to have the possibility of comparing answers obtained from men with answers obtained from women – gender is a relatively straightforward dichotomous variable (that is, one with two, and just two, elements).

2. **Age**
   Are you going to want to distinguish between age groups? If

so, are you asking for date of birth, precise current age or current age within an age band and how wide should the age bands be?

3. Social class

What about your respondents' social class backgrounds? This can be tricky and there is a vast literature dealing with it. Do you ask for occupation and relate it to government-defined systems for identifying socioeconomic position? Since 2001 in the UK, the National Statistics Socio-economic Classification (NS-SEC) has been used in government research. It contains eight classes ranging from higher managerial and professional occupations (Class 1) to those who have never worked or are the long-term unemployed (Class 8). More information can be found on the website www.statistics.gov.uk. What if your respondents are students? Do you ask them about their father's occupation? Or their mother's? Or do you ask the respondent to *say* what social class they belong to? If you do that, do you give them a prompt card with a list on it, or do you wait and see what they come up with? (Most people will say 'middle class'.) Unless the theoretical foundations of your study require it, you may well decide that the variable of social class is not worth the complexity and ambiguity that is inherent in it.

4. Ethnic identities

Ethnicity is a difficult area, partly because of the sensitivity of the topic (and therefore the pressure upon you to ensure that whatever you say in conclusion is based on valid and reliable evidence) and partly because the very nature of ethnicity is complex and becomes ever more so with each new generation that is born and grows up subject to the cultural influences of the land of their birth. There is a grave danger of polarising ethnic differences when the cultural frameworks that may influence them are more subtle than that.

5. Religion

Unless your study requires religious faith or church attendance to be a key variable, it is probably best avoided. In the modern world, the sociology and psychology of religion are highly complex, and it would, for example, be naive in the extreme to distinguish simply between churchgoers and non-churchgoers,

Muslims and Christians, unless you were working with a hypothesis that was specifically based on that distinction.

6. **Variables specific to your project**
This is a much more fruitful way forward. What are the variables that your research question will require you to write about and base your conclusions on? Are you sure that the questions you are asking will give you what you need? If you are planning to use some aspect of individuality (for example, happiness, professional experience, good looks, body shape) as a key variable, how are you going to assess it? Might you want to link some descriptive or exploratory questions together in order to emerge with a numerical score? (For example, the answers to a number of questions might be combined during data analysis to give you a dichotomous or scaled measure of 'contentment/discontent' or any other personal quality.) If you plan to use variables such as 'respect for the cultural heritage' or 'awareness of sexually transmitted diseases', have you worked out how you are going to rate them? I could go on and list hundreds of such examples, but the key point remains the same: you need to have thought about the practicalities of data analysis (coding, rating and dealing with ambiguities) long before you reach that crucial stage.

In an experiment or quasi experiment you need to be certain that the questions you plan to ask or the measurements you intend to use in order to evaluate outcomes will work equally well with all the groups you are comparing.

As long as you have properly carried out exploratory and pilot studies, you will find that all these matters are fully covered but if you have skimped on them, as many inexperienced researchers are tempted to do, you will wish in the middle of your data analysis stage that you'd planned it better.

In this chapter, I will take you, step by step, through the normal process of data analysis, although, as with everything else in a research project (large or small), the precise pattern of what you need and choose to do will be unique to you. Even if you and a friend were to decide independently to use an identical questionnaire or schedule, I'd lay odds of 100 to 1 that, unless you conferred, your respective analytical stages would contain substantial variations.

If you asked me to recommend just one book on ...
survey data analysis *it would be:*

Kent, Raymond (2001)
Data Construction and Data Analysis for Survey Research,
Basingstoke, Palgrave Macmillan

Step 1: Think design, think analysis

The design of your questionnaire or interview schedule should, in most respects, lend itself to ease of analysis.

Above all, in mailed questionnaires, you should keep to a minimum the number of open-ended questions that invite lengthy written responses, because they can prove problematic when you subject them to quantitative analysis. Within the framework of an interview schedule, you'll be able to accommodate your respondent's open-ended verbal replies because of the coding frame you provide yourself with and the control you maintain over the situation; you can convert verbal contributions into usable material, being careful not to distort or corrupt their meaning, and you can use probes to achieve clarification as and when necessary.

In a mailed questionnaire, researchers are tempted to include far too many questions that invite unstructured responses. A small number is fine, but, with time pressing at the analysis stage, you will quickly reach the point where you decide that you can't do justice to all such replies.

You wouldn't believe how many times I have been approached by people who tell me that they have 'just carried out a project'. They say they have lots of lovely data, but they are feeling at a loss to know how to deal with it. They wonder whether I couldn't just help them with the analysis and write-up. Ideally, they would like to leave me with an untidy pile of forms and hope that I will come up with the findings they are sure are there if only they can be dug out. I have learnt that a common problem with such material is that they contain a large number of lengthy answers to open-ended questions, and although I may feel sympathetic towards the request, I regretfully decline. Research – or good research, anyway – simply does not work like that. In my experience, such a project is dead in the water because of the apparent lack of careful planning and forethought. If you end up with unmanageable data and an overwhelming sense of helplessness, you can usually conclude that something was missing from the planning process.

Step 2: Living with your data

After you have completed the planning stage, and even as you are gathering your data:

- You will be doing preliminary mental analyses – getting a sense of the shapes and patterns that are emerging – often quite early on in the data collection process.
- You will be alert to any ways in which, despite all your preparation and piloting, the answers being given look likely to present you with problems of interpretation or analysis, for example if there is a significant tendency to 'add' an answer to what you had thought was a complete range of options.
- You will be thinking actively and making notes that you may want to build in to your eventual write-up.
- You will be deciding how best to handle the responses to open-ended questions: you will spend time with this data and see whether you can devise useful categories into which the replies, or most of them, will fall.
- You will keep your papers in good order, using a numbering system for purposes of identification. You may start to input data into your SPSS file, especially as you reach the end of the data-gathering process and while you are waiting for a few late questionnaires or interview schedules to materialise.
- You will check the completeness of your responses, for example some people just don't notice if you have printed your questions on both sides of the paper (perhaps you shouldn't have done), so that you find yourself with alternate blank sheets. Can you go back and ask them to complete the job? It's worth a try.
- You will begin to formulate your ideas for the task of analysis. Research is never a linear process, neither at the planning stage, nor at the point when the fruits of your efforts begin to emerge. You go backwards and forwards, testing ideas, perhaps

playing around with some preliminary data analyses by hand, seeing what works and what doesn't, thinking about it, and jotting down thoughts prompted by it. Data is live, it is original and it is the product of your own efforts: it deserves to be used to full effect, and to that end you should at this stage be devoting to it all your spare time and energy.

Step 3: Data entry using SPSS

SPSS is the Statistical Package for the Social Sciences. It was launched in 1989 and, with growing availability of access to PCs, it has become the standard analytical tool for most survey researchers. In order to use it efficiently, you need to have attended beginner's classes in it or to have access to a colleague, supervisor or technician who can help you get started. The program provides an on-screen, self-help tutorial and, like most software programs, it's relatively easy to use at a basic level, but you may need to seek guidance initially.

The first and in many ways the most important thing to emphasise is this: SPSS is a tool and it is only a tool. It may be more sophisticated than a bricklayer's trowel or an egg whisk, but in each case, the worker needs to have a clear sense of the nature of the job that needs doing. At the end of the day, it is the skill employed by the craftsperson that determines the quality of the end-product. SPSS will do all sorts of wonderful things when you ask it to and, with each version that comes out, the range and speed of what it can do gets better and better. But you still need to know what to ask it to do and how to interpret the product when SPSS has delivered its harvest.

So, let us assume that you have waited until all your data is in. (Data is a plural noun, the plural of datum, and as such it should command a plural verb. You will certainly find examples of researchers who write 'When all your data are in ... ', but, in truth, the singular verb always sits more comfortably with a noun that, in a research context, has taken on a meaning that implies a single (if grouped) entity.) You have in front of you a pile of, let's say, 250 completed questionnaires or interview schedules. You've checked them all and you are satisfied that they are as complete as you can get them. They've all got a reference number by which they can be uniquely identified. This is the procedure (the details can vary between different versions of SPSS. I am using Version 12.0.1):

1. Create your SPSS file by clicking on *File*. Then on the drop-down menu click on *New* and *Data*.
2. Next you will need to 'define your variables' by clicking on the *Variable View* tab at the foot of your screen. This enables you to create, within your new file, columns headed by each of your variable names and to distinguish their respective qualities.
3. Start to input your data. You'll find that you begin very slowly, but in no time at all – certainly by the time you get to record number 30 or 40 – you'll be going much faster. Be careful to be accurate. At the end, if you want to be a true professional, you should do a 1-in-10 accuracy check to see whether there is a worrying level of errors. You might like to link up with a colleague so that you can help each other do respective 1-in-10 checks: one person reads out, the other watches the screen.
4. To help you at this stage and later, you will need to have access to one of the many detailed guides to SPSS. Some universities produce their own SPSS handbooks, and there is an embarrassment of riches in the bookshops.

If you asked me to recommend just one book on ...
SPSS *it would be:*

Pallant, J (2005)
SPSS Survival Manual, 2nd edn, Maidenhead, Open University Press.

Now you've converted all that research effort, all those conversations, all that administrative process into ... what? A set of numbers – probably with some words in there as well. Your data is ready to be processed.

Step 4: Don't despise your frequency distributions

You would be amazed how many times I have had to say to students when they turn up with a rough draft outline of their work,

'But where are your frequency distributions?' Frequency distributions (FDs) form the bedrock of your study: in respect of each question that you asked, how many responses did you get to each of the options available?

Some novice researchers think these descriptive statistics are too boring to quote; they want to move straightaway to more complex calculations. It's as though, having lived with the exercise for so long, they lose sight of the importance of giving the reader – to whom the material is completely new – a clear view of the basic facts.

So, no matter what other analyses you plan to pursue, get SPSS to give you frequency distributions for all your variables. Print them out and think about what they mean. Write notes. Turn them into neat tables or draft charts using Word or Excel.

For example, a student, Kay Verdon, asked a convenience sample of 160 students, 'What did you have for breakfast this morning?' The frequency distribution, after editing and conversion to MS, looked like this.

Student breakfast:	N	%
Hot food	2	1.3
Cereal and/or bread or toast	34	21.3
Tea or coffee	18	11.3
Nothing	105	65.6
Other (chocolate bar)	1	0.6

You should check to see that the numbers all add up. The percentage column might sometimes come to 99.9 per cent or 100.1 per cent, as it does here. Don't worry about it, that's OK.

You will probably need to decide how to handle any 'don't know', 'no information' or 'not applicable' responses. Sometimes they should be included, sometimes not; in the latter case, reference is usually made to them at the foot of the table.

You may wish to enlarge on the bare information contained in the table; for example, my student commented that the two who had a hot breakfast had had a traditional fry-up in one case and scrambled egg in the other. She also went on to explore reasons given by her sample for the answer 'nothing': a quarter of the men said they 'felt nauseous', while 29 per cent of the women chose to take a shower instead of eating.

As you edit, you will be starting to decide which frequency

distributions you might want to incorporate in your report. Don't include too many because they can disturb the visual and interpretive flow of your narrative; it will be appropriate to 'bury' some of them in the text rather than present them as tables. The proportion of frequency distributions you use may depend on how well you formulated your research question at the outset: if it was tightly formulated, you will only have a few and will need to use most of them; but if you had pages and pages of questions because you didn't clarify a specific research question at all, then you will end up with a multitude of rather dreary 'facts' that will make your report difficult for the reader to interpret. My youthful first research report was, I am ashamed to say now, like that.

Although all your SPSS data and workings can be saved in an SPSS file, I also tend to store the finished workings neatly in a Word file so that they can easily be incorporated into the text. (As always with computing, make sure you have portable disk backup copies of everything – including the SPSS data file. And don't forget to keep saving your work as you go.)

Step 5: At this point, life gets more complicated

A very few studies may do no more than make use of frequency distributions, but most projects require the analysis of data to be taken some way further than that – perhaps, at an advanced level, involving a great deal of data manipulation. SPSS has made this a lot easier than it once was, but deciding what to do next still depends first and foremost on the researcher's own questioning spirit, conceptual awareness and a willingness to learn what is possible and how to achieve it. It also, of course, depends to some extent on the nature of the research question that is being asked.

There are two distinct patterns to your likely next stage of analysis:

1. One leads to the preparation of statistics based on the information you have obtained in respect of one variable and how it compares with the information you've obtained from another: Step 6 describes this process. Further down the line, you can also explore the impact of a third variable on the relationship between the other two (Step 7).

2. The second pattern uses analytical techniques that are linked to either numbers (for example, age, money, or any 'score' that the researcher has built in to the analysis) or the ranking of qualities in some kind of meaningful numerical order (for example, five chocolate bars, ranked 1–5 according to the expressed preference of samples of men and women). The researcher can explore differences in averages among separate groups within the overall sample or test out whether there are similarities (correlations) or differences in the numerical patterns displayed by identified groups or subgroups. I will consider each of these processes in Steps 8 and 9.

Step 6: Cross-tabulations

When you have studied carefully your frequency distributions, you may want to see what happens if you look at two of them together. For example, in the student breakfast example, the hypothesis might have been: 'There will be a gender difference in breakfast eating patterns'. Of course, you could hypothesise which way the difference will go but, in an exploratory survey like this, you don't have to. Or you could adopt a null hypothesis: 'There will be no difference between men and women in breakfast eating patterns.'

My student, Kay Verdon, interviewed equal numbers of men and women, and we know from the frequency distribution that 65.6 per cent of the total sample told her that they ate nothing for breakfast. Was this result the same for both men and women?

As soon as you ask a question like that, you need to create tables that have breadth as well as depth; columns as well as rows. We call them 'cross-tabs'. You have to decide what you want, but SPSS will deliver the results at the touch of a button, as it does with our student's modest example below.

What did you have for breakfast?	Men	%	Women	%	Total	%
Something	36	45%	19	24%	55	34%
Nothing	44	55%	61	76%	105	66%
TOTAL	80		80		160	

SPSS will carry out a significance test for you (but see the note on inferential statistics at the end of this chapter, together with Step 10 and Chapter 15), and this leads to you adding at the foot of the table the results of a Chi-square calculation:

$$\chi^2 = 8.004, df = 1, p<.01.$$

This means that, within the limits imposed by the quality of your sample, the figures are seen to be statistically significant, putting you in a position to say that, so far as *this* sample is concerned, there was a difference between the genders: women were more likely than men to have nothing for breakfast.

You may now be able to see why it is advisable to gather the fruits of your work in a Word file as well as in an SPSS file. This allows you to play around with the table – deciding whether to omit some cells, for example, and settling on which way round the columns and rows should run.

You will want to include percentages linked to each cell. Here I have got rid of the decimal place, which is good practice when the total number in each group is less than a hundred. The way in which you calculate the percentages depends entirely on the way you worded your analytical question. Our student asked whether there was a difference between the genders, so the logical approach was to calculate the proportion of men who had no breakfast compared with the proportion of women.

If, as is often the case, your main aim as a student is to *explore* your chosen topic and provide descriptive analytical data about it, then the presentation of frequency distributions and cross-tabs – checked for statistical significance – will probably take you as far as you would wish to go.

Step 7: Third variable analysis

Once you have produced your cross-tabs, you may want to move a step further. This will depend largely on whether your sample is big enough, but, if it is, you will be entering the realm of third variable analysis.

Here, to illustrate the point, is another example from one of my students. Susan Clark set out to explore the use of mobile phones among men and women of different ages. The student gathered a convenience sample in two urban areas, and found initially that there was no significant difference in mobile phone usage between the groups she was targeting.

However, in one of her questions she asked people whether they felt embarrassed about using their mobile in public. (The study was done in 2001; the situation may well have changed by now.) She found, predictably you might say, that the younger group (aged up to 30) were significantly less likely to feel embarrassed than the older group (40-plus): only 14 per cent of the former compared with 33 per cent of the latter (p<.05). Similarly, Clark discovered that more women were embarrassed than men: 32 per cent compared with 8 per cent (p<.01).

But the question arose of whether these statistics tell the whole – or even the true – story. What happens if you explore in different 2 × 2 cross-tabs the men and women separately and in sequence defined by age? The results were illuminating:

- There was no difference between young men and young women: they were overwhelmingly unselfconscious about the public use of mobiles.
- Nor was there any gender difference in the older age group: they were split roughly 50/50.
- The men of all ages were equally comfortable with the public use of mobiles.
- But when Clark examined her female sample, a very different story emerged, and a large and significant difference (p<.01) was demonstrated. Young women were perfectly comfortable with the use of phones in public; but women over the age of 40 were not. Indeed, it was largely this female subgroup in the total sample who led the author initially to argue that there was an age difference in the comfortable use of phones in public.

Now, you may say that these findings are all very obvious. But that misses the point. Whatever the social irrelevance of the finding (and it is actually the kind of conclusion that commercial companies are keen to obtain), the methodological lesson to be learnt is that the initial table was misleading. There is no *overall* difference between the age groups – just among young women and older women. Similarly, the difference identified between men and women doesn't hold good at a younger age; in other words, to argue a gender difference among young people on the basis of the original figures would have constituted a spurious argument – even though the original cross-tab led in that direction.

Third variable analysis is an essential tool in the development of theories around your subject and it can prevent you making inappropriate general assertions that turn out on further exploration only to apply under given limited conditions. Of course, age and gender are not the only independent variables that can be manipulated in this way (although they are the most common). Others frequently drawn into the equation include social class, ethnic identity, educational background and voting intention.

There are computer programs that take you far beyond third variable analysis – but that's for another time and place.

Step 8: Comparing numerical values – measures of central tendency

The concept of the 'average' is widely understood. In statistics, the 'average' can be represented in three ways: the mode, median or mean. The mode is a crude indicator and is the most frequently occurring score in the frequency distribution. The median is the middle score in the FD; it divides the sample into two equal parts. The mean is the most frequently used measure of central tendency and is computed by dividing the sum of the scores by the number of cases that contribute to that sum. The mean is almost always the right measure to use, although the median may be preferred if the FD includes some wildly extreme scores at either end of the scale.

Here is an illustration of how the three measures of central tendency can vary in a single project. A student, Abigail Cooke, set out to discover whether women are more frightened of spiders than men. She asked a convenience sample of 126 to complete a 10-point fear scale (in which a rating of 10 indicated 'terrified') and produced this bar chart showing the results.

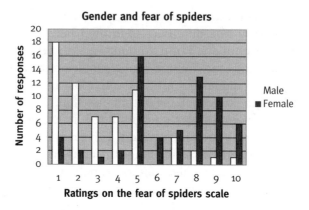

Gender and fear of spiders

There were equal numbers of men and women in the sample, and the measures of central tendency were as follows:

Measure of central tendency	Men	Women
Mean	3.3	6.5
Median	2.2	7.5
Mode	1	5

Although, at first sight, on the basis of these figures the appropriate conclusion would appear to be obvious, it cannot be asserted until a significance test is carried out.

Comparison of means as a technique of research analysis is more common in projects that are linked to the world of academic psychology or to one or other of the natural sciences. The approach is dependent on the availability of data that reflects numerical values, for example age, precise details of income, productivity levels, body measurements, scores on a rating scale or figures obtained by the completion of a personality or other test. The arithmetic values are entered into SPSS. After you have asked SPSS to compute an average figure (normally a mean or median) for the total sample, you can instruct it to do so for the subgroups within your sample and to carry out probability checks to see whether the differences identified between any of the subgroups are statistically significant.

For example, Caitlin Thoday, another student, hypothesised that 'first-born children will score lower on a simple extraversion questionnaire than later-born children.' She gathered a random sample of 100 university students, and administered a newly designed six-question personality test drawing on Eysenck's early work (1958):

- The sample was equally divided by gender: 50/50.
- 48 per cent of the students were first-born; 45 per cent were born second or later; 6 per cent were only children; and one was a twin.
- Mean age was 22.9 and the mode was 20.
- The extraversion score (escore) ran from a low of zero to a high of six.
- The mean escore for the whole sample was 3.18.
- Testing the hypothesis, the student reported that first-born children had a mean escore of 3.15 compared with 3.24 for second and later borns.
- The difference was not statistically significant.

The hypothesis was therefore rejected. As a good student researcher, Thoday examined the answers given to each of the separate component questions but, using the Chi-square test, she failed to find any significant differences between the responses made by the two groups. She looked at the possibility of gender or age influences but found none.

This illustration neatly demonstrates that not all research produces positive results. Students understandably get excited when they succeed in demonstrating significant differences; conversely, they express disappointment when they don't. But that is to misunderstand the nature and process of the research enterprise. Every result has meaning, and negative findings are just as important as positive findings, although if they are unexpected, then the researcher will normally move on and try to explore why that was so. For example, in her work, Thoday wondered whether the reason was to be found in the instrument used or in the fact that her sample was made up only of university students.

Step 9: Comparing numerical values – correlations and rank order

The second principal way of analysing number-based data is to ask whether the pattern demonstrated in one data set is similar to or 'correlated with' the pattern demonstrated in another. Some complex analyses of this kind are commonplace in economics and quite frequently found in most areas of academic research. For entry-level students, it is generally advisable to seek supervisory guidance because it isn't always obvious which measurement systems or which ways of testing probability levels are appropriate; on the other hand, I've often found that different statisticians give you different advice.

Correlations can be based on raw data: for example, in a sample of 100, SPSS will give you a quick correlation between IQ score and the rating achieved when answering questions that produce a measure of 'quality of life (QOL)'. I have no idea what such a calculation would deliver, but a perfect positive correlation = 1.00; a completely random relationship = 0.00; and a perfect negative relationship = –1.00.

An alternative approach and one that is much simpler to use early in one's research career is to think in terms of a rank order correlation. The best way of explaining this will be to describe the work of another of my students. Natalie Start gathered a convenience sample of 50 male students and 50 female students; the inclusion criterion was for each of them to have experienced an intimate relationship for at least 12 months. On the back of an exploratory study, Start identified 10 factors and asked her sample to rate each item for its importance in maintaining their 'own intimate relationship as "rewarding"'. She offered a four-point scale.

Having secured her data, Start calculated the rank order of the stated importance of each of her 10 factors, and she divided the sample between men and women. She obtained the following results.

Factors	Rank order for females	Rank order for males
Trust	1	2
Friendship	2	1
Feeling comfortable	3	3
Commitment	4 =	6
Emotional support	4 =	9
Sense of humour	6	5
Chemistry	7	7
Physical attraction	8 =	8
Good sex life	8 =	4
Similarities	10	10

Start carried out a Spearman's rank order correlation coefficient exercise, which gave her a positive correlation of 0.721 which was statistically significant. She was therefore able to conclude that, despite some apparent differences in respect of the emotional support and sex factors, both men and women viewed the foundations of a successful relationship in very similar ways.

Of course, as you become more experienced in research data analysis, there are many more ways of proceeding: the analysis of variance (ANOVA) is one, and factor analysis is another. But it is important that you develop your skills steadily and that, with each new calculation you make, you ensure that you understand what it means. That can be a challenge, but it's no more than your hard-earned data deserve.

Step 10: Probability

I have already referred in passing to the topic of probability. Why is it important? How should you handle it in your data analysis?

The appearance at the foot of tables or in the body of the text of what look to the layperson like hieroglyphics and the process of having to 'do sums' worry a great many students. But the reality of probability theory, at a basic level, is straightforward. Provided you learn it step by step (which is the way to learn anything, of course), then it is a stage of data analysis that you will be pleased you've done once you've done it. Moreover, probability theory is, in some form or another, relevant to all types of research activity.

Statistics *can* be extremely complex and intellectually demanding, and people's natural ability to deal with numbers varies hugely. But probability theory is more about logic than numbers; you need to understand why some apparently 'obvious' findings are not obvious at all. Indeed, they may be wrong.

The commonest way of exploring probability issues in practice is to toss a coin. While I am sitting here at my computer, I have done just that – with a £1 coin, a 2p coin and a 10p coin. The results (I promise you) were as follows:

Coin	Heads	Tails
£1	5	5
10p	3	7
2p	7	3

You can do just the same – and draw up a similar table.

Now, you know and I know that coins have an equal likelihood of falling either heads or tails, but, in 10 attempts, only the pound coin, in my experiment, obeyed that expectation. And many a naive researcher, obtaining the sorts of differences shown for the 10p and the 2p coins in my table would get very excited and claim that 70 per cent of group A (it could be women, footballers or law students) liked such and such (chocolates, sex on Sunday afternoons or getting drunk – not necessarily in that order), whereas only 30 per cent of group B (men, cricketers or history students) liked these same things. To the naive researcher, this might seem a legitimate conclusion to draw.

But, of course, it isn't, because coins don't fall 5/5 out of 10 every time. We know it from our experience. Just as we know, if we are card players, that deals from packs of cards can deliver some very peculiar hands. But 'knowing something' is not enough. And probability testing is the established way by which scientists check when we can and can't say that group A really has behaved differently from group B.

The sophistication of probability testing in areas of hard science – affecting, for example, the safety of bridges in civil engineering, the effectiveness of (and the harmful side effects induced by) some new drug or clinical procedure, or the costs of investing heavily in a newly developed fertiliser – is very complex indeed. And the rules about when you can and can't use which probability tests are widely debated in academic journals. But at the entry level of research, when you want to draw conclusions based on often imprecise data, some of those rules are a distraction. (See the note on inferential statistics at the end of this chapter.) If you move forward into higher levels of research activity, then you will also move forward to a more advanced or more rigorous exercise in probability testing. But in Chapter 15, I introduce you to eight significance tests that can be used using SPSS. You don't need to employ them for frequency distributions, but for cross-tabs, for comparing means and for correlations, they are essential tools of the trade.

Step 11: Dealing with open-ended questions

I have already referred to open-ended questions and the need in survey design to keep them to a minimum, but how should you handle those open-ended questions that you felt were indispensable? Their analysis is a task more akin to some aspects of qualitative research, and I shall deal with it in the first part of Chapter 12. For the moment, suffice it to say that the responses to open-ended questions in a survey can sometimes be coded and can therefore be treated as structured material. Alternatively, you can diligently digest them all and write a narrative section based on your absorption of their content. Or you can draw on them selectively to provide illustrative quotations threaded into relevant parts of your text.

In any case, in your road map, you will need to have allowed sufficient time to enable you to read the material and work through the responses, entering them on file, organising them structurally, and reaching some conclusions about their meaning.

Step 12: Drawing your analysis to a close

You should now be ready to begin work on your write-up, which I discuss in Chapter 13. In major studies, the professional researcher often finds that, at this stage, the mind also turns to the need for ways in which further light might be thrown on some of the results that have emerged – perhaps by means of further investigation using different methods or by carrying out yet more detailed analyses of the survey data to hand. In time-limited studies, this is less likely. Once you've completed your data analysis, you'll be ready to breathe a sigh of relief (or pause for breath) and then move on to the final phase of composing your report and delivering it as a finished product.

a note on inferential statistics

Researchers are faced with the need to draw conclusions – or make inferences – on the basis of necessarily partial data. Statistics as a science has been developed to tell researchers how

a note on inferential statistics *continued*

much reliance they can place on the inferences they wish to make: that is, how confident they can be that the conclusions drawn from their sample truly reflect the situation in the population from which the sample was drawn.

Some statisticians argue that tests of significance can, or should only be used if:

- the researcher has used a simple random sample (or a sample that mimics the properties of a simple random sample) selected from a complete sampling frame of the population of interest
- the response rate (at both respondent and item levels) is complete, that is, 100 per cent.

Inferential statistics provide an estimate of the probability that, if the phenomena (correlation, difference between groups and so on) exist in the population, the sample data would take the form observed by the researcher.

This position presents clear and dispiriting implications for undergraduate or other entry-level researchers in the social and psychological sciences because very few students will meet the sampling requirements specified.

Such statisticians argue that students should not be misled into thinking that inferential statistics can be used on population data, non-random samples, random samples with non-response, or any other situation that fails to meet the strict criteria specified. The mathematics doesn't work and the numbers produced are either incorrect or just irrelevant.

However, in my teaching career, I have come to accept that the purity of statistics cannot always be upheld when exercise projects are being carried out by students needing to learn about the nature of research and the methods employed in the pursuit of knowledge.

The plain fact is that, in the social and psychological sciences, statistical tests of significance are frequently employed in situa-

a note on inferential statistics *continued*

tions that fail to conform to the strict requirements just outlined – especially in non-experimental studies that compare, for example, differences between men and women, young people and older people, right-wing and left-wing voters.

It would always be better to meet the strict criteria required for statistical purity, but it is not always possible, and the argument for nonetheless employing inferential statistics is twofold:

- It is better to have an approximate measure of significance than none at all – so long as due caution is emphasised
- It is better for students to experience the *process* of testing for significance and to understand both its meaning and its shortcomings if the strict criteria have not been fully met.

Of course, where research is focused on the 'heavy end' of programme evaluation – the testing of potentially dangerous pharmaceutical products, for example – it goes without saying that the most rigorous standards of random sampling must always be employed.

The use of qualitative methods in research is almost always discussed in theoretical terms. There are particular reasons for this:

1. Although qualitative research – broadly defined – has a long history, much of the intellectual argument for its expanded use emerged in the second half of the twentieth century and was linked to perceived weaknesses in quantitative research. Particular aspects targeted were the partial view of complex social reality that survey research was seen to be delivering and the extent to which this limited perspective was largely driven by the researcher's own perception of the field being investigated. Concern was felt that the interviewee's subjective perspective was not adequately accommodated by quantitative methods.

2. Qualitative research uses its gathered data to create theoretical ideas, compared with experimental research that starts with a theoretical position and accumulates data in order to test its validity. The two methods have quite different research objectives.

3. The roots of qualitative research as we know it can be related to some complex areas of philosophical, psychological and sociological discourse revolving around questions such as:
   • How do we know what we know? How do we know what other people feel?
   • Is what people say different from what people do?
   • How can researchers interpret their findings without bringing into play their own prejudices, perspectives derived from their own gender, age or life experiences? Feminist writers in particular had a sense that masculine perspectives tended to be predominant in sociological

empiricism and theorising and that this demonstrated the lack of objectivity in traditional research methods.
- If we categorise people, say as black, young or disabled, and then use these categories to compare them with other people, do the comparisons have a legitimate meaning? In particular, is the meaning that researchers impose upon them the same as the subjects of the research would recognise for themselves?

It is not the primary aim of this book to consider this debate or these issues in detail, but rather, in Part 3, to approach the task of 'doing' qualitative research in a determinedly down-to-earth fashion. For the beginning researcher, the nature of the problems that have to be tackled in a qualitative methods approach, although in many ways different from those confronting the beginning researcher doing a survey or experiment, are nonetheless primarily practical.

If you ask me which method is better – quantitative or qualitative – I can only respond by saying that I find the question to be, if not meaningless, then misleading. I have carried out dozens of research projects and read hundreds of student research project reports, and I know that, whatever the method employed, research can deliver interesting and useful findings capable of influencing practice or policy and potentially making a contribution to the development of theory. I know, too, that both methods require a high degree of self-discipline and a capacity for attention to detail – qualities that characterise members of the research community in any field of endeavour.

Of course, provided adequate time and other resources are available, both methods can be employed side by side in the same project and be administered by the same researcher.

Quantitative and qualitative research are both legitimate vehicles for 'finding out' about social reality in whatever spheres of human life are the focus of your interest. But they find out different things. Those who speak or write dismissively of one or the other are flouting a fundamental rule of academic life in an open society: intellectual curiosity is the driving force of scholarship and science, and any method of exploration that delivers valid and informative results can fuel it – subject only to restraint by the principles of morality and human rights.

Both methods provide valuable learning experience for students because of the wide-ranging demands they make on researchers' own thought processes and the consequential contribution to the development of skills likely to be of use in all sorts of career routes – professional, managerial or academic. If, through the use of qualitative research, you can improve your understanding of complex issues and relationships, then the experience will almost certainly stay with you and pay dividends in the complex world of work and professional life. Elements that you will learn and that will have relevance far beyond the narrow world of social research include:

• How to access sources of evidence

• How to explore the disparate feelings and experiences of other people

• How to view individuals in their situational context

• How to organise and manage complex exploratory data

• How to interrogate, interpret and analyse verbal data

• How to write up a report that accurately reflects the evidence obtained.

To understand something about the nature of knowledge and to have learnt, by doing, what can and can't be concluded from a single research exercise will teach you a profound lesson that will stay with you for many years.

9 Studying a small sample

You've decided to explore people's feelings, thoughts or experiences in some depth. First you must learn about the principles and practice of studying a small sample. Although major qualitative research studies – carried out at doctoral level, for example, or with a view to preparing a book-length research report – may over a period of time gather samples of considerable size, it is normal for entry-level research practitioners to equate the use of qualitative methods with relatively small samples. This will be reflected in this book.

Why study a small sample?

Small sample studies have many advantages for students – both practical and theoretical. What are they?

The practical advantages are:

1. Gathering a sample of strangers is quite stressful to some people, so that working with a sample of between, say, 5 and 20 is, on the face of it, less problematic than organising a survey sample of between 50 and 120 – or more.
2. Most qualitative research methods make few if any statistical demands on the student. If you're one of those people inclined to say 'I've never been any good at maths' or 'I hate sums', then the temptation of doing an arithmetic-free research project is pretty irresistible.
3. There is a seductive appeal about being able to 'get involved' in face-to-face encounters as quickly as possible.
4. And you may feel relieved that you have avoided a lot of the painstaking brain work that is needed in the preparation of detailed survey schedules or questionnaires, together with all the exploratory testing, the pre-piloting and the piloting that goes with it.

The theoretical advantages are:

1. Reflective approaches to research are in tune with many students' preferred way of thinking. Qualitative research feels more 'human' than methods that can sometimes be portrayed as reducing everything to tick boxes and tables.
2. Allowing the interviewees to talk at length with the researcher rather than merely responding to a series of pre-planned questions suggests that the material obtained will be in some way closer to the reality of the interviewee's life.
3. If qualitative research is used as it should be, the student is able to explore respondents' feelings and experiences in ways that go beyond the crudity of traditional categories such as age, gender or ethnicity.
4. There is the possibility that the person being interviewed can exercise more democratic responsibility in the encounter. To some extent the interviewee can direct the flow of conversation, so avoiding the risk that the researcher's own background sets the agenda in an autocratic way; and if you provide the interviewee with a copy of your draft analysis of the encounter, you can invite and obtain subjective feedback.
5. If the method involves elements of observation (as it might well do), the researcher may be less reliant on what the subject *says* about what they do, and instead can actually view what they *really* do. This gives a sense of increased validity to the data-gathering process.

Identifying your research question

Small sample studies have a well-established, important and valid part to play in research. They can be used, and have been used many times, as the exploratory phase of long-term quantitative research projects, after which detailed plans can be drawn up for more structured or experimental stages of the enquiry.

But, very commonly at student level, small sample studies have been shown to have value as ends in themselves because of the way, when they are used cleverly, they throw light on feelings, prejudices and subliminal ideas that it is difficult to tap into by more structured methods. They allow respondents to supply the researcher with wide-ranging perspectives on complex issues. Almost any topic can be explored through working with a small sample, but these 10 concrete examples might help to start you thinking about your own field.

1. What does it feel like to live in an urban area with high levels of vandalism and deprivation?
2. What does it feel like before, during and after doing a bungee jump?
3. What kind of leisure time or sports facilities would people like to have available to them in their area? What factors might affect their likely usage of them?
4. Why do boys and/or girls of school age truant?
5. What is the experience of adopted people when they go in search of their birth parents?
6. In what ways does the presence of low back pain (or asthma, or being deaf, or any other physical condition) affect aspects of your life?
7. Under what circumstances do people say they drive *within* the speed limit?
8. What are the experiences of bloggers in pursuit of their hobby?
9. What does it feel like when your husband/wife/partner leaves you after years of being together?
10. By what process did hard drug users become so?

You will see that I continue to advocate the importance of having a research question clearly in your mind. Not all qualitative methodologists agree with this advice and it does depend a bit on the theoretical framework or the field in which you are working. Mason (2002, p. 17) uses the plural term, 'research questions', and refers to the idea of identifying an 'intellectual puzzle' or 'something in particular' around which you will 'develop an empirically and theoretically grounded argument' (p. 121).

There is, I think, a distinction to be drawn between a qualitative research study carried out by an experienced professional and one undertaken by an entry-level research student. My experience as a teacher tells me that, in student-led qualitative research, failure to identify an initial question can lead to inefficient drift and an inferior end-product. The absence of focus and any clear objective can result in a rambling series of descriptions and anecdotes, but making no clear point.

It is still possible to have at the back of your mind the classic anthropological theme, 'What is going on here?', so that the precise framing of your question can evolve as you proceed through data collection and analysis. But, when time is limited and methodological skills are not yet fully developed, having a precise starting point encourages you to draw a boundary around your task, while leaving you free to explore unanticipated aspects of your own research question.

Qualitative research is dynamic and interactive

The way in which you set about obtaining an answer to your research question is completely different from how you would tackle it in survey research. Indeed, because of the dynamic and interactive nature of qualitative research, the question itself might well evolve in the course of the project, although if this happens, you must be sure to keep a clear record of how the evolutionary change came about and what revised question it leaves you with. Moreover, your starting question will generate other questions that you may need to pursue in order to answer the original question more completely.

One monumental mistake that you could, but mustn't, make is simply to ask your interviewees the research question. It should be firmly there in your mind, and when you come to write your report, you will aim to provide an answer to it, but, rather like a detective, in interview with your respondents, you will approach it in a more roundabout, more clandestine fashion.

If we take question 7 in my list of hypothetical research questions (driving within the speed limit), different people would approach it in different ways, but if I were doing it, I would want to start with a generalised discussion about the trials and tribulations of modern motoring, in the course of which speed restrictions would be expected to be mentioned – if not by the respondent, then by me. That would lead into the more common question, 'Why do we (all) break speed limits?' and then, and only then, into the real question area: 'What are the restraining factors that serve to keep you within the law?' Quite how you explore that, how much detail you go into, to what extent you try to get the respondent to discuss their feelings about 'breaking the law' in this way, whether you start to use prompts in order to cover areas not mentioned by the respondent ... all these things will form part of your planning process and will evolve in the course of data collection.

You can see from this example that the boundary between qualitative and quantitative research can become quite porous. Methodologies are not like religious faiths or political allegiances: in research, you should always feel free to use whatever method enables you to obtain the end-results you aspire to. So, in this example, you may well reach a point where you want to produce a prompt card in which the various deterrent factors as previously identified are offered to the interviewee with the request that they be rated on a scale. This isn't by any means always so, and sometimes there are good methodological or theoretical reasons for not crossing the boundary in this way.

Strategic sampling

In qualitative research, samples may be made up of people – either as individuals or in groups. But one of the unique aspects of the method lies in the fact that your sample can and probably should consist of a wide range of different elements:

- Your core sample: the people who make up your pivotal target group, their beliefs, attitudes and social position
- Other people related to those who form your pivotal target group and their relationship with your research question (for example, in research question 4, you could organise interviews with a small number of parents and teachers as well as with truanting children themselves)
- Experiences, not solely as described by your interviewees through narrative accounts of their lives, but also sourced in texts and records (for example, in question 8, in addition to interviewing experienced bloggers, you may wish to do a content analysis of a sample of blogs)

- Periods of time or moments in time critical to your research question (for example, in question 2, you might expect to attend and observe a bungee jump in progress)
- Structural elements that surround your area of interest (for example, in question 1, you might look at, describe and analyse an example of the architecture and layout of buildings in sites known for their high rates of vandalism)
- Institutions relevant to your question (for example, in question 5, you could interview the staff of an organisation that facilitates contact between adopted people and their natural parents)
- Places (for example, in question 3, you might choose to review some existing leisure sites and find out about levels of usage)
- Media-generated material relating to your question (for example, in question 9, you could do some content analysis of the coverage in newspapers and magazines of advice given to people whose longstanding marriages were at risk of breaking up).

From these examples, you will gather that it is not always clear at the outset who or what will be included in your research sample. The interviews themselves may suggest alternative lines of enquiry, and a crucial part of the methodological skill that you will develop will alert you to the possible additional approaches that might prove fruitful as your data collection process evolves.

The system of sampling you are employing has some similarities to purposive sampling, although a better label for it is *strategic sampling*. This more satisfactorily distinguishes it from the probability and non-probability sampling methods used in quantitative research. You are aiming quite explicitly to select people, objects, situations or experiences that will help you explore your question, enable you to develop theoretical ideas and give you the opportunity to test them before reaching a conclusion.

This flexibility of planning, more than anything else, is the joy of qualitative research.

a hypothetical example of strategic sampling

We'll use one of the suggested topics that I listed: What does it feel like before, during and after doing a bungee jump? And, for

a hypothetical example of strategic sampling *continued*

the purposes of the illustration, don't let's worry too much about resource constraints.

1. Find an experienced bungee jumper. In a university, that shouldn't be too difficult. There may even by a student union club devoted to the activity. I know of one site on the viaduct of a disused railway line, and an alternative approach would be to take yourself off to that place on a summer weekend and seek a volunteer for your project.

2. Work out a way of interviewing your bungee jumper in relative privacy. Take him/her through the history of their involvement in the sport. How did they come to do it in the first place? Does it stem from an interest in other adrenalin-pumping activities? What was the first jump like? Did they experience any after effects? What is it like now?

3. Using snowballing, track down a first-timer, and be with them before, during and after their first jump. Stick with them like a television reporter, interrogating them as they go, and perhaps recording their comments on tape.

4. Find a specified number more – male/female, sporty/not-sporty, frightened/not-frightened. Keep going with your explorations. These will represent your *core sample*.

5. Perhaps talk with significant others (parents, partners, children) in the lives of your bungee jumpers. How does it affect them?

6. If you're really clever, get a friendly medical student to carry out some tests on two or three bungee jumpers before and after a jump. (That's the point about qualitative methods: you can use your imagination to explore any aspect of the topic that seems relevant. Don't imagine that there are any set rules to forbid your imaginative aspirations.)

7. Explore, in particular, whether the act of bungee jumping has any effect on their lives or behaviour afterwards. Is it addictive?

The same research approach could be used in respect of leisure parachuting, hang-gliding or marathon running. Why do people do it? What effect does it have on them – and those close to them – before, during, immediately after, and even six or twelve months later.

exercise

Now identify a research question suitable for the use of qualitative methods, and outline – as in the example above – how you might pursue the idea of strategic sampling in order to answer it.

Gathering your core sample

Qualitative research sampling procedures are not as clearly defined as they are when you are gathering a survey sample intended to be accurately representative of its population. Mason (2002, p. 144) goes so far as to say that she does 'not think it is possible to provide a recipe which sets out how sampling should be done in every qualitative research project, or even a set of common principles'.

You are certainly not seeking to obtain a random or a representative sample. In that sense, the process has some similarities with the gathering of a convenience sample in quantitative research. But it is important that you avoid any unintended bias in your sample. What you are after is a kind of controlled bias – strategically controlled to enable you to obtain a valid answer to your research question.

Your core sample should be large enough to include:

- a range of people that will allow you to explore different and comparative experiences relevant to your question
- some who, you know in advance, will present data that may challenge the assumptions you find yourself making. If, for example, in a study of truancy from school, you are edging towards a conclusion that identifies a particular type of boy or girl truant, you should go out of your way to try and track down for interview some truants who don't fit that pattern, together with some children who have similar characteristics to many truants but who have no history of truanting.

It all depends on the specificity of your target group, but with most small sample projects you should aim to obtain as wide a range of people as you can secure access to in the time available. The core sample size may be anything from 1 to 20: the smaller the sample, the more detailed, intense and sophisticated will be the process of exploring psychosocial reality. As you edge up into the teens, you will find yourself increasingly tempted to drift ever more steadily in the direction of quantitative methods: you will tend to want to say in your final report that 'seven people said such and such, compared with six who said the opposite'. You must resist this.

A common method of gathering a small sample is through *snowballing*. First you identify one or two people who fit the criteria you have specified for your target group, interview them, and then, when you've concluded your research-driven conversation, ask them if they can suggest one or two different people who might meet your requirements. If that works successfully, your life – at least at this stage – will be very simple; but sometimes you have to be more creative in your sampling methods. For example, Caitlin Thoday (2003), in her doctoral study of drug users, spent time hanging around with likely groups in order to gain a level of trust. She talked about the research she was doing and recruited people who showed an interest. She reported that this was an effective method of gaining access to a 'hidden group' engaged in illegal acts. Thoday says that such informal and 'fluid' recruitment was essential for her project 'as people were understandably suspicious about the nature of the research' and what she was going to do with the information she was gathering. Some feared that she might have been an undercover police informant.

What factors to take into account in gathering your sample

The factors you will want to accommodate when drawing up your sample will vary from project to project. But in order to get a reasonable spread of expressed views, you may want to think about chronological age, gender, relevant experience, social class and/or occupational group and ethnic identity. Having an appropriate coverage optimises the quality of your material, but it does not allow you to draw conclusions about the differences between the elements within your sample. For example, if in your sample of 15, you have two Egyptians and one Indonesian, the responses they give may enhance your overall findings from the respondent group as a whole, but you will not, *absolutely not*, be able to say that they are in any way representative of their national populations as a whole, nor will it be permissible to compare their perspectives with others in the group – except (as with all the members of your sample) by identifying them as situationally positioned individuals with unique identities. The rules of probability apply equally to a qualitative research sample as they do in any other methodological approach, and they prohibit any such conclusions with numbers as small as that. Qualitative research theorists would also point out that any attempt to move in that direction is entirely alien to the experiential nature of your explicit research objectives.

With qualitative research, your aim is not to emerge with findings that are statistically representative of a given population but rather to explore subjective patterns of personal, group or organisational experience, to gauge the meaning they have for the people involved, to contrast this with the views that others have of them, and to take proper account of situational context.

majorities and minorities are equally important

One particular illustration of the different approaches adopted by quantitative and qualitative researchers relates to the labels we put on people. Survey researchers often make data comparisons based on gender, age, ethnic identity, social class, and other systems of classification. Within a given framework, this is fine: Do girls do better at primary school than boys? Are certain ethnic groups better at running marathons than sprints? Are men more likely to achieve managerial status in industry? Why do criminal statistics consistently show stark gender differences? If one or other of your parents is a doctor, are you more likely also to become a doctor? There are perfectly respectable statistical exercises to be carried out in order to explore these questions, and the answers *in their own terms* are meaningful.

But what qualitative researchers would say is that such studies do not tell the whole story. They don't do justice to the exceptions – the labelled individuals who don't fit the predicted stereotype. They don't explore the extent to which physical, mental, cultural and psychological variables influence the differences. They don't consider what it feels like to achieve or fail to achieve.

majorities and minorities are equally important *continued*

Interestingly, though, social psychology suggests that the kinds of generalisations that quantitative researchers identify (for example, there are many more male binmen than female, many more female nurses than male) help ordinary people to make sense of the world around them. We all seek shortcuts in our interpretations of social reality; we like to think that we live in a world that is not totally random but which contains patterns within it. Qualitative researchers, by contrast, thrive on the identification of exceptions – what does it feel like to be a female refuse collector or a male nurse? How does it affect the way you play the world and the way the world treats you?

The strategic approach to research planning

As we shall see in the next three chapters, a particular characteristic of qualitative research lies in the fact that the processes of sample-gathering, data collection and data analysis exist side by side. They interact with each other. You may start with your first target individual for interview, but, even as you are analysing the resulting material, you set about approaching a second person and adapting your interview approach in the light of your experience with respondent number one. You will have an idea of how many core interviewees you are going to need – if only to enable you to draw up a programme of likely interviews in the time you have available – but, using tactical initiatives, the addition of secondary interview targets or alternative data sources (such as documents, situations or places) will also need to be time budgeted for. Subject to resource constraints (principally a lack of time), only when you have data saturation will you be able to decide that your sample is complete: that is, when you feel you have gone as far as possible towards answering your research question, and that further explorations will add little or nothing to what you have already obtained.

exercise

Let us assume that your research question is 'What do people use their cars for?' The background to this is the political and environmental debate about whether we are approaching the time when travel by car is going to have to be restricted. The policy-makers and environmentalists tend to assume that the only use people have for their cars is to make a journey from point A to point B, and that if alternative modes of transport were easily and plentifully available, then many would be happy to change their habits.

But is that assumption valid?

First stage: think about or discuss within your group what use members make of cars (if they drive one) and what it means to them. Then, in the light of that exploratory discussion, think of three or (at most) four topics that might throw light on the question. Decide how to achieve a small strategic sample of, perhaps, six people willing to let you carry out a series of interviews for the purpose of this exercise. Because it is an exercise, keep the interview short – a maximum of 10 or 15 minutes.

Think about and discuss what you have learnt.

If you asked me to recommend just one book on ...
qualitative methods *it would be:*

Mason, Jennifer (2002)
Qualitative Researching, 2nd edn, London, Sage

Introduction

All qualitative research methods begin with the assertion that social researchers are located in a subjective context, and cannot lay claim to neutral or scientific objectivity. Because of this, although the methodological process follows a familiar sequence, it is preceded by a crucial and distinctive first stage:

1. Recognise who you are, where you come from and how this may affect your view of the subject and your understanding of the material obtained.
2. Identify a research question.
3. Consider the *nature* of that question.
4. Decide on the method or methods you are going to use to find an answer to the question.

In qualitative research, the range of data collection methods stretches from interviewing and observation to the use of artefacts, documents and records from the past; from visual and sensory data analysis to ethnographic methods. The various methods can be encompassed in case studies, multidimensional explorations, action research programmes, group discussion, clinical research or in pursuit of customer feedback.

In each case, there are issues to be tackled and skills to be learnt in order to emerge with relevant and trustworthy data. Methods of data analysis can include strategies for analysing talk and text, structured techniques for the interpretation of observed behaviour and the use of computer software programs to reduce some of the repetitive tasks that qualitative methods can require.

I shall turn to some of the more complex methods in Chapter 11, but here I will concentrate on small sample interviewing. This is the method that most students or entry-level researchers turn to when they decide that qualitative research offers an attractive way forward for them.

The distinctiveness of working with a small sample is important to grasp from the outset. Your aim is to emerge with feelings, ideas, described experiences, opinions, views, attitudes and perspectives that have a breadth and depth to them extending beyond that which a structured questionnaire would deliver.

Again, the central principle has to be asserted: one method is not superior to the other. Each method delivers different things:

- Survey methods using a random or representative sample enable you to test ideas and arrive at conclusions that are based on evidence that you can reasonably claim reflects the position of the population from which the sample was drawn – albeit interpreted through a perspective that you, the researcher, have imposed upon it.
- Small sample interviewing enables you to arrive at conclusions that are specific to the sample, but which give a reflective or explanatory depth to the subject being explored, and which – in the wake of detailed analysis – can include complex interpretations of how each person's perspective relates to that person's psychosocial context.

If you asked me to recommend just one book on ...
qualitative interviewing *it would be:*

Rubin, H J and Rubin, I S (2005)
Qualitative Interviewing: The Art of Hearing Data, 2nd edn, London, Sage

How will you present yourself?

So, you have decided on a research question and settled on a target small sample to enable you to obtain an answer to that question. You have gained access to the population and secured whatever permissions are needed.

You are ready to start, but one of the most important aspects you have to deal with at the outset is how you are going to present yourself. In most forms of qualitative research, you will need to achieve a greater degree of closeness to your information providers than is normally the case in survey research. You want them to accept you as somebody they are prepared to talk to openly and sensitively.

In quantitative research, the interviewer needs to have the appearance of someone who is courteously and professionally efficient. In pursuit of the role, you would normally dress quite smartly and maintain a serious manner in your dealings with the strangers on whose willing cooperation you are dependent.

In small sample studies, you will need to give more thought to your presentation of self, because your aim is, as far as possible, to merge with the background in which you are working. One very experienced research methods teacher (Dr Ali Pickard of Northumbria University) has described how she was doing a naturalistic study with urban school children. Initially, when she was negotiating access in school, she had no difficulty dressing for the process of negotiation with the head and class teachers – she just wore her normal smart academic attire. But when she moved on to work closely with the teenagers, she found their initial suspicion of her (still dressed to impress the head teacher) quickly melted away when she changed her style of self-presentation to a more informal and downmarket mode of appearance.

You shouldn't underestimate the seriousness with which your interviewees may approach the encounter. You might be nervous (at least to begin with), but at least you are aware of what you are doing and what you are hoping to achieve. Your interviewees may know that you've asked to talk with them, but it will be, in their eyes, an unusual encounter and one with which they may not feel entirely comfortable. Depending to some extent on the subject matter, the occasion may seem to them to have some of the characteristics of the confessional, a job interview or a police interrogation.

Very often your smart office clothes will be right, but equally often, depending on the nature of your target group, you will have to adapt. It is easy to get this wrong; if you do, it can look patronising or just plain silly. But if you want to encourage people to give you their life story, including the dangerous or unhappy bits, then you need to show yourself as somebody they can feel comfortable with, and you probably don't want them to confuse you with other professionals – social workers, benefits staff or tax fraud investigators, for example. Some of the classic studies in the history of qualitative methods – Whyte's *Street Corner Society* (1981) or Yablonsky's *The Violent Gang* (1967), for instance – involved the sociologists living like their subjects, and there are examples of researchers being admitted to a psychiatric hospital in order to study it from the inside. This is the ethnographic tradition and the principle holds good in appropriate instances.

Having a base

Having a suitable base for interviewing is not always easy to achieve. Market research interviewers sometimes hire hotel rooms for this purpose, but students must either hope for sympathetic help from their departmental teachers or else use their initiative. Sometimes it is possible to interview respondents in their own home, although avoiding the telly, the kids, the spouse or the saliva-dripping dog can be problematic – as any community nurse or probation officer will tell you.

In small sample enquiries, you must be able to engage with your interviewees in a setting that is reasonably comfortable and familiar to them, free from disturbance and conducive to a conversation in which they feel free to talk about possibly emotional, confidential or sensitive matters. With qualitative research interviewing, it is quite common for apparently 'safe' discussions to move into more 'dangerous' or upsetting territory and it is essential that these should be allowed to flow without interruption if they are of any conceivable relevance to the question.

Not long ago, for example, I agreed to be interviewed by one of my undergraduate students who was doing her project on what it feels like to be an only child. Halfway through the interview, I burst into tears – not something I do very often and certainly never in the presence of a student. I was glad that the interview was taking place in a private and neutral setting. If the interview had been in my professorial room, the dynamics of the occasion might have been quite different; and if it had been in the student coffee bar, it probably wouldn't have happened because the whole tenor of the encounter would have been more superficial and controlled.

Unstructured or semi-structured interviewing with a small sample

Straightaway, we can acknowledge one of the central tenets of small sample interviewing: that the questions you employ, the topics you focus on and the methods you develop in order to achieve the best flow of responses will not be cut and dried at the outset. Each research encounter will be different. Qualitative research relies heavily on your own performance as an interviewer and your own skills as an analytical interpreter of the evidence you accumulate.

These are your basic guidelines for the initial phase:

- You are not expected to have it all 'sorted' before you begin to gather usable material.
- But you don't want to look foolish because of your amateurishness, nervousness or a lack of preparedness.
- Therefore, as with any research, you need to engage with an exploratory and preparatory phase, in which you might initially start with someone either already known to you or whom you have been led to believe would give you a sympathetic and 'helpful' hearing (or you can even use a student-colleague or friend as a simulated interviewee in a role-play situation). With that person, you may be able – depending on the nature of your topic – to seek methodological feedback that will enable you to improve your approach work.
- You can use the material you get from this exploratory/preparatory phase in your analysis and write-up. There is no strict boundary between exploration, piloting and 'proper' data collection in small sample interviewing. Once you have embarked on the data-gathering phase, beginning with your first tentative interview, then everything you see, hear and write down is treatable as evidence. There isn't a 'starting block' in the way that there is in mail questionnaire, experimental or survey work.
- In the interests of self-training, you can extend the exploratory/preparatory stage for as long as you like (and although this is heretical in some experts' eyes, you can even include a pilot stage in order to satisfy yourself that you have got the approach spot on).

- Because of this 'organic development' aspect of qualitative research, researchers sometimes have trouble satisfying the requirements of governance or ethics committees, especially in settings more accustomed to dealing with scientific research projects. They tend to want to see a fully piloted research plan set out in detail before permission is given.
- This can best be thought of as a *strategic approach to research* because you know where you want to get to, and you are able to use *tactical initiatives* to achieve that end.

The impact of the research interviewer

The specialist texts on qualitative methods lay great emphasis on the potentially prejudicial influence of the researcher's self, both on the process of data collection and its analysis. Taken to an absurd conclusion, this could have the consequence of suggesting, for example, that only women should research women's issues and only Sikhs can accurately analyse the dynamics of Sikh culture. (But even such a conclusion is flawed because the existence of a sense of identity between the research analyst and the subject population does nothing to counteract the partial perspective that, it is argued, any researcher is prone to, nor does it deal with the challenge of 'getting inside' the personal view held by each single interviewee.)

In its extreme form, the message conveyed by those who emphasise the power of the analyst's self in research interviews has two elements:

- There is no such thing as objective reality because everything is understood and interpreted through the eyes, ears and brain of analysts from a specific social context
- Everything is relative to everything else: there is no validity in observations, no reliable truth in described experiences and no conclusions to be drawn from what one person tells another.

Such a view, of course, makes a nonsense of any recordable research, and, although the caution that it induces is useful, the evidence does not support it all the way. Good qualitative researchers will acknowledge the power of self, but they will also employ professional skills in order to gain access to the perspectives of those whom they are interviewing.

The cautionary note is a useful one to keep in mind throughout the research process. There are particular risks of researcher bias if you are embarking on a project in a field where you already feel 'at home'. In such a context, you need to be especially careful because of the extent to which you may think you already know what you want or expect to find. Very often, students choose a topic that reflects their own life experience: being a single parent or a migrant from another country, being a committed Green, having a disabled person in their family, being enthusiastic about cars or football or cooking or architecture. In such instances, the obligations on the researcher are twofold: to embark on the exercise as though you know nothing (to 'feign naivety'), and to work hard at being open to interpretations and patterns that differ from your own prior assumptions. You should also use the strategic sampling approach to identify and interview individuals who you know hold views different from yours.

If you do research in fields about which you know little or nothing, or in which it is logically impossible for you to 'have awareness' of how it feels on the inside – if you're a woman researching a man's world, for instance, or vice versa – then you don't have to feign naivety. You are naive. But, of course, you will still have preconceptions. Suppose you're a law student interviewing social workers, or a radical politics student interviewing policemen or accountants. You would be unusual if you didn't have quite high levels of prejudice or presuppositions about these occupational groups, but, *as a researcher*, you have to put them to one side. It may be difficult (you may even feel that it's dishonest or unprincipled), but the fundamental requirement in all research is that you enter the process prepared to allow the data to determine the outcome. You can minimise your prejudiced starting point by ensuring that your neutrality is emphasised, that your manner takes on the mantle of an independent academic researcher, and that your own views are not allowed to intrude upon the encounter in ways that will counteract the legitimacy of what your interviewee may want to say.

In your work, you must be aware of your self, but you must also do everything in your power to put your self to one side and focus totally on the independent worlds of the people you are interviewing and observing.

One example of this might be found in the way you use language. Caitlin Thoday notes that when she was doing research with drug users, she had to be really careful about the words she used. In order to achieve rapport with her interviewees and have credibility in their eyes, it was crucial for her to use the correct current street names for the various illegal substances: 'Using out-of-date or out-of-context names left you vulnerable to being laughed at or not understood.' You obviously don't want that to occur when you're in the field. Thoday found that the best way to overcome this problem was to talk to interviewees informally and spend time observing them before beginning an interview.

ten rules for running your interview

1. Present yourself, to the greatest degree possible, in a neutral fashion. Partly because of the impact of reality television, people do understand about the role of a researcher. They know that, in the modern world, people can ask questions – sometimes, there are sinister implications, but sometimes there are not. And it is your aim to emphasise that you and your enquiry fall into the latter category.

2. You must give yourself an identity. Who are you? Where do you come from? Why are you doing this? If you are honest and frank with the interviewees, there is more chance of them being honest and frank with you.

3. Acknowledge openly the extent to which you are similar to or different from your target sample. But don't do it in such a way that this might influence what your interviewees talk to you about or the angle they put on it.

4. Ensure that no mental, emotional or moral barrier is erected between you and your interviewee. You have to adopt an accepting position. Your interviewees are the experts in their own lives; they have lived with themselves day in, day out, and if you encourage an open flow of conversation, they will share some of that expertise with you. Make sure that they

ten rules for running your interview *continued*

understand that all you want is for them to be themselves and to share with you their own feelings, opinions and experiences. Emphasise the anonymity of their contribution.

5. Allow the interview to run a natural course. You will have your semi-structured topics in mind, and you must try to ensure that they all get some coverage. But the order in which you deal with them is immaterial.

6. Try to make the interview as comfortable as possible. If someone listening in thought that you and your interviewee were having an entirely ordinary everyday-type conversation, then you could claim to have scored. It's easier said than done, of course, but what you should try to avoid at all costs is a situation in which you are asking a sequence of questions, as though you were carrying out a survey.

7. Your contributions to the encounter may not all take the form of questions. You can achieve fruitful responses by making comments (of a non-judgemental kind, of course), throwing in a single word, or even by nodding and smiling silently in the style of a good television interviewer.

8. Sometimes, you may get a sense that the interviewee is growing weary of being the sole provider of information. All conversation should involve some degree of social exchange, so you shouldn't be too coy about adding your two-pennyworth. But if you are an easy talker, don't fall into the trap of taking up too much of the interview time. That time is precious, and your talking is only useful insofar as it facilitates the contribution of your interviewee.

9. A qualitative research encounter may provide a rather unusual experience for your interviewee. It offers an opportunity for the person involved to talk freely about something quite important, but about which they may not normally feel free to air their views or feelings at such length. It can involve a degree of self-analysis, and may sometimes spill over into emotional territory. In some projects this will be almost inevitable: studies that focus on, for example, the death of a child or parent, some aspect of mental illness, or failed aspirations in

ten rules for running your interview *continued*

the interviewee's life – these are intensely powerful factors. In such instances, the researcher must be prepared for the possibility of tears or even anger in the course of the interview. At the very least, it is useful to have a clean pack of paper tissues handy; this has the benefit of showing helpful concern whilst leaving the interviewee free to cope with the legitimate emotion that has been displayed.

10. All interviews should have clearly defined beginnings, middles and ends. When you come to the conclusion, make sure that the closure is courteous and not too abrupt; offer your thanks and make sure that you don't have to rush away to another appointment, leaving the interviewee with a feeling that they have been cynically used for your own ends.

What kinds of questions are suitable for use with a small sample?

The method is especially clever in situations where the researcher wants to be able to explore complex and unpredictable areas of thought, feeling, behaviour or experience.

Here are some real-life examples from different courses:

1. What does/did it feel like to be the parent of a child who dies in childhood? Studies that set out to dig deep in a field of intense emotion like this are ideal for the qualitative methods approach, but are inevitably demanding on both interviewer and interviewee.
2. In urban developments, what steps are taken to protect aspects of the cultural heritage? This allows for detailed exploration of the complex conflicts of interest that may be involved.
3. Do you like your occupation? Work satisfaction is a highly complex subject and, as such, lends itself to qualitative exploration.
4. OK, so you've got 16 different sets of prescribed medicines in your home (tablets, creams and so on). Tell me how you manage them and what you use them for.

5. I know you've tried a number of different diets. Would you like to tell me about them? What you liked about each of them? What you didn't like? How easy or difficult it was to maintain them? The question is: What makes a diet easy or difficult to maintain?

6. Do you ever use a condom? If it varies, give me some examples of when you do and when you don't. Sex education programmes – and the media advertising that supports them – tend to make assumptions about the rational nature of people's approach to sex. Their effectiveness (even their worthwhileness) depends to a significant extent on an understanding of the reality of human behaviour in this sphere, and a qualitative researcher is particularly well placed to throw light on that.

7. When did you last buy a new washing machine/car/television set (or any other major 'replacement' item). (Assuming that it was within your memory span), can you outline for me how you came to make the decision? In a question of this kind, you are trying to tap into the micro-processes that lead to a major decision. This is tricky and probably best carried out in the immediate wake of a purchase being made.

8. What is your experience of living together with other students? You'll need some factual descriptions to begin with. What are the kinds of things which make for a happy or unhappy atmosphere? Can you describe one time and place when the atmosphere was happy? (Is 'happy' the right word?) Can you describe one time and place when the atmosphere was unhappy? What part did the interviewee play in all this?

exercise

Can you think of a question in your own area of interest that would lend itself to this kind of exploratory and reflective treatment? Who would you be interviewing? And what tactical initiatives might you need to take?

the meaning of words

In any interview, the risk of misunderstanding what is said is always present. Whatever research method is chosen, the researcher is faced with the task of clarifying and defining concepts:

- What do specific words mean to the subjects of the research?
- Do the interviewees mean what the researcher means by them?
- Do different people interviewed or observed mean different things by the use of the same words?
- How is the meaning of the data gathered affected by the respondent's and the researcher's cultural, class or regional background? Or their ethnic identity? Or a language barrier?
- What other sources of language bias might there be in the way the researcher is going about it?

Recording your interview

There are three ways to keep a record of your interview. You can use written notes; you can audio-record the interview; or you can video-record it.

Deciding about this, and preparing to act on your decision is the stage when, all of a sudden, qualitative methods start to look less simple than they did at the outset.

In theory, you could be terribly grand and take along a 'secretary' as a third party to keep a note of your interview – even doing so in shorthand. Dream on! Not only would such an arrangement be beyond most students' capacity to arrange (although, unless you are a 72-year-old mature student, you could always ask your mum!), but the mere presence of a third party would be an unhelpful intrusion in an encounter where the establishment of rapport and the protection of confidentiality are crucial.

A written record of the interview requires you either to take notes during the conversation (you'll be surprised how much you improve with practice) or to write down as much as you can recall immediately after the encounter – again it's surprising how skilful you can become at what is sometimes called 'process recording'. As the project evolves, you may begin to impose a topic-related structure on your recording, so that you can pre-plan those parts of the interview to which you pay most attention. But you mustn't allow this to get in the way of your objectivity or your openness to the unexpected remark – or a strategic change in direction.

Audio-recording is very common in qualitative methods. You will need to practise the technique, including the best script to use in order to obtain the interviewee's permission. If you sound nervous or uncertain about the use of audio, this is likely to be apparent to your interviewee, making it more likely that they'll say, 'Oh, I think I'd rather not, thank you.'

Make sure your machinery is working and that the microphone is picking up both of your voices. Good modern equipment is highly sensitive, but it is still possible for you to go to a great deal of trouble and then not be able to hear what your interviewee has said. Disaster! (Talk to any journalist and they'll tell you a story of when they'd gone to great trouble to arrange an interview with an important and busy person, only to get back to the office to discover that their audio-record of it was blank.)

An additional advantage of audio-recording is that it serves as a learning tool for you. As you listen to the playbacks, you (and your supervisor) will be able to judge when you failed to pick up on a potentially fruitful cue, when you interrupted the interviewee in a damaging way, or when your own 'self' intruded too much upon the encounter. With audio-recording, you can concentrate almost 100 per cent on managing the conversation although if it's a long interview, you will need to be prepared to change the tape cassette or disk. When you listen to the interview afterwards, you will hear much more than you could have written down, and you will be staggered to recognise how much of what was said you failed to appreciate at the time. The analysis of your tapes can be problematic because of the sheer scale of the task.

Video-recording is a theoretical possibility, and it would certainly give an important added dimension to your analysis (allowing you to observe non-verbal cues – in yourself as well as in your subject), but in most instances it isn't practical because:

1. It either involves the presence of a third party on camera, or the use of a studio-type setting with videoing being done from a control room, or a pre-set, stand-alone camera with the inter-

viewer in charge of it. All three possibilities contain elements that run the risk of distorting the nature of the occasion.

2. Under such circumstances, it would be almost impossible to claim that the interview was taking place in a naturalistic setting – hence putting it in conflict with one of the underlying principles of qualitative research.

3. The method has connotations, reinforced by TV drama and documentaries, that give the interview the appearance of a police interrogation – not a good message to convey.

Some of the ideas on offer

Jennifer Mason (2002, p. 46) neatly encapsulates both the nature and the challenge of qualitative research methods when she says: 'I see research design as a skilled activity requiring critical and creative thinking, rather than as a product which can be displayed and copied'. It is a process that is difficult to get right the first time you do it; and your teacher or supervisor has precious little influence or control over how you fare in the field.

Because qualitative research is primarily designed to tap into the situational reality experienced by your interviewees, the range of ideas that sociologists and others have suggested tend to be variations on the same theme.

Focused interviews

An interview is a conversation with a purpose. And in a research project, it is you, the researcher, who defines that purpose. Focused interviews ensure that you retain a high degree of control over the topic while granting your interviewees full scope to determine the nature of the responses. They involve a standard sequence of events:

1. First, in your planning phase, you decide that your research is focused on a specific experience that some people have had – breaking a leg, reading the *Sun* every day, being burgled, having seen a particular film, done a degree in biochemistry.

2. You gather a sample that fits the focus of your project.

3. Through a literature survey, exploratory discussions, observa-

tion and creative thought, you identify probable sub-topics that your target sample may have views and feelings about. From this, you design a flexible checklist to guide you, always allowing scope for additional (and unexpected) material that may be offered by your interviewees.

4. You engage the sample in interview, aiming to keep the focus of your topic firmly at the top of your agenda but maximising the opportunity for your interviewees to express their experiences, feelings and opinions without attempting to structure their words in any way.

5. You will find that your interviewees contribute additional dimensions to your chosen topic, and, in turn, you can then draw on these in your subsequent interviews. In this way, your interviewing frame gains richness and depth as you proceed – thanks to the active involvement of your subjects.

The focused interview is a good starting point for inexperienced qualitative researchers because it offers a reassuring degree of structure. It goes some way to counteracting the tendency of beginning researchers to try to cover too much ground: if you religiously complete stage (3), you will find that you give yourself an advance idea of how specific your focus needs to be in order to emerge with relevant and worthwhile findings.

Narrative approaches: 'telling my story'

Here's a good example of a narrative approach in research interviewing:

At Sheffield Hallam University, some teacher training entrants are students who have previously failed in mathematics or have a weak mathematical background. But most of them go on to become confident and effective mathematicians, some even achieving first class honours. The researchers (Angier and Povey, forthcoming) interviewed a small cohort of such students (having a weak entry profile followed by success on the course), and their report consisted of the stories they constructed about these students: What was it about their time at Sheffield Hallam that seemed to make the difference?

This is a perfect example of the strength of qualitative methods – allowing the researcher to explore the meaning that a particular life experience (in this case a very important one) has had for a targeted group of people. It doesn't set out to 'prove' anything. It aims to emerge with illuminating findings that help to make sense of complex psychosocial interactions.

Reflexive interpretation

In qualitative researching, the role of the interviewer is recognised as central to the encounter, and reflexive interpretation of the interview takes fully into account the part played by the researcher – when agreement with the interviewee's sentiments was expressed, when the interviewer experienced discomfort, impatience or anger. The analysis pursued in this way challenges the idea that the words of the subject can be interpreted in isolation from the nature of the interaction between two people.

Using pictures, vignettes or scenarios

A potentially rewarding way of tapping into the respondent's feelings is to offer additional stimulus as a basis for conversation:

- You can show pictures, maybe asking the interviewee to express an opinion or indicate a preference. One student, Joanna Austin, showed interviewees pictures of four young women in different styles of dress for working in an office. In this way, she was able to demonstrate the way in which people had stereotypical views of what kind of a person each would be in a working environment: one was labelled assertive, the second laid-back, the third caring and the fourth a gossip.
- You can use vignettes in order to tell a story to interviewees with a view to prompting a reaction. One approach that has been used in the study of race prejudice is to recount a brief episode in which either a black person attacks a black or white victim or a white person attacks a white or black victim. In all other respects, the details and the wording of the story are identical. Black and white interviewees are targeted and are asked questions about their opinions of and feelings towards the characters in the story. Each interviewee only hears one

version of the story, but the results from large samples allow comparisons to be made in respect of the different versions. The preparation of vignettes is a difficult art form.

- You can use scenarios. These are similar to vignettes, except that they are designed to involve the interviewee actively in the story. For example: 'Your partner vomits on the roadside during a night out clubbing. What effect does that have on your relationship?'

Although the techniques lend themselves particularly to a reflective response, it is perfectly possible to use them in a large-scale social survey.

11 There is more to qualitative research than interviewing

When you have a project to do, you should always choose the method likely to throw the most light on your research question, although your choice may be constrained by what is feasible, given the limitations of time and other resources.

Although small sample interviewing is the most common means by which students gain their first experience of the art of qualitative research (and it *is* more of an art than a science, although it has elements of craft about it too), there is more than one way of accumulating qualitative data.

Ethnography and the anthropological tradition

The ethnographic approach is the oldest of the qualitative methods and lies at the heart of the academic discipline of social anthropology. Traditionally, anthropologists studied cultures in foreign lands, but in the second half of the twentieth century there emerged a new body of literature based on the application of similar methods to contemporary settings in the developed world, such as hospitals, commercial offices and local government departments.

The ethnographic approach is not an easy one for the beginning researcher. I shall always remember that one of the worst marks I got as an undergraduate was for an ethnographic account of life in the Paris office of Gaz de France, where I'd been sent for 10 weeks to gain work experience. I wasn't well briefed; my modest understanding of the French language meant that I couldn't follow much of the informal conversation; I hadn't been taught how to make notes in a usable fashion; I had little or no experience of any office environment; I failed to engage the participants in exploratory conversations; and, above all, I struggled (and failed) to make sense of all the 'noise' that was going on around me. My anthropology teacher commented that I had read too much into the lunch-time antics of the office in which young men chased young women around the desks to little or no apparent purpose (or so I thought). It was a hard lesson to learn for a naive student.

Full-blown ethnographic methods require time, space and the availability of skilled supervision if they are to be done well.

Ethnographers frequently combine data obtained through various observational methods, such as naturalistic observation and participant observation, as well as that obtained through the examination of documents and interviews, in order to describe the context and meanings of everyday social situations. (Shaughnessy et al., 2000, p. 100)

At a more modest stage of research experience, ethnographic methods can be employed successfully if the investigator has a clear idea of what is being sought, for example, 'exploring whether and how staff members organise their working environment for their own benefit'. This, of course, conflicts with the *holistic* tradition of ethnography, but it is that very idea of holism which often gets in the way of good qualitative work being done by students. So much of the process of learning to do research is like learning to play the piano: you have to practise your scales and produce polished renderings of simple tunes before you can hope to play a concerto to concert-performance standard.

An ethnographic approach requires you to:

- have a setting in mind where you will carry out your fieldwork
- secure appropriate access
- recognise that you are, in the first instance, asking the question, 'What is going on here?' and 'What are the cultural influences that are driving it?'
- identify one or more precise questions to focus on
- acknowledge that what you find will be at least partially different from what anybody else might find because of your own cultural, political and psychological preconceptions or background
- accept the idea that you will be a part of what you are observing and reporting – and that your presence in the field will have an impact on what goes on
- have a high-quality system worked out in advance for recording your observations – notebook (paper and/or elec-

tronic), diary, portable audio recorder
- develop and commit to draft the central ideas and themes that emerge from your observations from the moment you enter the field.

Participant observation

Participant observation is the method you employ when you have decided to use an ethnographic approach. It normally requires you to have a role within the setting quite other than your role as researcher:

- If it is a work setting (for example, an art gallery or a museum), then you might arrange to have a job as a porter, a secretary or on the reception desk. The role should be one which gives you involvement in or access to those areas you want to observe.
- In a youth club or in any charity setting, you could become one of the volunteer helpers.
- Being a participant observer in an informal group setting – for example, among binge-drinking teenagers, football supporters or wheeler-dealing commercial operators – is more difficult, but not impossible.

When you have made arrangements for your participatory role, you will need to decide which of two methods you will be employing:

- One method requires you to conceal your research function. So far as your working colleagues, customers or service users are concerned, you are what you appear to be – an employee, a volunteer or a colleague.
- The more usual approach, especially at student project level, is for your research role to be made explicit in all instances where it is appropriate to do so. (When the approval of ethics committees is needed for your research to go ahead, you will be expected to choose this option.) With this approach, you have the advantage of being able to discuss what you have observed with the subjects who form the focus of your study – to ask questions, seek clarification of inexplicable activities,

explore motives, feelings, attitudes and opinions. Because you have been upfront with people about your research identity, you need have fewer qualms about behaving in a researcher-type way. You do, though, have to be careful about this because you might make people nervous about what you are writing – and that, in turn, will change their behaviour and their relationship with you.

Another approach possible in major studies is for the researcher to be employed within the project *as* a researcher. Often this happens in action research projects, and it would be misleading to describe such researchers as anything but participants in the project because they are expected to feed in the fruits of their work in order to facilitate dynamic developments in practice. The potential for tension between the researcher and the activists is uncomfortably real. (When I was the chair of the management committee of such a project, I sometimes despaired because of the conflict and suspicion that characterised the relationship between the radical activist practitioners and the ethnographer-researcher. It was an experience that I have never forgotten and one that I wouldn't willingly repeat.)

If you asked me to recommend just one book on ...
observation *it would be:*

    Lofland, John and Lofland, Lyn H (eds) (2004)
    Analysing Social Situations: A Guide to Qualitative Observation and Analysis, London, Wadsworth

A modest model for participant observation can come through student placements – in schools, social care agencies, health settings, kitchens, commercial offices or factories. But, given my Paris experience, I would suggest that, although the question 'What is going in here?' remains valid, the focus in a student project context should always be much narrower. This is particularly important in instances where the student researcher has little or no prior experience of the given setting. The focus should either be provided by an experienced academic supervisor who knows the scene, or – more probably – should be determined by the researcher in the first week or two of the attachment following preliminary observations, exploratory discussion with insiders and – ideally – a consultation session with your supervisor.

The chief tools that you will employ will be a notebook, laptop, index cards and audio recorder. Whether you use pen and paper or electronic equipment, the methodological model is the same: you make a record of what you see and hear, and steadily (and probably quite quickly) begin to classify your observations under headings that make sense to you. It is that self-directed interpretation of the experience that gives the exercise its personal dimension, but there is a risk that it introduces a powerful bias, especially if you have gone into the project with strong preconceptions.

Surprisingly often, the end-result is implicitly contentious, especially if it is focused on a sphere of life that is inherently controversial – a psychiatric hospital, for example, a prison or any other 'closed' institutional setting. But even observation of ordinary workplaces can produce descriptive accounts of behaviours or relationships that the parties involved would prefer to keep hidden. For example, your work might observe that the minutes of meetings are manipulated by people in positions of power, that gossip networks operate in ways that undermine trust, that attitudes towards customers or service users are disparaging or that scapegoating or discriminatory behaviours are rife.

Responsible researchers will normally expect to feed back their findings at an early draft stage to those who are the subject of their observations. This allows participants to dispute what is said, although it does not give them the right to demand changes in the text.

Insider research

Insider research, sometimes called clandestine research, has an important history in the field. One of the most widely read examples is that of Cohen and Taylor's account (1972) of the realities of life in a top-security wing of Durham Prison. The authors, as young academics, had been given a part-time visiting teaching role in the prison, and they used the material they got from their classes to describe how high-risk prisoners serving long sentences devised the ways and means of coping with their situation, of achieving 'psychological survival'. It was, and remains, a readable study and it made a significant contribution to criminological theory – but it was believed that the authors had not told officials what they were doing, much less sought permission for it. The word in the Home Office was that they might never again be allowed to carry out research in government-controlled penal settings.

This illustrates a key point about insider research. Information is power – and all organisations in the public or private sector like to keep control over the levers of power, including the right of access to inside information. The growth of governance restrictions in the public sector and the reluctance of commercial companies to grant researchers free access to internal systems both impose significant constraints on social research.

There are two kinds of insider research:

- Legitimised research in which the researcher's role is known to a small and selective number of gatekeepers – but not to those who are the primary target of research observations.
- Research that is carried out without anyone at all knowing about it until a final report is prepared and published.

In some settings, insider research can be dangerous, and is equivalent to undercover work carried out by police, army or the secret service. You can imagine that such work among hardcore drug or paedophile groups will pose serious moral dilemmas to the researcher; and in revolutionary settings, criminal gangs or proscribed political groups, the risks can be life-threatening.

Methodologically, the approaches to insider research do not differ markedly from similar work that has gone through standard approval procedures. Note taking, organising and indexing observations, constantly and actively reviewing ideas and theoretical perspectives as they emerge, and, from an early stage, preparing sections of a draft report to reflect your findings: these are all familiar activities. The difference lies in the need to protect your clandestine presence in what may be a highly charged situation. It may preclude the idea of feeding back your findings to the target group in order to invite their comments. It calls for a particular kind of personality and is not a recommended approach for the entry-level researcher. It is tantamount to spying, and if your cover is blown, the whole project may collapse in a heap as you are required to remove yourself from a setting in which you will be seen to have flouted the conventional rules of loyalty and trust. You may even have signed a document agreeing to do no such thing.

It is ironic that, in many countries, senior politicians frequently publish their memoirs and that, when they refer to what has gone on in cabinet meetings or committees, their work has all the characteristics of insider research.

From the point of view of theory development and practice improvement, there is much to be said for insider research – especially in monopoly-type settings such as government departments or large industrial or commercial operations. Political and public interest in restricting the potential for bureaucratic waste or counteracting the known tendency for staff to safeguard their own interests is a reason for arguing that insider research may be the only way in which such malfunctions can be exposed and tackled.

Non-participant observation

If you are doing non-participant observation, to misappropriate Jean-Paul Sartre's words, 'you are a camera'. You are the passive, if reflective, observer of a chosen subject area, and the research techniques you employ will be designed to impose an element of structure on what you see:

- First of all you must decide what it is that you are observing – and why.
- Normally you will be observing a facet of ordinary activity – children playing in the street, car-drivers seeking parking space, shoppers deciding what to buy, traffic wardens on duty, hospital patients in the waiting room, drinkers in a bar. Generally, you are restricted to activities that are on public display and which you can monitor unobtrusively.
- Or you may set up an artificial situation and watch what happens – as in the televised *Big Brother* format or in management games during staff selection procedures.
- Contrary to the principles embraced by some types of qualitative research, your subjects will probably have no explicit say in what you observe or how you interpret their words or behaviour. They are active in their own world, but possibly oblivious

to your research role.

- You will bring your own presuppositions and preconceptions with you and these may influence what you choose to observe, what you 'see' and what you record – even though you will take careful and disciplined steps to counteract the risk of researcher bias.
- You may use video systems to record the sequence of events, but if your target observations are widespread and complex, the camera's focus will give you only a limited view.
- With strategically positioned microphones, the quality of audio pick-up will vary with the sophistication of your equipment.
- You will need to decide whether to share with your targeted subjects the analysis that you carry out and the interpretations you place on what you have seen and heard. But in the wake of that, you will also have to take a view on how to handle the responses your subjects make to your analysis and interpretation and what weight to place upon them. What happens, for example, if you are convinced you saw something occur that your subjects categorically deny? Of if they contradict the interpretation you have placed upon it?

You cannot, even with a camera, observe everything that happens. Decide at an early stage – probably after some exploratory and pilot work – just what it is that you are going to concentrate on. There are many established techniques which you can use. These are two of the most commonly used:

1. The Bales (1999) interaction system of measurement is one way of recording interpersonal contact. Who talks to whom? For how long? What verbal and non-verbal cues occur? For best results with Bales, you must have a hypothesis – perhaps relating to core variables such as gender, status or age. Without a hypothesis or a specified and precise question, the results that emerge may give you a detailed number-driven account of group interactions, but you will be left struggling to decide what conclusions to draw (see also Perakyla, 2004).
2. Sociometric gridlines allow you to establish the nature of the relationships (positive, negative or neutral) between different dyads, trios or groups within a larger network. In committee meetings, I've sometimes used the method as a way of passing

the time: Who speaks the most? Maybe one person only ever speaks when a specific other member has just spoken – and then to disagree with what has been said: Why? Can you identify themes or moods or ideas that link members who seem to form a group within the group? Who remains silent? Does anyone emerge as a scapegoat, attacked by all? Does someone play the role of peacemaker? Who gets angry and why? Is there a key figure whose contributions have a powerful influence on the others? It can be a difficult model to use and keep up with in real time, and you need to be clear what any likely outcome might mean. Denzin (1970, pp. 118–20) describes how sociometric methods can be employed in both qualitative and quantitative contexts.

You can develop your own system, depending on the nature of your interest. Gender analysis, for instance, gives you a starting point and can be used in any setting – a children's nursery, a shop counter, a protest meeting in the community hall. Your aim will be to settle upon questions concerning the politics of gender and, for this, you will almost certainly have to use unstructured observation and interview techniques in an exploratory phase. Once an interesting question has been identified (Is there a gender difference between who plays with which toys? Who gets pushed aside at the counter or at the pub bar? Who plays the most assertive role in a meeting?), you will work out ways of counting and interpreting relevant instances, and taking note of surrounding circumstances on each occasion.

exercise

Go to a railway station, position yourself close to the arrival platform, and observe the nature of the greetings between travellers and those waiting to meet them. What is the range of behaviours that you can observe? Can you classify them into different groups? Can you differentiate between the behaviour of the person waiting and the traveller?

The main argument in favour of non-participant observation is that it allows you to research what people *do* rather than what they *say* they do. Not all actions or locations lend themselves to the method, but, used as a short exercise, it provides an effective test of the student's skill in planning and implementing a research project. Moreover, in the light of your observed data, you can link it with other qualitative research approaches – like interviewing men and women about their gender-related experiences.

learning a lesson from the novelist

On radio, the novelist Anthony Powell has talked about the different levels of technical difficulty in writing about conversations involving, in turn, two people, three people or five people, with the hardest task of all doing justice to what is going on between people in a crowded bar or party with dozens of men and women milling around, having more or less significant conversations and encounters – simultaneously.

When I heard Powell talking, it immediately struck me that what he was describing had echoes for the social researcher observing different situations. It is one thing to give a single individual the opportunity of responding to questions in, as it were, one dimension. It's quite a different challenge to watch and listen to what two or three or more people say to each other and how they respond. Or, again, to see and monitor what happens in a group – whether it be a group of children playing in a nursery, an unstructured encounter between two gangs on the street, or even, if they talk among themselves, a group of people brought together specifically to provide the researcher with a set of opinions on proffered topics. You can't ask people 'Would you mind saying that again, please. It sounded very important.' (Well, you can! But what they tell you they said won't be the same as what they actually said in the first place. And your query will intrude inappropriately on what is meant to be a naturalistic setting for you to observe.)

learning a lesson from the novelist *continued*

Advanced qualitative research tries to deal with these challenges, although there are those who would argue that top-quality novelists sometimes do it better. The difference is, of course, that, whereas the novelist can create an imaginary dialogue, the researcher has a principled obligation to reflect only what is seen and heard.

Focus groups

Focus groups have been used in the commercial world for many years and, more recently, by political parties wanting to design their policies, not by ideology, but by tapping into the feelings and wishes of 'the people'.

If you asked me to recommend just one book on ...
focus groups *it would be:*

Krueger, R A and Casey, M A (eds) (2000)
Focus Groups: A Practical Guide for Applied Research, London, Sage

Traditionally, focus groups have been employed to:

- explore how consumers might react to the development of new products or planned advertising campaigns
- find out how, when and why people use a particular service (like a leisure centre, a library or an advice bureau) – or why they don't use it
- obtain customer feedback about the quality of a service received
- discover, within an organisation, whether staff morale is good or bad, and what makes it so (Greenbaum, 1998).

Once the group is in place, the researcher's job is to ensure a good flow of relevant conversation. In order to achieve that, you will need to have a series of items that you can prompt the group to talk about without interrupting the flow.

How do you get to this point?

1. Identify your research question.
2. Identify a relevant group and bring them together. The ideal number is eight, although some commercial operators set about gathering anything up to 20. If you are relatively inexperienced in the process, a group of six, seven or eight is comfortable to manage. You are not aiming for representativeness, but it is usual to use purposive (or strategic) sampling in order to guard against uncontrolled bias in your material.
3. You can gather as many groups as you wish, but, for a student project, four, five or six will give you as much material as you are likely to need. After that, diminishing returns begin to set in, with each additional group giving you relatively little new material.
4. Find a warm, comfortable, convenient setting in which to entertain your group. Market research companies tend to hire a hotel function room for the purpose and provide refreshments (tea, coffee, wine, soft drinks, water) on arrival: this helps to break the ice. Give people name labels – but only with their first name on. (If people are ultra-sensitive about their anonymity, you can always give them a fictional name.) This enables a participant to say 'I agree with what Sue said a moment ago ...'. Sit them in a circle or round a small table. You should be a part of the circle.
5. Begin by explaining what it is all about, how it works, how long it will go on, and what the house rules are. Two useful ideas are to ask people to be courteous to each other and to indicate that there is an expectation that all those present will be free to contribute equally, which allows you to cope with any member who begins to dominate the exchanges.
6. Introduce your first topic. You may, at any time, use visual aids in order to prompt discussion. Publishers, for example, might want a focus group to look at the dust jackets or titles of books; magazine editors might want feedback on the layout of a page. Don't intrude on the group's deliberations more than is absolutely necessary in order to get through your predetermined agenda. You may wish to give the group a time schedule so that they spend an appropriate amount of time on each of the topics you have chosen.

7. Provided you have planned the exercise carefully and selected a group with knowledge of your material topics, you will be surprised how little direction you have to give. In such circumstances, three principal topics (possibly with prompts for further clarification) will probably be as many as you should aim at, although you can have as many as six.

8. Groups can last for anything between 20 minutes and two hours: a lot depends on the material you are giving them to talk about.

It is normal for focus groups to be asked to agree that their discussions be audio-recorded. You need high-quality audio equipment in order to pick up all the contributions when you come to transcribe them, and you should spend some time beforehand trying it out in dummy situations. It can be difficult to identify voices when you play the tapes back, so having an additional note-taker present (sitting outside the circle) is often helpful.

Market research companies often offer a modest payment to group members, but if your participants have a vested interest in the topic, they will not expect that. On the other hand, they are providing you with a service and some symbolic recompense would not go amiss.

Examples of target populations that might be suitable for a focus group and possible research questions could include:

- School children who have received teaching in a foreign language: 'What factors make it easy or difficult to learn?'
- Residents of a neighbourhood plagued by vandalism: 'What experiences have you had and how do you think the vandalism could be reduced?'
- Holiday-makers on a particular package tour: 'Did everything go well?'
- American tourists in London: 'What was good and bad about your stay?'
- Customers of Marks & Spencer (or Argos or Asda or Lidl and so on): 'What are the advantages and disadvantages of shopping in this store?'
- Regular attenders at concerts held in the same venue: 'What do you like and dislike about the experience on different occasions?'

the art of successful focus group management

- Be actively interested in all the participants and their contributions
- Be familiar with the questions
- Use good listening skills
- 'Manage' the group confidently
- Encourage everyone to participate
- Find a way of capturing and sensitively dealing with the points that are raised but are not taken any further
- At the end, summarise the discussion and thank everybody for their contributions

But:

- Don't be a participant in the discussions
- Don't put forward your own views
- Don't comment critically on any of the contributions
- Don't let the group get stuck on any one point
- Don't allow one or more members to dominate the discussion
- Don't take sides in the debate
- Don't interrupt

Source: Adapted from internet guidelines issued by Cornwall County Council.

Content analysis

Analysing documents takes you close to the territory of the historian and the student of literature, but you can conduct content analyses of anything that is written down or otherwise recorded – film, TV programme or website.

For example, Chavez (1985) analysed American newspaper comic strips and revealed that only 4 per cent of the female characters were shown in working roles, despite the fact that about 70 per cent of all women in the US are employed outside the home.

If you asked me to recommend just one book on ...
content analysis *it would be:*

Neuendorf, Kimberly A (2002)
The Content Analysis Guidebook, London, Sage

At one extreme, content analysis can be relatively modest. For example, you will use content analysis techniques to organise and make sense of the questionnaire answers you get to open-ended questions. But content analysis can also be monumentally ambitious, as with studies that have set out to identify discriminatory attitudes towards other nations by painstakingly reviewing the verbal content of different newspapers in one country.

There are four stages to the task:

1. Identify your research question – either by prior decision (as when you are dealing with the answers to an open-ended question in a questionnaire) or as a result of exploratory work within the framework of the study. It is likely that this stage will go hand in glove with decisions made about the data sources that are to be analysed: they can be newspapers, books or magazines, advertisements, video-recordings, websites, graffiti on lavatory walls or tombstone inscriptions.

2. You may need to determine a sampling method – perhaps on different levels: for example:
   - complete units: which copies of which newspapers will you analyse?
   - parts of the whole: which items within each sampled newspaper will you analyse – the leader page, the front page lead, the letters page, the agony aunt piece, the ads – classified or display? (Each of these options might lead you to draw very different conclusions.)

   You should be able to claim that the data you emerge with is representative of the source and its content.

3. Next, you have to determine the categories of analysis that will govern your coding process. Will you be focusing on single words? On the repetition of phrases? Or will you attempt to extract and interpret 'meaning' from blocks of text? Advocates of a quantitative approach to content analysis argue that this

is the best way of achieving a high degree of reliability in the conclusions drawn, but those favouring a more reflective approach argue that just 'counting words' offers only limited systems of interpretation. It is difficult to teach the skills of content analysis in abstract; all researchers have to feel their way into the method by using a mixture of creative artistry and disciplined logical thought.

4. Once you have determined the foundation stones of your analysis, you will create a coding frame suitable for your purpose. It will need to be flexible, because, as with small sample interviewing, you will find that your understanding of both the process and the substance of what you are looking at will evolve as you progress.

You may need to distinguish between explicit meaning and implicit meaning. Some studies have employed content analysis in order to highlight discriminatory attitudes or behaviour, and they have frequently used imaginative ways of serving their theoretical ends. For example, Weigel et al. (1980) watched television drama and measured the time before the first black person made an appearance and the amount of interaction across races that occurred. Similar analyses have focused on the expressed nature of women's roles as portrayed in advertising or the way in which different occupational groups (nurses, policemen, accountants) are represented in television or radio drama.

The interpretation of implicit meaning is not straightforward. Here's why:

• You will need to have been rigorous in the analytical process in order to claim that you have not been guilty of prejudiced data selection.

• You must be careful about the interpretations you put on the representation of data; if the findings are potentially controversial, a safe way forward would be for you to ask one or two independent analysts to make their own interpretation alongside yours.

• You must remember that the origin of the material you have analysed is itself biased – TV plays, newspapers and even advertisements are written by individuals from a particular background. You need to be careful about the extent to which you generalise from what such media people produce to what society at large might say or feel.

Case studies

Case studies offer student researchers a golden opportunity to focus attention on topics relevant to their field without being tied to what they may see as too narrow an approach to methodology.

Case studies can be about:

- *Individual people:* The classic examples are from mental health studies or from post-Freudian therapeutic fields. The researcher identifies a child or an adult, and builds up a detailed profile that describes aspects of behaviour, reviews earlier life and considers the family setting. Somebody with an eating disorder would make a good subject for such a case study.
- *Individual people in a social context:* For example, the life of an elderly or disabled person living in an inhospitable urban environment or in residential care. The case study would aim to get beyond the stereotypical view of such people and locate them in a historical and situational context.
- *Dyad or family relations:* Another classic area of case study research has taken marriage (or its equivalent) as the starting point, and has looked at the nature of the relationships within the marriage and between the couple and other members of the family.
- *Groups:* Studies of street gangs are the traditional example of such a case study, but any interacting small group – in an office, leisure or sports club or, in many ways an ideal target, a time-limited holiday group.
- *Middle-range workplace settings:* Classrooms have been a frequent focus of case study research among educationalists, and committees (if you can get access to them) provide fruitful opportunities, although you would additionally need to be able to monitor what occurs on the fringes of the committee, before, during and afterwards.
- *Businesses or public sector organisations like schools or hospitals:* This is the heavy end of case study research, and is normally undertaken by generously resourced teams of professional analysts and financial consultants.

Case studies can employ any of the qualitative methods on offer – with observation, interviewing and document analysis the most likely elements to be brought into play.

If you asked me to recommend just one book on ...
doing a case study *it would be:*

Yin, Robert K (2002)
Case Study Research: Design and Methods, London, Sage

The main practical requirement when carrying out a case study is to have or move quickly towards a clear question in your mind. To take the six spheres of potential activity listed above, a possible question might be:

- *Individual people:* What is the effect of this individual's behaviour on their own position? (You will be tempted to ask the rather more ambitious question, 'Why are they behaving like this?', but others better qualified than you have probably already tried and failed to get an answer to that question.)
- *Individual people in a social context:* What is the effect of their environment on this individual's thoughts, feelings, attitudes and behaviour?
- *Dyad or family relations:* What is the nature of the effect that each party has on the other in this close family context? Or, more modestly, what do they think of each other, and how do their feelings manifest themselves?
- *Groups:* Who provides leadership? How is what the group does determined?
- *Middle-range workplace settings:* What factors hamper or facilitate the achievement of explicit objectives in the setting?
- *Businesses or public sector organisations:* Why is this company, this department not functioning as well as it should be doing?

The case study method offers you an excellent opportunity to learn how to apply qualitative research methods of a wide-ranging kind.

N = 1 explorations

N = 1 projects are a hybrid of experimental and qualitative methods. They tend to be used predominantly in the clinical, therapeutic or behavioural sciences, and they involve a sequence of questions: If you do something to a person (or a situation), what effect does it appear to have on that person (or situation)? If you stop doing it, does the 'effect' disappear – or not? The method is sometimes referred to as an ABAB approach, reflecting the fact that, within ethical limits, you can repeat the sequence (application, followed by withdrawal) several times to see what happens.

Because you are focusing on just one person or situation, you can comfortably employ qualitative-style interviewing techniques in order to complement the experimental findings and obtain verbal feedback about people's experience of what you have done.

A doctor might say to a patient; 'Here are three creams to try out on your skin rash. I want you to use an N = 1 approach to see which one works best – but you must do it very scientifically. Use one for ten days, then stop for ten; use the second for ten, then stop; and finally use the third for ten days. Come back and tell me what the results of this N = 1 experiment reveal to you.' The patient could also be invited to keep a careful record of the practical difficulties of following such instructions and of any unwanted side effects.

You can use the same approach in testing what makes for the best office or working environment: better lighting, more or less heating, the availability of a free drinks machine. Of course, you have to bear in mind the results of the classic Hawthorne experiment in which every change that was made, for better or worse, led to an increase in productivity because the staff appreciated being made the centre of attention by management (Roethlisberger and Dickson, 1939).

12 Analysing qualitative data

The analysis of qualitative data is one of the most exciting research tasks. With perseverance and an organised approach, you will emerge with a good analytical account of the evidence you have gathered, some reflections on the nature and meaning of that evidence, an acknowledgement of the possible influence upon it of your own subjective starting point and conclusions that flow naturally from your examination of the evidence.

In order to get to that point, it helps if you take three factors into account:

1. **Overlapping stages.** The job of qualitative data analysis is not ring-fenced. The various stages that you work through while practising qualitative research are 'all of a piece': your planning and data collection processes (which overlap with each other) very largely predetermine the *potential* quality of the end-product although its *actual* quality will depend substantially on your skills as a disciplined and imaginative analyst, theorist and author. Of course, the link between data collection and the finished report is present in any kind of research project: 'rubbish in, rubbish out' or RIRO, as the maxim has it. But with qualitative research, your *thinking* is the thread that runs right the way through all the stages of the project. You don't just do the interviews and observations and then, at the end, say to yourself, 'Right, what have I got?' By then, you will already have a fair idea. And what you have got will be largely predetermined by what you've already done.

2. **Qualitative research is different.** The special nature of qualitative research is something that you must bear in mind. A common mistake in qualitative data analysis is to behave as though you have done a survey; being tempted to describe and 'add up' what different respondents have said in the course of their conversations with you. Such a tendency, however, almost always means that you end up with the worst of both worlds:

you didn't gather the kind of sample that allows you to draw reliable (or even tentative) survey conclusions, and you risk missing the opportunity of delivering interpretive findings 'in the round' – exploring, for example, what you have learnt about your respondents' interactions with their social situation, their reflective feelings and how they view the links between present and past, together with other people's perspectives on your primary question.

3. **You need time.** In order to do justice to all the hard work you have put into the project, you must allow adequate time for the final stage. With a submission deadline to meet, there is a real risk that you will sell yourself short. Make sure you have time to get all your gathered material into a form suitable for analysis and give it the attention it deserves as you work on your draft report. Like many researchers before you, you may discover at this point that you have no choice but to work round the clock in order to emerge with something you will be proud of.

If you can take these factors in your stride, the likelihood of you producing a report that is 'better than satisfactory' will be greatly enhanced.

Let us, then, work through the different kinds of data analysis, starting with the very simplest – which doesn't mean it's always easy.

Content analysis of the answers to open-ended questions

Open-ended questions are used in both quantitative and qualitative research, but their proportionate significance in the project as a whole is likely to be very different in each case. In quantitative research, the answers you receive are generally quite brief, but the initial principles of analysis are common to both methods.

There are two degrees of complexity. First – and not truly qualitative at all – the answers can be very short, maybe just one word in length. You are required to make a list and then group them and subgroup them in whatever way the subject matter suggests. Very often, they may be responses to a relatively simple 'why?' question: Why do you go shopping at Tesco? Or an equally straightforward 'what?' question: 'What was it about this morning's lecture that you found (a) helpful and (b) unhelpful? (In a small sample qualitative methods study, you would certainly want to explore beyond and behind such answers; it would be a waste of an opportunity not to do so.) Having grouped the answers (remembering that there may well be multiple answers from any one respondent – many reasons why you shop at Tesco, for instance), the quantitative and the qualitative researchers would vary their handling of the material. If these are the answers given by a large sample within the framework of a survey, your aim will normally be to quantify them and structure the material in tabular format – possibly using some of the verbal material in the text. In a small sample study, you would not only be likely to have probed beyond the one word/one sentence responses but you would also try to avoid all reference to numbers (including phrases like 'A majority said ...'); instead the data should be used reflectively and in narrative format – allowing the reader to get a sense of the nature and meaning of the responses offered.

Second, there are responses, usually of more than one sentence, which contain material that falls fully into the category of qualitative methods. For example, on a customer comment card (in a hotel, for example), there may well be space for responses that could extend to a hundred words or more. These will need to be analysed in two quite different ways: on the one hand, there may be some counting to do, but there will also be a need for interpretive analysis, relating to levels of satisfaction or dissatisfaction, praise, anger or disappointment, and so on. You need to develop analytical frames that identify the targets commented upon – housekeeping, food, service, comfort. Don't edit words out: assume that every word matters. If you have the numbers in your sample to justify it, count as necessary; in any case, aim to produce written analyses that accurately reflect the facts and feelings which your data reveal. Mark with highlighter pens (or highlight on screen) any quotable quotes that you might wish to use.

Interpretive content analysis of complete interviews

The type of analysis that you perform will vary according to the nature of the research you are doing, the type of questions you are trying to get answers to and, perhaps, the disciplinary framework within which you are working. For example:

- In sociolinguistics (where you may be exploring the use, context or purpose of certain words, phrases or sounds) or in reflective exploration of feelings within the framework of theoretical psychology or sociology, you will almost certainly require a word-for-word typed or written transcription and, at times, access to technical systems of understanding.
- In any study of respondent opinion designed to get beyond the superficial views that characterise some kinds of social surveys, it may be possible to vary the levels of analysis at different points in the recording depending upon the apparent relevance of the material that is flowing. Such an approach would suggest the selective use of word-for-word transcription, together with edited summaries of those parts of the interview that contribute less fully to the central issues. This kind of editing process can only be done if it is the researcher who is producing the transcription – because only the researcher is in a position to make such editorial judgements.

A transcription is a complete manuscript record of what was said by all parties during the course of an audio-recorded interview. Producing it is a time-consuming task and sometimes, because of the inaudibility of the recording or because two people are speaking at once, a rather difficult one. Senior researchers may be fortunate enough to have a budget that enables them to pay a secretary to do the job for them, but for many students it's a case of DIY. The transcription should not attempt to edit or render grammatically correct what was said; it should include unfinished sentences, interruptions and swear words. If there are significant pauses, these should be indicated. Symbols can be used to indicate non-verbal pauses or 'meaningless' sounds. Mostly, they are not 'meaningless' at all.

Obtaining a full transcription of interviews in every case may be regarded as the ideal goal, because it means that you have in front of you the total body of generated verbal data. But the task is expensive of your time, and the benefits may not always be proportionate. Often, with submission deadlines looming and provided that the nature of the question to which you are seeking an answer makes it appropriate, an edited but detailed account of each interview will serve your purpose. On the other hand, it has to be said that *listening* to your tapes over and over again is time-consuming and by the time you've done that four or five times during the editing process – and struggled to track down the piece of conversation that you really want to quote precisely – you might end up feeling that an initial commitment to transcription would have been worthwhile.

Normally you should try to get the transcriptions done as soon as you have completed each interview. That way, not only do you spread the load of what is always an onerous job, but you are more likely to be able to remember or decipher snatches of mumbled conversation that don't come over too clearly on your audio-recording.

Let us, then, assume that you have produced a word-for-word transcription. What next? At this stage, the mental quality that is a prerequisite in all researchers – an alert and creative attention to detail – is brought into play. (Remember that genius is proverbially said to be 'an infinite capacity for taking pains'; and if you are blessed with that character trait, it will serve you well in any kind of research analysis. I always think a slightly obsessional personality is a positive asset – even a career requirement – in a researcher.)

Eight key factors in qualitative data analysis

1. Remember that the aim of qualitative research is to explore individual or situational perspectives and gain an in-depth understanding of personal feelings and experience. Keep asking yourself if you are delivering the goods in this respect.
2. Remind yourself of your research question(s), and keep coming back to it (or them). You are allowed to introduce secondary ideas (and formulate additional or supplementary questions) as they emerge from your data; sometimes these may unexpectedly take over the lead role in your write-up – and you need to be alert to that possibility. But if you allow your thoughts to become too diffuse, too detached from your research question(s), you will find it difficult to structure the emergent conclusions as they develop.
3. If you are analysing the transcription from one interview

before you have completed your interviews with other people, you should make a note of any issues that emerge during analysis that you will wish to explore further in succeeding interviews. This dynamic and circular relationship between data analysis and data collection is a fundamental difference between qualitative and quantitative research methods.

4. It is purely a matter of personal choice whether you work on screen, with a handwritten manuscript, or by making marks on a hard copy transcription sheet. In the latter case, you must make sure that your copy has wide margins, double-spacing and is on one side of the paper only; you should have a good supply of pencils or pens in different colours and some coloured highlighter pens. With on-screen analysis, you can use font colour systems and text highlighting to classify portions of text and establish links between them.

5. The main task that faces you – that of emerging with an accurate account of what your interviewees have shared with you – can best be tackled by creating, in respect of each interview, a two-column table on your screen. Your transcription or interview summary should be stored in one column and your parallel commentary in the other. The most effective way of proceeding is to give yourself a large number of rows (added to, as necessary) into each of which, in the left-hand column, you put a short block of transcribed text. You can then easily use the equivalent right-hand column cell for recording your annotations against each block – either on-screen or in handwriting on the hard copy.

6. If each interview contains a series of semi-structured questions, the responses to these can be colour-highlighted, so that later you can look at every interviewee's contributions side by side – either by copying them into a different file or table or just reading them in colour sequence as you make notes. In the right-hand annotation column, you can jot down any thoughts about the responses (hesitations, ambiguities, misunderstandings, levels of assertiveness, defensiveness or emotional reactions).

7. A high-quality interview should go beyond the asking of semi-structured questions and seek to engage the interviewee in free-flowing conversation. It is this material that calls for the

greatest level of analytical alertness. It is easy to gloss over 'throwaway' remarks and apparently superfluous comments or to ignore emotional dimensions to the encounter – easy, but wrong. They should all be noted in your column under whatever headings are apparent to you. An unanticipated contribution by just one interviewee can sometimes change the balance of your conclusions quite significantly – provided you are wide awake and open-minded enough to hear it.

8. So, you've got your transcription broken down into short passages, each contained within a cell in your left-hand column. You've highlighted the answers to specific questions. What next? This coming stage is the hardest of all, but also the most crucial. It is the stage which, if successfully completed, distinguishes successful qualitative research analysis from the mere presentation of anecdotal interview extracts. It is universally agreed that the stage involves three separate processes:

- The first requires you to enter in the right-hand annotation column a detailed commentary on the data as it is recorded. This is a *thinking* process, an opportunity for you to *react to* your interviewee's material. Even if some of the interview content looks straightforward (and students often feel disappointed about that), you should nevertheless actively pinpoint all the elements in it; and if there are sections where you feel that there is more to it than meets the eye, then you should say that – while indicating by colour-coding that you are making an interpretation that may be speculative.

- The second process requires you to identify the principal emergent ideas in each piece of transcripted data. Bryman and Burgess (1994) talk about the building of 'typologies and taxonomies'; Robson (1993) speaks of 'counting, patterning, clustering and factoring'; while Walliman (2001, p. 262) is more down to earth, referring to 'interesting issues raised and new questions resulting from these'. What you are really doing, though, is creating a coding frame, into which (most of) your accumulated data will gradually fit. Whereas in survey research, the coding frame is based on the questionnaire or research schedule that you started off with, with small sample, open-ended interviewing, it is the words of the interviewees that determine the shape of it.

You, as the data analyst, act as the intellectual intermediary between what was said and what it means *structurally* within the context of your research question.

- The third process occurs when you have a number of transcripts to work on side by side. This is the stage when you begin to identify and reduce to manageable proportions the central themes that will drive your report. You may wish to go down the road of concept generation or theory development, but more probably in many small-scale explorations, the focus will be on the presentation of an accurate account of what your various interviewees, when reviewed together as a strategic sample, enable you to say about your original research question and the additional themes that you have accumulated. Good study reports can be built around 'why?' questions: Why did the interviewee vote for a particular political party? Why do some student teachers succeed better than others at keeping order in the classroom? Why do people buy second homes or overseas property? Why do students drop out of university? Why do people spend money they haven't got? All these questions have theory links, but the student researcher will deliver a successful report if, say, five or six topics are identified from the full range of interviews and the material offered by interviewees in respect of each topic is put together reflectively, accurately and informatively. That, in turn, will lead to the drawing of conclusions, which is the goal at the end of this third process.

Let me try and illustrate how this final stage of qualitative research analysis works by briefly quoting two examples of student work.

being an only child

Fiona Watts asked 'What does it mean to be an only child?' and interviewed 17 people between the ages of 6 and 64. Interviews were reflective and respondents were allowed to lead. Watts found that after only three interviews themes were beginning to arise, and from that point she began to focus in greater depth on these themes while still being alert to the emergence of new themes.

being an only child *continued*

The researcher noted three main themes that related in almost every interview to the experience of being an only child:

- An awareness of the importance of a support system
- A tendency to be more independent and self-sufficient
- The relationship with a parent or parents came over as being particularly important.

Two less prominent themes were identified:

- Feeling the centre of attention and/or feeling under pressure to perform
- Better relationships with adults than with other children.

Overall, Watts concludes that, although there have traditionally been negative stereotypes about only children, many of her interviewees viewed the experience in positive terms.

sexual infidelity

Emma Tarrington interviewed 10 male undergraduates in their early twenties in order to explore with them the question: 'Why are men unfaithful in their sexual relationships?'

The interviewer made handwritten notes; interviews were rewritten into bullet-point format; and the relevant information was colour-coded. Information that couldn't be linked to other interviews was uncoded. Fourteen codes were identified and, following further analysis, five major themes emerged:

- Taking advantage of opportunities
- Situational infidelity
- The need to feel desirable
- The effects of a long-distance girlfriend
- The presence or absence of an expression of guilt.

Tarrington found it difficult to know what 'meaning' could be put on the evidence she had accumulated, and she felt that no one factor was paramount. 'One conclusion that we can be confident

sexual infidelity *continued*

in making is that infidelity is not simple,' but she concluded that 'each individual appears to have a reasonable rationale behind his behaviour'.

What should now be clear to you is that the task of data analysis cannot be reduced to a perfect formula. Its success depends on:

- how well – and how intensively – you interact with your data
- how well you organise your written analyses of the transcripts
- how cleverly you identify the five or six themes to emerge from your data
- how well you incorporate and do justice to the different perspectives that your interviewees offer you.

a cautionary note

In the analysis of qualitative research interviews, two temptations must be resisted. First, don't fall into the trap of 'counting numbers'. It is almost always inappropriate to refer to the fact that 'six people said this and four said the opposite', however seductive the idea might feel. The reason is partly to do with probability theory: in small samples, the kinds of differences you identify are unlikely to stand up to scrutiny. But it is mainly because that is not what the methodology is designed for: your aim is to bring to the surface the reflective thoughts and experiences of a strategically selected group of people and the light they throw on an identified practical, policy-related or conceptual question.

The second trap is much harder to resist and reflects a common shortcoming in student-produced qualitative research reports. Don't think that you have done enough just by presenting a long stream of quotations from your various interviews. By all means, in the course of your analysis, identify 'usable' quotes, but when you have done so, you still have to complete the three separate processes identified in factor 8 above: *thinking, creating structures and identifying themes*. You will find it easier to avoid the

a cautionary note *continued*

simple 'listing of quotations' trap if you constantly return to the task of reminding yourself of your research question – even if it has been revised in the course of data analysis. A high-quality report will lead the reader smoothly and seamlessly through the evidence that is presented towards the thematic conclusion(s) that constitute(s) the project's end-result. (Avoiding this trap will also result in final project reports being much shorter than they often are, because it will lead to a reduced tendency to include far too many lengthy quotations.)

Observation

Think about this: the analysis of an audio-recorded and transcripted interview, which I have acknowledged requires your full concentration and creative skill, is itself a kind of observation. You are, in retrospect, observing yourself in communication with another person. You may be focusing on the words of the interviewee, but, in accordance with the principles of qualitative research theory, you are also paying attention to your own performance and its impact on the situation.

The analysis of any true observation study, because it usually focuses on interactions between more than two people and because you are probably unable to hear or monitor everything that occurs, is necessarily both more complex and yet less complete. Inexperienced students should be wary of embarking on such a project without good supervision.

There are many analytical models designed to be used in observation studies, but, as Bell (1999, p. 164) wisely remarks:

the sad fact is that, in spite of all the tried-and-tested methods that have been employed by experienced researchers over the years, there never seems to be an example that is quite right for the particular task. Inevitably, you will find you have to adapt or to devise a completely new approach.

I stand by my golden rule: if you have a clear research question and one that deters you from trying to watch anything and everything that occurs, then the tasks of both data collection and data analysis will be achievable.

Whatever it is that your participant or non-participant observation project may be focused on (a meeting, a demonstration, a club activity, shop interactions, traffic movement, crowd behaviour), you should have – usually following a question-seeking exploratory stage – a question to answer. You may seek the answer by watching or listening; you may use audio equipment or a video camera; you may yourself be completely invisible, inconspicuous or fully involved; the subjects of your interest may or may not know what you are doing; and – strange as it may seem – the data you gather can often be subject to both qualitative or quantitative analysis.

Qualitatively, it is best to design your own analytical framework. These are some of the things you can do:

1. Devise a way of identifying dominant or submissive people – or indeed any other adjectival category of person that lends itself to an accurate or measurable judgement on the basis of your observations.
2. Analyse the interactions that take place between the participants.
3. Identify any open expression of feelings (anger, pleasure, pain, resentment, hostility, sadness).
4. Monitor visually the role of one identified person (maybe, for example, the behaviour of the solitary male in an all-female group, or vice versa).
5. Take note of situational events that impact on the members of your group.
6. Check out decision-making processes.

One approach, in particular, lends itself to a time-limited student project. It requires you to test out your research question either by observing natural behaviour in an appropriate setting or by adopting an experimental approach in order to engineer and monitor reactions. Television programmes that confront innocent citizens with artificially created absurd or antisocial situations are using this model; the question they invite the viewer to ask is 'How will people react if they see, for example, a car being vandalised or crushed under a heavy metal weight?'

observing behavioural dominance in children

Jeanne Schofield secured access to a preschool playgroup and obtained consent to set up a video camera. She recorded 13 children at play with the aim of analysing the presence of dominating and non-dominating behaviour. Each observation lasted 20 minutes, twice a week for three weeks. She made written notes at the end of each observation.

The researcher adapted an established rating scale (Fawcett, 1996) in order to code the behaviour. It had four points from 'very dominant' to 'very cooperative'. The ratings were based on observations of language, tone of voice, facial expression, body language and physical contact.

Schofield recorded 208 interactions in all of which 40 per cent involved some dominant behaviour. She found that boys were significantly more likely to engage in dominant behaviour, whether in play with other boys or in cross-gender interactions. However, she was able to compute that the gender difference was primarily caused by the extreme dominance of just two boys out of the eight observed.

Schofield discovered some of the problems that observation research can encounter:

- Intrusiveness: she felt that some of the children's behaviour reflected their awareness of the presence of the camera.
- Technological shortcomings: the omnidirectional microphone used meant that general 'noise' in the group masked specific verbal exchanges.
- Bias: she was not able to use an inter-rater, and was sensitive to the possibility that her interpretations might have been subjectively influenced.
- Retrospectively, she wondered whether she might have been better to focus on a particular child.

If you are engaged in ethnographic, participant observation or insider research, it is not normally possible for you to make your record of events at the same time as they are occurring. The data that you analyse, therefore, is drawn from your own log, diary and notebooks. The way that you organise the analytic process will be driven by your research question, but it can often be subdivided by reference to six key words:

1. *Who?* Who are the key figures? Who interacts with whom? As in a theatre programme, you can draw up a list of dramatis personae and each name can have its own data entry.
2. *What?* What activities take place? What emotions are on show? What is the social structure within the setting? What pleasure and pain are felt?
3. *Where?* Where do the events you are observing take place? What does it look like? Do different kinds of events take place in different places? Is there any sign of territoriality – locations to which some of the players have access and from which others are excluded?
4. *When?* In what order do different events occur? Is there a daily, weekly or seasonal pattern to events?
5. *How?* How do different people achieve their ends, cope with negative experiences or manage their feelings? How functional or dysfunctional is the setting as a whole, or some discrete part of it?
6. *Why?* This question comes, not during the main phase of analysis, but at the end – when you are trying to interpret what it all means: How do you explain some of the things that you have recorded? What meaning do they have for the particisipants (you may have to go back and ask them) and the setting as a whole? If you want to draw analytical conclusions or make recommendations for change, what does your data allow you to suggest?

Observing an experiment

Observation as a methodological technique can be combined with an experimental research design. Social psychology student, Georgina Key, asked the question: 'If a pregnant woman tries to go through a narrow door at the same time as people are intending to come through it in the opposite direction, will the people stand back and let her through?' She hypothesised that they would. In a number of city-centre stores, a pregnant-looking young woman role-played the action, and the public's reactions were observed and their behaviours noted down. A great deal of preparation and piloting were needed to achieve the desired effect in the planned scenario.

The experiment was carried out 200 times: on 100 occasions the model wore her very convincing pregnancy kit (hired from a fancy-dress shop); on 100 she was her normal slim-line self.

The results were twofold:

- There was no significant difference in behaviour within the sample as a whole.
- But when the gender of the other person was taken into account, there was a difference – but in the opposite direction to that hypothesised. In practice men were more likely to defer to the non-pregnant woman than to the pregnant-looking woman. Although this may be thought to display a shameful lack of courtesy, it is, of course, explicable by evolutionary theory: the pregnant woman is self-evidently 'not available' and therefore less worthy of male attention.

Key has one fascinating cameo comment. Five teenagers pushed rudely past the pregnant model and then stood outside chatting for a while. They suddenly noticed the observer standing there making notes and they went and asked what it was about. 'When the observer explained, the group all claimed that if they had been involved they would have deferred. Little did they know that they had been' – and had not done what they said they would.

This example clearly illustrates the argument for and the advantage of observation studies: by using them, you avoid the need to ask people what they *would* do in hypothetical circumstances; instead you are able to record reality as it happens. In this example the analytical stage was straightforward and unambiguous: count the numbers of people who stood back and those who kept on coming; distinguish between male and female members of the public; note any differences that seemed to relate to age or whether the 'other' consisted of more than one person. Test them for statistical significance. The conclusion drawn, therefore, was unashamedly quantitative, but the method was qualitative insofar as it relied on observations of real life.

Focus groups

You, as the investigator, have been responsible for setting up a focus group; you have your own research question(s) firmly in your mind; you have given the group its task(s); and, very often, you have retained the right and responsibility to prompt the group members in their deliberations so that they fully cover all aspects of the question to which you want some answers. The situation has been structured by you, and this makes the creation of an analytical framework easier than in unstructured observations.

You have a list of topics or questions that make up the focus group's agenda. The group members are not normally told of these in advance, and you may introduce them into the discussion in random order, but your analytical tool will contain them in an organised fashion – each topic given its own computer file or large sheet of paper. There should not normally be more than six topics, and fewer than that can be advantageous.

The key to good focus group analysis is to recognise that the process does not exist as a distinct stage but interweaves dynamically with the data collection task. Your analysis begins the moment your first group comes together. As the investigator, you will be managing the group as it engages with the questions you present to it, but you will simultaneously be absorbing, thinking about and mentally organising the material the group members give you in return. This enables you to adapt the prompts you make in each succeeding group in order to throw more light on the key issues as they become clearer in your own mind; it also provides you with a clue as to how many more groups you need to run before diminishing returns set in.

In your analysis sheets, question by question, topic by topic, group by group, you will need to consider the following:

1. What opinions are emerging?
2. Are there dominant opinions, or is there a wide spread of different opinions?
3. Beware of the disproportionate influence of any member with an assertive personality; ensure that you draw in the less confident talkers in order to avoid emerging with a seriously biased misreading of the group's *overall* view.

4. Don't be too eager to identify or press for consensus: there isn't a topic in the world on which everyone agrees. This is a very common student error. You should be wary of any draft sentence that begins 'The group felt/thought/expressed the view that …'. Your aim is not to emerge with some kind of view held by a democratic majority, but to allow the full range of reflective opinions to be represented.

5. In order to avoid another potentially dangerous error in focus group analysis, you must be careful to ensure that your interpretations are neutral and in no way influenced by your own opinions or your original expectations of what the focus groups might come up with.

6. Can you detect any pattern to the differences of opinion that present themselves – by age, gender, estimated social class? You won't be able to write conclusively about these and you won't prove anything on the basis of two or three groups but it is legitimate to refer to such tentative thoughts that might, theoretically, lend themselves to further study – either in a survey or in new focus group exercises.

7. Distinguish between opinions expressed spontaneously and those which only emerged in response to prompts.

8. Be especially alert to ambiguities of opinion, non-sequiturs and examples of internal inconsistency. Most people don't always think logically or honestly.

9. Take particular note of intensely held opinions, emotional outbursts or vigorous disagreements within the group.

10. Has the group provided you with examples that might be used to illustrate your analysis?

11. Move towards a point where you can differentiate between two or three 'big issues' that have emerged, which you will wish to give headline coverage to in your report, and the more diffuse or supplementary expressions of opinion. (One of the many mistakes I made in my early research career was to write long reports in which everything was presented as though it were of equal importance, with the result that readers tended not to notice the bits that mattered; I came to realise that it is the author's responsibility to guide the reader towards the conclusions that deserve to be emphasised.)

Professional focus group moderators usually have an assistant accompanying them who welcomes the participants, acts as host and observer and takes notes from a position outside the group. Superior analyses can be achieved if the moderator and assistant moderator share in the task of reviewing the data; this makes it less likely that the one-person analyst will miss something glaringly obvious or impose a biased perspective on the record. For the student, such an arrangement is not normally possible, but, if it can be arranged, the involvement of a colleague (or supervisor) in at least a part of the reading process will go some way towards simulating it.

Case studies

Depending on the precise nature of the case study (which can be focused on a small group, a work setting like a factory floor, a community like a village, a street or even a small town, a health centre or a classroom, a developing situation in the community like an open air meeting or concert, a dyad, a family or a single person), the research analyses may include the exploration of background statistics, the review of documentary evidence and data from interviews, groups or observations. In other words, the methodologies involved are those which have already been discussed. The distinctive feature of case studies is that the data relates to a specified period of time – an hour, a day, a week, a month, a year or more. Some of the classic studies of social anthropology were case studies of a discrete community; Sigmund Freud's work was based on case study material drawn from his work with patients; generations of social workers and counsellors have been taught how to follow suit with a particular focus on family dynamics; and social historians have made use of the case study approach.

For the student, the key to a successful case study is to start out with a sharp focus. Often this is best done if the starting point is the introduction of an innovation in the 'case' – the arrival of a new boss in an office, the administration of a new therapeutic procedure, a change of diet, the arrival of a new group of students within the framework of an established course programme. In this way, especially if you can include a before-and-after dimension, the analysis can be concentrated on the apparent impact of the new development:

- Outline the personal or situational factors before the 'innovation'
- Indicate what effect it was thought the innovation might have
- Record reactions to it, attitudes towards it, interactions prompted by it, expressed views about it
- Record its apparent impact – including both positive and negative aspects.

Another approach is to focus your research question around a particular issue: What interpersonal or other tensions are apparent, how are they handled and what is their impact on the case study situation? How unified are the people in pursuit of a homogeneous goal? Obviously, the nature of the case study context will lead to wide variations in the appropriateness of different questions.

Triangulation and multiple (or mixed) methods

The analysis of your data in a multimethod or triangulated approach is not, initially, problematic. You simply pursue each task step by step in an organised fashion. But difficulty can arise at later stages when you need to relate different pieces of evidence to each other and incorporate them into your write-up. Sometimes, it is appropriate to keep the findings separate, allowing them to build up a cumulative portrait of your subject. At other times, you will aim to interweave them, so that they contribute seamlessly to the drawing of a well-supported conclusion. You may recognise that these are the same kinds of strategic questions that novelists face when confronted with the task of presenting narrative accounts of simultaneous events occurring in different locations. You, like the novelist, must employ judgement, skill and imagination in determining how to proceed.

NUD*IST, NVivo and computer analyses

Software has been developed in support of qualitative data analysis, most notably, in the US, by Lyn and Tom Richards. Tom Richards is a computer scientist who designed and developed the NUD*IST software and has since taken it forward into NVivo. Lyn Richards is a sociologist who, like many researchers, felt the need for IT support in order to help with some of the more cumbersome and time-consuming processes that are involved in qualitative methods data analysis. The first packages came onto the market in the 1980s and they have continued to develop, with NVivo 7 launched in 2006.

The claim is that they have transformed the time-consuming and complex tasks of analysing qualitative databases 'by hand' and that they help the researcher:

- manage the literature review
- store data conveniently
- search the database and draw out thematic material
- maintain a research record
- import and export information into different software packages such as Word, PowerPoint and Excel.

Basically, NVivo is an enormously powerful database: it stores transcripted material and has powerful search and retrieve functions allowing researchers to handle very large data sets, perform complex searches at the touch of a button and organise material that might otherwise be overlooked.

Like all computer programs, NVivo is a tool that depends on the researcher having developed the skills to use it effectively. And it doesn't do your thinking for you.

Anything from open coding to inductive theory building needs a human being to bring creativity and originality to the data. Computers are unable to 'see' themes in the data, although once themes have been identified and classified by the researcher, the software is able to search for reoccurrences; it is in this respect that NVivo can be a very handy tool and save lots of time spent trawling through data. (My thanks to Caitlin Notley for her generous help with this section.)

If you asked me to recommend just one book on ...
qualitative data analysis *it would be:*

Gibbs, Graham R (2006)
How to Analyse Qualitative Data, London, Sage

PART 4 The last lap

13 **Writing your report**

I take there to be two self-evident facts about writing. First, there are many different ways of approaching the task. Professional authors – novelists, journalists, producers of official or commercial documents – all develop their own distinctive style. They will have picked up tips along the way from teachers, supervisors, colleagues. Most will have learnt to become alert to the techniques used in the written material that they read. For example, if you look at pieces of reputable journalism in the national press, you will see that, if the people involved are not famous, the opening paragraph or two will be designed to catch the reader's attention and the details of names and places are threaded into the body of the article rather than being put 'up front' – as you or I might be tempted to do. In regional newspapers, by contrast, the geographical relevance of any story to local readers is highlighted in the headline and the first few paragraphs.

Second, the shape and length of compositions will vary hugely, depending on the context, the purpose and the requirements specified by those in editorial authority. This is, of course, particularly so with regard to research project reports, where the word length is usually clearly spelt out by course leaders.

How to produce a successful report

You will already be familiar with the art of writing because of all the essays you have prepared over the years, but there are still five suggestions that will help to lay the foundations for you to produce a successful research report:

1. It is misleading to think that the writing stage only begins when you've completed your data collection and analysis. You should keep a report file or folder in active use from the very beginning of your work. At various points in the working process, you can draft a literature review, outline your aims

and methods, and, if you are using quantitative methods and therefore know well in advance the likely structure of your final report, even create a dummy outline of how you think your findings might look. If yours is a qualitative research project, you will find that as your topic categories, typologies or themes take shape during data collection and analysis, these will indicate the sections that will probably form the backbone of your draft report. Sometimes, however, the key concluding elements of your report only become clear at the very end of the analytical process, and you must avoid getting trapped by preconceived ideas or assumptions.

2. If you are actively thinking about your project all the time you are doing it (as most researchers say they do), you will find that you stumble across pertinent quotations in books, magazines, journals and newspapers. Write them down and keep the reference carefully.

3. It is important to keep a careful record of any quotations from other authors that you might wish to include. Be painstaking in noting down the relevant references – author's surname and initials, title of the book or journal article (plus, in the latter case, the name of the journal, volume and issue number), publisher, date and relevant page numbers.

4. You may find that phrases or allusions occur to you that might be suitable. But don't force them in. The other day when I was watching the birds feeding in my garden, a simile came into my mind about something that could be described as being 'like a bluetit with a nut allergy'. It grieves me that I haven't been able to find an appropriate context for it yet.

5. Many students like to present their report in a visually appealing manner. This is certainly a desirable demonstration of professionalism, and I would not want to discourage it. But it is important to emphasise that an attractive package does not compensate for any deficiency in content.

If you asked me to recommend just one book on ...
report writing *it would be:*

Murray, Rowena (2002)
How to Write a Thesis, Buckingham, Open University Press

The shape of your report

The primary requirement for success is a report that, within the limits of the word length specified, follows a predictable pattern:

1. Prelims
2. Introduction of the topic
3. Literature review
4. Research aim(s)
5. The methods used
6. Research findings
7. Discussion
8. Conclusion
9. References

Prelims

A contents page can be included behind the title page, and, at the foot of this, you should acknowledge those who have given you assistance – including your teacher and supervisor (even though it's their job to help you). If you are writing for publication, you will usually be expected to lead off with an abstract that provides a very brief summary of your work, and some journals will ask you to indicate four or five keywords intended to be of value in any computerised database system that might accommodate your report.

Introduction

Your introduction should be quite brief and might refer primarily to what is interesting, attractive, theoretically important or topical about the focus of the research you are about to present.

Literature review

The length of your literature review will be determined largely by the overall word length you are required to work towards. As a rough guide, it should normally take up about a quarter or a third of the total word space available. In many ways, the literature review is 'just another essay', and most of you will be well practised at the craft. It is, though, an especially important piece of writing and one that you should approach seriously. Its traditional purpose is fourfold:

- It properly ensures that you have briefed yourself beforehand, and that you are fully aware of what other research exists in your chosen field. In the context of some courses, you will be expected to outline the theoretical issues that link up with your chosen topic.
- It enables you to discuss the strengths and weaknesses of what other people have done and reflect on the relevant field of knowledge.
- It provides an established framework to which you can refer in order to indicate the extent to which you have drawn on previously published work for the design of your own project.
- It allows you to comment on aspects of your own methodology (in comparison with what others have done) or set your eventual findings alongside those already reported in the literature.

Sadly, in some instances, literature reviews have become something of a drudge and a formality and are of poor quality, which is a shame because they lie at the heart of the scientific tradition, which holds that all new research done, whatever the method or field, gains in value through being related to the existing body of knowledge and opinion.

Research aims

The section on research aims should be short, precise and accurate. In quantitative research, it will normally reflect the aims you identified at the outset, emphasising the research question you set out to answer. In qualitative research, your aims and the research question may have evolved during the project; if so, you should clearly indicate the nature and outcome of this process.

Methods

You should describe your methodology in detail. There is an unwelcome tendency sometimes to employ complex terms in an attempt to sound impressive or because you've been told that that is what you should be doing. If that is the requirement of your course and its teacher, then so be it. My own view is that you should aim to keep the account of your methodology simple and only use words that you fully understand:

- What did you do by way of preparation? Exploration, preliminary discussions with 'experts' in the subject, piloting?
- What kind of a sample did you gather? What are its strengths and weaknesses?
- What happened next? Reflective interviewing? A survey? An experiment or quasi-experiment? The use of an interview schedule? Observation? Mixed methods?
- How did you set about the task of setting it up and running it?
- What difficulties arose? There are *always* difficulties, and the mark of a good researcher is not only to be able to deal with them as they occur but also to describe and discuss them in some detail afterwards.
- How did you analyse your data? What computer programs did you use, if any? Don't hesitate to describe in detail the more mundane pen and paper elements or the on-screen file management procedures you used in the course of analysis. All researchers know that these are the elements that lie at the heart of the analytical stage. Again, what difficulties did you encounter?

The findings

The findings constitute the heart of your report. I shall return to the topic in a moment, but the main thing to say is that you should leave plenty of time to organise and write about the output from your data analysis stage. You should also be prepared, if you want a really high-quality report, to take your writing through several drafts before you are entirely satisfied with it.

The discussion

The discussion is, in effect, a spin-off from the findings, but, even in studies that have used qualitative methods (where it isn't always easy to draw a clear distinction), it should always have a section to itself.

The conclusion

The conclusion should normally be brief and it can sometimes be drafted as a final paragraph in the 'discussion' section. It is the most challenging part of the whole exercise because the conclusion contains the two or three sentences that you want the reader to remember about your work. You've reported your findings in detail and you've discussed them at length. But, in a busy world, just how would you sum it all up in 200 words? What is the single most important finding? Don't let it get lost in the body of the report.

References

Make sure that the references are accurate, alphabetically listed by surname, complete and in an acceptable style. You can, if you wish, use a numbering system, but most research writing uses the system that lists the author's name, publication date and page number at the appropriate point in the text – like this (Davies, 2007, p. 214) – and lists them alphabetically in a bibliography at the end.

The art of drafting

You may think that those who write for a living are able to produce a finished product 'just like that'. If so, you might feel that you should be able to do the same and that you are an abject failure if your words don't fall into place so easily. There may be one or two top-quality journalists who can pen 1500 words of supremely elegant prose at the drop of a hat (or speak it into an audio recorder or voice-sensitive computer), but the truth is that most people faced with a task of authorship quickly learn that it is a much lengthier process than they had anticipated.

It is wise to assume that, in writing your report, you will go through three, possibly four, draft versions.

Draft 1

Draft 1 can be really rough and messy. The important thing is that you get down on paper as much as you can of what needs to be included, with gaps labelled in such a way as to indicate the search procedures you have to undertake in order to fill them in. It can be shorter than the required word length, although it may not be. The beauty of having draft 1 is that it gives you a real sense of the shape and scale of the finished product, even if the sentences, the grammar and the spelling are not perfect.

Draft 2

Draft 2 requires you to work painstakingly through draft 1, editing sentences and phraseology, checking for accuracy, taking bits out, adding bits in, improving the shape of tables and charts, and – using the wonders of MS Word – juggling with the positioning of entire paragraphs or pages in order to ensure that the reader will benefit from a smooth thought flow.

Draft 3

Draft 3 involves doing draft 2 all over again. The main task may be much easier by now, although the basic fact is that with every change you make, the quality of the finished piece of work gets better. There may still be irritating gaps in your text that require you to spend time digging out missing material or even going back to your data to rewrite an unsatisfactory section. Another job to be done at draft 3 stage will be to check the word length and get the text to fit the specified requirements; linked with this, but of value in its own right, you can work your way through the manuscript just deleting superfluous words – like that word 'just' that I used there. You'll be amazed at how many cuts you can make without losing anything of value. Thirdly, you will need to ensure that your references are complete: there should never be a single proper name in the text that is not referenced at the end of your report.

Draft 4

Draft 4 is the last stage and is mainly about layout and structure, although you will still stumble across misspellings, missing words and infelicitous phraseology. Check that your tables and charts are located where they should be, your pages are not too crowded and your format conforms to any requirements that have been speci-fied by your course handbook.

One last detail: although you can and should, by all means, use your computer's spellchecker, remember that it isn't foolproof: if you have written 'now' when you meant 'not', the meaning of a sentence might well be the opposite of what you intended it to be – but the spellchecker won't detect it. You should always do (or get a friend to do) a proofreader's check on the text before you are finally satisfied that it is as near perfect as it can be.

a note on word length

I know that students have to work to the word length that their
courses require of them, but over the years I've become
convinced that the tradition in some departments of asking
undergraduates to deliver lengthy research reports or dissertations is a mistake. There are three reasons:

- It means that students don't learn the art of editing down.
  Take this comment – admittedly about his experience of short
  story writing – from the novelist Ian Rankin (2002, p. 2):

    I've managed to whittle stories down from 800 words to 200 – a
    struggle, but useful in that I came to learn just how much it is
    possible to leave out. There's no place for fat on a story: it has to
    be lean and fit.

- I've had the misfortune, as an external examiner, to have to
  mark hundreds of reports ranging from 20,000 to 40,000
  words long; and I've even heard of one course that asked
  undergraduates for book-length reports of 60,000. These have
  all been from short research projects contained within the
  space of a term or a semester or part of a one-year
  programme. What happens is that students just pad the dissertations out with unnecessarily long quotes from the literature,
  or, in the case of qualitative methods reports, they include
  long extracts from interviews without attempting to work out
  how best to communicate the meaning of their material to a
  busy reader.
- Most important of all, students become competent (more or
  less) at writing long reports, but they don't learn the writing
  and editing skills that would serve them better in their future
  non-academic careers by teaching them how to capture the
  essence of a complex piece of work in a way that is 'lean and
  fit'. This practice has probably contributed to the tendency in
  the public sector for official documents to be overlong and to
  have been produced without the benefit of editorial discipline.

Presenting your findings in a quantitative research study

Planning and carrying out your data collection often feels like the exciting and creative part of your project; the job of data analysis tests your tenacity, skill and concentration; but it is in the writing of your findings section that your work reaches its goal, its fulfilment. Some people feel a sense of anticlimax at this stage, partly because they've lived with their project for so long and partly because they think their results don't have quite the sparkling quality they had hoped for. Occasionally, when they turn to the task of writing up, some novice researchers think there is nothing of interest to focus on, and only spring to life when their supervisor points out something they've missed or not realised the significance of. It is always a good idea, at this stage, to share your work with somebody else – perhaps by making a brief presentation of your work to a small group of colleagues; you'll be surprised how often another person will notice something you'd missed.

In the first draft of your findings section, you should follow a conventional pattern. If time allows and the demands of editorial logic demand it, you can always reorder your material and present it differently in the final draft.

Start with a statistical outline of your sample. Present the frequency distributions that describe it – gender, age, ethnic identity and whatever other specific classifications your study requires you to pinpoint. You don't have to use tables in every instance. For example the gender split can be outlined simply within a narrative paragraph, inserting percentage figures in brackets.

presenting percentages

The use of percentages is normal in quantitative research reports. There is a purist view among some statisticians that, if your sample is less than 100, percentages are inappropriate; but this argument is outweighed by the fact that, even with samples of 30 or 40, the quality of comprehension is greatly improved, for the reader's benefit, if you translate numbers (or Ns) into percentages. In tables, you should use the symbol % at the head of the

presenting percentages *continued*

relevant column; in the body of the text, however, it is stylistically preferable to use the verbal form 'per cent'.

A common error is to introduce an element of spurious accuracy by using decimal places. For example, if out of a sample of 93, 69 interviewees are female, you may be tempted to say that women make up 74.2 per cent or even 74.19 per cent of the total. Perhaps you feel it gives an air of scientific accuracy to your project, but it's inappropriate and wrong. You should report simply that the sample was made up of 69 women (74 per cent) and 24 men (26 per cent).

If you use tables to present your frequency distributions, you should also include the relevant details in the text. For example, assuming that you have shown in tabular form the detailed answers to your question about ethnic identity, a linked paragraph in the text might read:

The greater part of the sample (69 per cent) described them-selves as white British; the two largest minority groups said they were white Irish (17 per cent) or African-Caribbean (8 per cent).

This draws your readers' attention to the ethnic make-up of your sample while leaving them free to check on the details by looking at the table.

The next stage will probably involve you presenting the heart of your findings – or at least (if your research has a number of aspects) the first of several parts of the heart. Because every project that is done uses different methods, asks different questions and presents different problems, there is always a sense in which only the student-author is in a position to determine how to handle the material in such a way that it is accurate, inform-ative and interesting enough to keep the reader's attention. Here are some guidelines.

How do I deal with my SPSS output?

You will have received teaching and guidance that allows you to input your coded data and to call on the many SPSS facilities designed to process it. You will see your tables and calculations on screen and you will proudly print them out. But at this stage, students often make the mistake of thinking that they should use the SPSS output just as it appears. For a successful high-quality report, that is not so. You must learn to think of your SPSS output as representing the rough workings characteristic of research in progress; its layout isn't meant to be used as your finished product:

1. The SPSS output will include abbreviations that you used to label your variations. It will refer to 'missing values'. It will structure the figures in quite complicated ways – ways that you will understand but which a busy reader won't have time to work out. And it will list several probability checks one after the other.
2. It is your job to convert all of this into a form suitable for public consumption: avoid abbreviations; restructure your tables so that they only include those elements that are essential and appropriate for your purpose; if necessary, carry out revised significance tests on the reformed tables; and indicate the result only from the significance test that is relevant.

A critical part of the researcher's skill lies in the ability to transmute the gobbledygook of an SPSS screen output into a simple table, bar chart or graph that instantly conveys the message you want to send.

Often the SPSS output is unbelievably complex, but not to labour the point, here is a simple example of a printout.

Crosstab

Count

		Subjects Gender		
		Male	Female	Total
Necessity to shop	Agree	13	3	16
	Partly agree	21	9	30
	Partly disagree	11	14	25
	Disasgree	5	24	29
Total		50	50	100

Chi-Square Tests

	Value	df	Asymp. Sig (2-sided)
Pearson Chi Square	23.858[a]	3	.000
Likelihood Ratio	25.576	3	.000
Linear-by-Linear Association	22.968	1	.000
N of Valid Cases	100		

[a] 0 cells (.0%) have expected count less than 5. The minimum expected count is 8.00

The student, Louisa Doggett, presented the data as a bar chart:

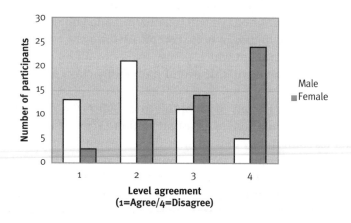

I only go shopping when I really need to

$\chi^2 = 23.858$, df = 3, p<.001

The same principle applies to all SPSS outputs: your aim should be to make your material accessible to your reader and presentationally attractive.

How do I present cross-tabs?

If your cross-tabs are small and relatively simple, the answer is clear. Showing the numbers is straightforward. But you will have to think about how to incorporate percentages in your table, and, in particular, in which direction, that is, along rows or columns, your percentages should run; it all depends on what makes the most sense in the context of your text. There are technical conventions about this, but it helps you to work out the meaning of your results if you think it through and decide for yourself. Which percentage figure do you want to compare with which other percentage figure? It is important to get this right, because your chief conclusions are probably dependent on it. Moreover, it is your job to help the reader understand what you are demonstrating.

You may feel that you want to include large cross-tabs. In modest studies based on a sample of less than 100, this is generally a mistake: it is unlikely that you will be able to use probability tests in such circumstances because of the statistical convention that says you need an expected five units in each cell if the χ^2 is to be valid. Moreover, the meaning of large cross-tabs is often difficult for the reader to interpret. They are an appropriate working element in the process of data analysis, but you should try to work out better ways of conveying the message that they contain.

One way of handling the problem is to combine variables. For example, instead of breaking age down into decades, once you have viewed your frequency distribution, you can combine them into two categories aiming to get close to a 50/50 split: perhaps '39 and younger' compared with '40 and older'. When doing this in order to employ the variable within a cross-tab, you must complete the adjustment before carrying out your probability-testing calculations; otherwise the temptation of combining them in such a way as to maximise your chance of getting a positive probability measure is very seductive. That act (sometimes called 'data dredging') is based on a misinterpretation of the theory that lies behind probability testing and is wrong.

How do I present scale scores?

The use of Likert scales (inviting respondents to indicate an attitude or opinion along a continuum) is very common in student research, usually based on four-point or five-point responses. The best way of dealing with these is to present the data in the form of bar charts.

You can, of course, obtain the chart from SPSS or by using the MS Word facility for inserting a chart, but an alternative way is to input the calculated figures into an MS Excel file. Here is the procedure, step by step.

producing a bar chart by using MS Excel

Open Excel and open a file, name it. Don't worry about labels for your data yet. Click on column A line 1: it will highlight. Insert your first total figure here, and then the remainder in order down the first column. Let's say you have results from along a 10-point scale.

Click *Insert*; click *chart*. For figures like these, you would normally want to create a histogram using columns: click on *column*.

Click on *next*; and *next* again. The titles page should be showing; if it isn't, click on the *titles* tab. Enter your chart title. Then enter the label for your x axis, the horizontal scale at the bottom of the chart. Enter the label for your y axis – the vertical line showing the numbers who scored on each point of the scale. Click *next* and then click on *new sheet*. Save it as an Excel file.

In order to transfer it to your Word manuscript, you need to click in the white margin area around the coloured chart, and then copy and paste to the appropriate position in your text. This is what it will look like – ready to incorporate into your text.

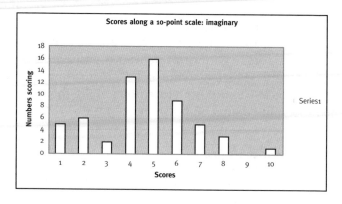

Most important of all: you will need to use your brain

Although quantitative methods research is science-based, writing a report is a cross between a work of art – the structure and contents and the words you employ, after all, are specific to you and depend to a large extent on your cultural background, your intelligence, your sense of logic and your literary skills – and a piece of craft work. There are tips you can learn, tricks of the trade that you will steadily absorb during a career and moments of enlightenment when you discover that something can be done better than you had initially thought of doing it. No one can programme you for that – probably the key to it is to give yourself plenty of time and come to terms with the art of drafting outlined in pp. 214–15.

Don't forget that if your project began with a research question, your findings and the discussion section should clearly indicate to what extent you have been able to provide an answer.

Presenting your findings in a qualitative research study

In qualitative research, the report-writing task begins from the moment you start to plan your project, not just in respect of the inevitable literature review, but because a crucial tool that you must use in your project is your day-by-day logbook or diary.

You have to be really disciplined about maintaining this record. It's not something that comes easily to most people (it is, perhaps, an activity that tends to be associated with our idea of the class swot, being geeky or having some kind of obsessional neurosis), but, without it, you will find yourself struggling to make sense of the process you are going through. So every day – perhaps at the end of the day when you can get some time to yourself – you should write an account of what you have done in the context of your project, who you have seen, where, what impressions they made on you, and how they have taken your thinking forward. This, of course, is in addition to any audio tapes, transcriptions or detailed notes you may have made in the course of your research encounters. The logbook will reflect developments in your thinking; in this way, it should gradually enable you to firm up the probable shape and structure of your draft report.

There is a standard sequential pattern that qualitative researchers learn to use as they move from data collection, through analysis, to the preparation of their draft report. It has two elements:

- The first we have already emphasised – the fact that, to some extent, everything overlaps with everything else: while you are still engaged in data collection (interviewing, observing), you will be analysing at least some of what you have already gathered; and while you are still engaged in data analysis, you will be working out how it is shaping up and making increasingly confident attempts at draft sentences, paragraphs and sections, using the categories you have begun to build on the back of your data. It would be misleading to suggest that this process is easy, but, provided you are patient, well organised and keep a clear head, you will be surprised how the mishmash of your raw data begins to metamorphose into a conceptually clear pattern.

- The second element relates to the fact that your data analysis process will have three specific stages, the third of which will flow directly into your draft report. They are:

1. The creation of data sheets describing and summarising the contents of your interviews and observations. We discussed this stage in Chapter 12.
2. Seeing whether you can identify ideas and conceptual categories that extend beyond any single interview or observation. Some of these you may have anticipated during the research planning process; some may be entirely unexpected – and you have to be alert to take note of these, especially if they contradict some of your own presuppositions. Some authors refer to this phase as involving the building of 'typologies' or 'taxonomies'; others prefer to talk about the identification of categories or the discovery of themes. Heretical though it may be to say so, the precise language is less important than the recognition that it is this stage which, more than anything else, epitomises the strength and challenge of successful qualitative research. The aim is to move smoothly from the point where your focus is on separate interviews or observations to a secondary level of analysis that enables you to recognise similarities and differences between the material provided by your data sources under three or four identified headings (or categories). It will include reference not only to the descriptive material about behaviour, relationships, attitudes or feelings that you have gathered but also to the interpretations that you as the researcher have put upon the evidence as you have accumulated it.

3. The final stage of analysis slips imperceptibly into the writing-up stage as you build on the identification of your three or four areas of interest and turn them into substantive sections that go to make up your report. When I am doing this, I aim to identify the three or four sections (perhaps using big Roman numerals, I, II, III and IV) and allocate each of them a computer file or a paper folder, so that the material that goes into each of them is quite clearly separated from the broader body of analysis. I am careful not to commit myself prematurely to too rigid a set of categories until I am absolutely clear that I have emerged, towards the end of the data collection task, with a structure that will both accurately reflect the evidence I have gathered and lend itself to a report with the necessary three or four discrete sections of text – with plenty of quotable material from my data sources, questions for discussion and tentative conclusions to draw.

As you turn towards the preparation of a draft, it is important to recognise that the nature of what you are looking to achieve may vary depending on the theoretical or practical context that forms your working base. Much of the qualitative methods literature originates from mainstream sociology, but many of the students who are using the methodology are operating in applied fields as diverse as environmental science, clinical medicine, nursing, marketing, public relations, psychology, law and criminal justice, sports science, social work or retail studies. Their focus of interest is likely to be more practical than theoretical.

Often the aim is to emerge with findings that throw light on consumer, client or service user experience of the organisation or on public attitudes towards aspects of the professional agenda. Sometimes comparisons are made between the customers or the users of a service and the professionals who supply it – in such instances, differences in the language used or the objectives identified by the two parties can provide an immediate foundation for theory-linked conclusions. Whatever guidance you find in the literature might be helpful, but it is always the case that you will have to translate it so that it fits your own setting.

The person who has gathered the qualitative research material is uniquely you – even if you have used a computer program to organise it. All the data is filtered through your intellectual self. There is truly *no* magic formula that allows you to duck out of the sustained period of mental concentration that is required if you are to make sense of what you have been given by your respondents or your observations.

So the lessons I would offer you are these:

1. Keep that logbook and ensure that you mentally interact with it from day 1 until you have completed your write-up. Even when you have settled on a draft outline or written a first or rough draft, you may still need to refer back to it in order to ensure that you have included all the lessons that are there to be learnt or perhaps to pick up a crucial quotation that you had omitted.

2. Use theory (whether grounded theory or any other kind) if that is what you are required to do and if you find it helpful. But if your aim is to obtain quality feedback on the impact of policies, the use of services or consumer experiences, then the idea of 'theory' may prove to be inappropriately pretentious. The quality of your research is not diminished if your report concentrates on reporting the reflective views of your respondents on matters that might benefit from being put into the public arena. Theory is fine in the right place, but its advancement is not a prerequisite in all instances of good student research.

3. I suggested early in this chapter that you should, from an early stage, begin to write down a possible structure to your report. It can be endlessly amendable, but to have a short draft outline is reassuring and entirely realistic. The qualitative research findings section might look like this.

Introduction to the findings
Topic/category/theme 1 identified – with the evidence
Topic/category/theme 2 identified – with the evidence
Topic/category/theme 3 identified – with the evidence
(Possibly topics/categories/themes 4 and 5 identified)

There is, of course, nothing sacrosanct about having three, four or five categories; I would, though, caution against its being more unless you are engaged in a bigger exercise than is normally the case at student project level. One of the commonest faults about project reports is that authors try to say too much in a shallow way, simply regurgitating everything they have heard in a rather higgledy-piggledy manner. This is neither good research nor is it good reporting.

4. You should never use qualitative research data in your write-up in the same chronological order as that in which you gathered it. Instead, once you have identified your topics and carried out topic-related mini-analyses (including the possibility of returning to the field for supplementary data collection in order to explore issues that might need clarifying or to use a different methodological approach to view the issue from another angle), then you can engage in the preparation of drafts that allow you to feed in the relevant material obtained at different stages of your data collection phase.

5. Keep a watchful eye on word length constraints. You'll be amazed how quickly you use up the allocated space. Never exceed the word limit.

6. Use quotations from your respondents *functionally.* Don't reprint great lengths of spoken text unless it serves an appropriate purpose. And use quotations or extracts in such a way that the reader is not left to do the analytical work or provide the commentary that you should do as the research investigator and author.

7. Ensure that your full report has a nice flow to it. One section should lead seamlessly to the next; the logical order should be – surprise, surprise – logically appropriate; and you should build up to your one, two or three conclusions in the wake both of the evidence you present and the analytical discussion you subject it to.

8. And if your project identified one or more questions either at the outset or later, make sure that you go as far as you can towards offering answers.

If you asked me to recommend just one book on ...
writing up a qualitative research report *it would be:*

Holliday, Adrian (2001)
Doing and Writing Qualitative Research, London, Sage

Postscript: Over to you ...

Having reached this point in the book, you have covered all the essential ground that will enable you to produce a successful research report. I recommend that you keep going over the material again and again as your work evolves. Unless you have a superhuman memory, you will need to constantly prompt yourself to ensure that you are taking all necessary steps to deliver a high-quality end-product.

Part 5 introduces some more advanced material for your selective use: in Chapter 14, you will find a glossary of terms used by qualitative researchers, while Chapter 15 provides easy access to eight tests of statistical significance.

I hope that you might find our website useful and interesting – www.palgrave.com/sociology/davies/.

By accessing it, you will be able to reinforce some of the lessons I have presented in this book, but you will also be able to enter into debate and discussion on any and every methodological issue – with a special option that relates methodology to your own disciplinary or subject area. Examples of completed student projects can also be found there.

I have always described myself as a journeyman academic, and one of the core values that I have held fast to is the idea that, in its essentials, the *process* of research, while involving concentration and hard work, is relatively simple and straightforward and that, as a researcher, you need constantly to remind yourself of the simple rules, nuances and tricks that enable you to turn a tiny slice of social reality into a form that, through words and numbers, accurately, if partially, reproduces it for other people's consumption. In the pages of this book I have tried to share that starting position with you.

But of course, in all the subject areas employing social research methods, the interaction between intellectual curiosity and the way an empirical or interpretive methodological approach is used means that, beyond the starting gate, life can, and usually will, get more complicated. Even in the most modest of projects, questions can arise – to be asked, perhaps, by a good supervisor – that require you, in the search for answers, to enter areas of either theoretical complexity or statistical analysis. In Chapters 14 and 15, I invite you to venture tentatively down these tracks.

14 A qualitative researcher's briefing sheet

ten golden rules in qualitative research

1. Get organised. Stay organised

Doing qualitative research is a complex and fluid activity. From the moment you start thinking about your project, give yourself a good filing system – both on screen and to accommodate all those handwritten notes you will be making. Divide your work into its constituent parts; and keep all your records up to date.

2. Have a research question clearly to the forefront of your mind

Write it down somewhere prominent – so that you never forget it or ignore it – and think of it as an intellectual puzzle.

3. Don't be afraid to try out your emerging thoughts, ideas and analyses on other people

Talking about your project helps to focus it. Take particular note if other people don't seem to understand what you're saying.

4. Use a controlled sampling technique

Your sample need not consist of only one targeted group. You can stretch it in ways that allow you to throw light on your question from different directions. You can interview third parties, seek out documentary evidence and engage with groups – in order to answer your question and solve your puzzle. This is strategic sampling.

5. Learn to recognise nuance as a key dimension in the feedback you receive

What you hear or observe has two dimensions to it: that which is apparent on the surface and that which your skilled ear, eye and brain will tell you lies beneath the surface.

ten golden rules in qualitative research *continued*

6. **Keep retracing your steps in order to strengthen the body of evidence that you are accumulating**
   Your work pattern will involve constant overlaps between data collection, analysis and write-up. If necessary, return to the field to check out your emerging ideas and conclusions.

7. **Stay flexible. Stay open-minded**
   You can never predict the shape or direction that your research will take. Never go into a research project determined to demonstrate something you already are sure to be the case.

8. **Keep a pen and paper always handy**
   Your brain will interact with your data at all sorts of times, and you need to be able to jot down ideas and analyses as they occur.

9. **Don't be tempted to drift towards a pseudo-quantitative method style of analysis**
   Your objective is to emerge with a report that suggests interpretations of human thought, feeling and behaviour. It will not involve numbers or proportions.

10. **Don't just 'let the quotations speak for themselves'**
    Your aim is to identify a number of themes or concluding assertions based on and supported by the evidence you have accumulated from all your various sources.

The language of qualitative research

A rather crude – and undeniably tongue-in-cheek – way of distinguishing between quantitative and qualitative research is to say that the problem with the former is that it involves 'doing sums' while the snag with the latter is that it uses long words.

The vocabulary that has been built up by qualitative research theorists reflects the fact that the methodology is inextricably linked to major debates in the world of social science and philosophy. They primarily concern the problem of knowledge:

- How do we know what we know?
- Is knowledge 'real'?
- Is what 'you' know the same as what 'I' know?
- What happens when something that is 'known' proves to be wrong?

Some of the greatest names in modern Western philosophy have grappled with these issues since the early twentieth century.

The debates spilled over into sociology when it was noted that the traditions of survey research require us to put our trust in what people say. At best, this involves a simplistic reliance on the meaning of words and, at worst, requires the researcher to live with 'facts' that are not facts at all but verbal distortions or dishonest claims bearing little or no relation to social reality. This realisation led towards an acknowledgement that one person's 'social reality' is quite different from somebody else's.

The issue impacted on psychology in a rather different way because critics held that traditional approaches to the analysis and measurement of human attitudes and behaviour (for example, by the use of yes/no inventory methods) would often misrepresent the complexity of human nature, or touch on only one aspect of it. They are also vulnerable to untruthfulness.

From the mid-twentieth century, qualitative research advocates began to explore ways in which their investigations could combat and improve upon what were seen as the shortcomings of survey research in sociology and inventory-testing methods in psychology. Those efforts continue to this day, and the challenge for the student researcher is to work hard to understand what it is about the qualitative approach that gets behind and goes beyond the methods and assertions that characterise the quantitative approach, and to what extent there is a continuing need for both methods.

A concise glossary

Abductive research strategy

Blaikie (2000, p. 25) has described a philosophical approach to research that is said to more satisfactorily describe the method used by qualitative researchers than either the idea of deductive or inductive reasoning (q.v.). The abductive research strategy reflects the way in which theory is generated side by side with data collection and analysis, with the researcher moving back and forth in the field in order to construct theoretically sound positions that accurately reflect the nature and range of the empirical evidence. It is broadly in line with interpretivism.

Action research

In action research, the researcher is normally an integral member of a team commissioned to bring about some new development, a change in policy or a challenge to existing practice. It can operate at government level or in the context of a campaign group, for example in support of a group of mothers striving to bring about the provision of improved local childcare facilities. The philosophy of action research stems from the idea that 'knowledge is power', but sometimes problems can arise if the researcher's findings don't coincide with the action group's policy aspirations. The action researcher can use both quantitative and qualitative methods.

Classificatory systems: categories, taxonomies and typologies

This conceptual and practical idea lies at the heart of qualitative research analysis. Instead of starting off with a classificatory framework (for example, a quantitative research project in psychology that sets out to measure the relationship between intelligence and impulsivity in offenders), qualitative researchers aim to formulate their own classificatory systems on the back of the data that emerges from their interviews or observations. In the light of their analyses of early interviews, the aim is to formulate three or four categories relevant to the psychosocial reality that the project is seeking to explore. Depending on the nature of the exercise (and perhaps on the experience of the researcher), these can take the form of taxonomies or typologies or they can simply provide the working framework of topics that will form the backbone of the research report.

Conversation analysis (CA)

At one level, conversation analysis is just that: the researcher examines transcripts of conversation and attempts to superimpose meaning upon them. But a vast technical literature has been developed around the subject of the 'social organisation of talk', and Silverman (1998, p. 273) confesses that 'the way in which CA obtains its results is rather different from how we might intuitively try to analyse talk'. He offers what he calls 'a crude set of prescriptions about how to do CA':

1. Always try to identify sequences of related talk.
2. Try to examine how speakers take on certain roles or identities through their talk (for example, questioner–answerer or client–professional)
3. Look for particular outcomes in the talk (for example, a request for clarification, a repair, laughter) and work backwards to trace the trajectory through which a particular outcome was produced.

Deconstruction

The philosophical position of deconstruction is closely linked to many of the more advanced ideas associated with qualitative research – especially the notion that meaning in any text or piece of speech is essentially problematic. But, although the argument is useful as a corrective to any unduly naive approach to textual analysis, it is also itself problematic because, pressed to its logical limits, it leads in the direction of claiming that *any* analysis of the written or spoken word is ultimately of limited value because of the inherent scepticism that attaches to any independent attempt to decipher meaning.

Deductive reasoning

The philosophical idea that underpins the style of research in which the investigator begins from a theoretical position and sets out to test it by gathering and analysing data. It is sometimes called the hypothetico-deductive method because, in experimental research, the researcher normally outlines a hypothesis based on the theory, and then uses empirical methods to see whether it is confirmed or not.

Discourse analysis (DA)

A research method that focuses solely on verbal systems of communication whether in text or through interview transcripts. The method emerged from the work of linguistic philosophers who identified the social and psychological significance, not only of words used, but of the verbal interactions that occur between different parties.

Emancipatory research

A form of action research (q.v.) designed to enable identified individuals or groups to analyse problems in their social situation and to empower them to take steps to rectify them.

Empiricism

The idea of empiricism has never been the same since Mills highlighted the shortcomings of 'abstracted empiricism', whose practitioners, he wrote, 'seem more concerned with the philosophy of science than with social study itself' (1959, p. 57). Even today, a quick look through some of the mainstream journals in psychology and elsewhere will demonstrate that the genre is alive and well. But Mills was not attacking empiricism per se; on the contrary, he argued that, linked clearly and intrinsically to relevant theories and creative thought, empirical activity is the bedrock of knowledge and understanding. One of the risks that qualitative researchers run is to allow their own assumptions to drown the empirical need for them to pay due attention to the evidence that their data presents. Empiricism is better defined as a commitment to respect the evidence that any properly planned and managed research project delivers and to locate your interpretation of it within the world of which it is a part.

Epistemology

A philosophical concept concerning how you know what you know and the methods you choose to use in order to test the validity of 'knowledge'. Epistemologists 'are occupied with the grounds and the limits, in brief, the character, of "knowledge"' (Mills, 1959, p. 58).

Ethnography

Ethnography is the study of human behaviour and relations within a cultural context. The approach has become subject to debate, partly because of our contemporary awareness that simplistic notions of culture (such as those which satisfied the early anthropologists working in 'foreign' settings) can be misleading – indeed, the very notion of 'culture' is increasingly recognised to be problematic.

Ethnomethodology

A style of research that concentrates its attention on the processes people use to organise their understanding of the world around them. Its primary focus is on language.

Feedback research

Although some sociologists frown on the idea, the fact is that small sample research can be carried out in such a way that it is exempt from the imperative that the principle of grounded theory (q.v.) imposes. Studies in both the public and private sector that use qualitative methods to obtain user or customer feedback on service provision are widely believed to have value, even if their theory base is 'given' rather than being subject to grounded exploration. It is always important to acknowledge the theoretical assumptions that underlie a planned project, but at student level, in particular, the qualitative research disciplines of design, planning, execution and analysis can be used to obtain feedback on any form of established practice.

Grounded theory
Seen by many as illustrating the stark difference between qualitative research and experimental research (in which data is collected to test a pre-stated theory), grounded theory emerges from the data. The process requires the researcher, during the data-gathering phase of a project, to examine the material as it builds up and to place it into categories – to classify it. Once this process has been started, the researcher returns to the field to gather more data and see whether the additional material fits into the established categories or whether (as is often the case) the classificatory system needs to be adapted to accommodate the fresh data. The next stage, in which the researcher is required to move towards the generation of grounded theory, is extremely difficult and may often be a step too far in a student exercise. Silverman (1993, p. 153) has pointed out that, even in the published products of qualitative research, there is a tendency towards the drawing of anecdotal conclusions, with little or no claim to theoretical rigour.

Hermeneutics
Hermeneutics is the research activity of interpreting whatever in the target situation is seen, heard or sensed. The 'hermeneutic circle' consists of the original data and the interpretive transformation of it by the researcher.

Hypothesis
Although it is more usually associated with studies in which a hypothesis (for example, the idea that variable A is related to or affects variable B) is subjected to rigorous testing generally using a controlled experiment or quasi-experiment, it is perfectly legitimate

for a hypothesis (that is, an assertion about the 'truth' of some psychosocial fact) to be explored or even tested through the use of qualitative research. A hypothesis is a testable proposition.

Inductive reasoning

The philosophical idea that is related to the style of research in which the investigator employs a doctrine of curiosity to gather data relevant to a predetermined subject area, analyses it, and, on the basis of that analysis, postulates one or more theoretical conclusions.

Interactionism

Interactionism focuses our attention on the way in which we explain the nature of interpersonal relations and the meaning that both actors and observers may put upon them. Methodologically, either interviews or observation may be employed, but Denzin (1970, p. 216) argues that participant observation offers the best chance of emerging with the most complete understanding of the interactions that are taking place in any given setting.

Interpretive phenomenological analysis (IPA)

A broad term that describes the standard approach to data analysis in qualitative research: looking for themes in the early emergent data; making connections between them; seeking further evidence (confirmatory or conflicting) through second-stage interviews or observations; the elucidation of confirmed patterns; and an attempt to infer meanings from the completed analysis.

Interpretive reading of your data

A reading of the data that looks beyond its literal form, and allows you to construct a range of meanings that can be inferred from the literal content – the social and psychological rules which the speaker(s) or the visual images reflect, their view of the situational context within which they are operating.

Interpretivism

The interpretive approach refutes the idea that any investigator can adopt a truly neutral approach to research. Denzin and Lincoln (1994, p. 13) argue that all research is 'guided by a set of beliefs and feelings about the world and how it should be understood and studied'. The consequence of this argument is to say that all knowledge is relative to the person interpreting it, but the qualitative researcher aims to overcome this risk by assiduously and continuously checking a postulated theoretical position against the evidence that the investigation throws up.

Kinesics
The study of how people use their body movements to communicate with those around them – either explicitly or implicitly. It incorporates but goes beyond what is sometimes referred to as 'body language'. The interpretive analysis of body movements is known to be problematic, and cultural differences of meaning must always be taken into account (Marshall and Rossman, 1995, p. 126).

Literal reading of your data
A reading of the data that concentrates on its presented form: the words and sentences used, its flow, the shape of the dialogue. The literal reading is a good way to begin your analysis, but you will normally want to move on to interpretive and reflexive readings.

Microanalysis
Used when the researcher's focus of study is language or any other form of communication. The researcher pays attention to the smallest details of what is said or hinted at and at the nature and shape of interactions reflected in the text. Video or audiotaping of the data is essential for this system of investigation. Video taping is essential if the analysis of non-verbal behaviour is planned.

Narrative analysis
Narrative analysis is the broad term used to describe a research act that aims to obtain from the subjects detailed accounts of their lived experience. In practice, many such projects have focused their attention on vulnerable or marginalised subjects, thus giving them an emancipatory emphasis (q.v.), but the method can be used with any group of people – including those in privileged or powerful positions.

Narrative inquiry
The narratives that emerge from interviews are situated in social worlds, and it is the task of the researcher to encompass both the lived experience of the subject being interviewed and the way in which it interacts with the external world.

Nuance
When interpreting research data, the investigator is expected to pay

particular attention to the subtle differences in shade or meaning that the subjects' use of language, sentence construction, pauses and reactions to what others (including the researcher) might say. The analysis of nuance is not easy, and there is clearly a risk that the researcher's own presuppositions and subjective view of the world may influence the interpretation. Great care should be taken.

Ontology

The pre-methodological question that asks how we perceive the social world. It is based on the argument that, because of our gender, age, upbringing and life experience, we all view those around us in unique ways. This fundamental fact has implications for our ability to achieve research neutrality, not only in the conclusions we draw, but also in the topics we choose to study, the way we go about the data collection task, and what we see, hear and interpret during the time of analysis and write-up. 'No research or story can be ontologically neutral' (Mason, 2002, p. 154).

Phenomenology

Phenomenology is a major product of twentieth-century sociological theory developed in order to explain and explore the way people view the world in the light of their own experience, the way they interpret other people's words and behaviour through the medium of their own subjective understanding of the world, and how this affects patterns of human interaction. Its thinking underpins many of the methodological imperatives that have been built into qualitative research.

Positivism

The *Oxford Encyclopedic English Dictionary* definition of positivism emphasises its origin in the philosophical view that 'every rationally justifiable assertion can be scientifically verified', but the term has come to be used by some qualitative researchers in order to speak or write derisively about or dismiss as flawed the scientific approach adopted by quantitative researchers.

Proxemics

The study of how people use and relate to space (territory). The method normally relies on observation, but interviewees can be asked to talk about their experience. Where do people sit in a meeting? How does open space in a housing estate influence behaviour? How close do people stand to each other? What about the placing of deckchairs on a beach? How does the use of space vary between different cultures?

Reflexive reading of your data
A reading of the data that takes into account the part that you have played in the generation of that data – your role in an interview, your writing of field-notes, your selection of the sample.

Reflexivity
In clarifying the nature of your role as research analyst, it is important to recognise the 'reflexive' element in what you do. Beyond the literal understanding of what you see or hear, and beyond the interpretive attempt to get beyond the literal surface of what you receive, there are questions about your own role, the impact you have on the situation and how you may be perceived by the subject of your interview or observation. You as the researcher are a player in and an influence upon the situation that you have created.

Reliability in qualitative research
Because qualitative researchers do not normally employ any formal or precise systems of measurement, the concept of reliability is related to the rigour with which the researcher has approached the tasks of data collection and analysis and the care with which the report describes in detail the methods that have been employed – including, especially, some discussion of how critical decisions were made. Often, the term 'reliability' in this sense is equated with methodological 'accuracy'.

Semiotics
An interpretive approach to the analysis of texts, speeches or media content that seeks meaning from a study of the interrelationships of language and structure within an acknowledged cultural framework.

Strategic approach
The use of a strategic approach means that the researcher, having settled upon the research question, will gather whatever samples are necessary to throw light on the question. Creative flexibility will be employed, and the precise direction of the data collection process will emerge only as the project develops. Tactical initiatives (q.v.) may lead the researcher in unanticipated directions.

Symbolic interactionism

A view of human behaviour arguing that all social interaction is dependent on the extent to which people share a symbolic view of each other and the world around them, characterised through their use of language and non-verbal communication.

Tactical initiatives

Methodological steps taken in pursuit of the strategic approach (q.v.) to find an answer to a question using qualitative research. Tactical initiatives may relate to sample-gathering, methodological style and exploration of the relationship between different variables.

Taxonomies, *see* Classificatory system

Telling a story

One aim of qualitative research interviewing is to enable subjects to tell their own story, but it has to be recognised, not only that the interview process itself will run the risk of fracturing the story that is there to be told, but also that subjects may tell different stories to different interviewers – depending on whether they see the researcher as male or female, young or old, a member of their own cultural group or an outsider. Stories, therefore, are not only subjectively specific to the teller; they are, in some degree, also specific to the listener – both because of the impact of the situation on the interviewee and the way the researcher interprets what is heard.

Theory

Although the word 'theory' may be used in a variety of ways, its most common and most useful meaning in the research setting refers to the relationship (often causal) between two variables: for example, 'When there are clouds overhead, it is more likely to rain than if there are not', 'If you are a convicted offender, you are more likely to be arrested for another offence than if you are not'. The variables can be people, objects, thoughts, feelings, behaviours, consequences. In qualitative methods, the idea of theory has tended to be dominated by the notion of grounded theory (q.v.), and, as Silverman (1993, p. 153) has pointed out, this has tended to mask the fact that it is at least as important to test theories as to generate them. Indeed, it can be argued that there is little point in the constant generation of theory, whether grounded or not, if the testing process is ignored.

Triangulation

Triangulation refers to the use of a variety of methods in one project (including those drawn from quantitative research) with a view to exploring the research question from different angles. Triangulation can be planned at the outset or it can be settled upon in the course of the project as new questions arise.

Typologies, *see* Classificatory system

Validity in qualitative research

In all types of research, the concept of validity relates to the question of whether the end-results of your analysis are accurate representations of the psychosocial or textual reality that you claim them to be. In qualitative research, however, extensive discussion and debate has reflected on one aspect of the concept: the extent to which the subjective involvement of the researcher must logically introduce a unique dimension to each research representation, with the result that the 'validity' of any one study refers to the interactive and interpretive reality of that project as distinct from the focused qualities represented by the data per se.

A cautionary view

Qualitative research derives from twentieth-century sociology and a longer tradition in philosophy, but that is not the framework that all who choose to do small sample research either come from or feel comfortable with. Some are in psychology (a discipline that gets short shrift from many of the major qualitative research theorists, but which is now expanding its interest in small sample work), social administration, management studies, environmental science, geography and a wide range of other applied disciplines – in health, criminal justice and business studies. If they have not done mainstream undergraduate courses in sociology or philosophy, some students from these fields must wonder what they have let themselves in for when they turn to the foundation literature in qualitative methods.

So let us be clear. It is perfectly possible to carry out a one-off, small sample study with only modest acquaintance with qualitative research writing, although you do need guidance.

The key question to answer is 'Why are you doing this research?' You may be interested in your subjects' reflective perspective on their situation, but you may also simply want to have customer or user feedback on a product, service provision or some treatment.

If you can bring yourself to read carefully all the entries in the concise glossary, you will detect that, while qualitative methods research has huge strengths, it is not entirely without its problems or its disputes – especially if you push the logically sceptical critique to its limits. All 'knowledge' – whether subjective or objective, qualitative or quantitative – is flawed, limited and subject to refutation. Some survey research can be truly dreadful in its mundane quality or the naive assumptions that its author makes; the routine use of published inventories in some areas of psychology is particularly open to abuse. But qualitative research, too, can disappoint when the researcher puts too much faith in unsubstantiated and untested respondent assertions as evidence. Its weaknesses are:

1. There are times when, in small-scale projects, you find yourself having to take the work and the words of the researcher on trust.
2. The discipline's emphasis on the impact that the researcher's own cultural background can have on the data-gathering process introduces a degree of relativism that can make a mockery of the idea of achieving reliable and trustworthy evidence.
3. A naive researcher will stop short of the thematic analysis that is an essential final step in any successful project.

In social science as in the natural sciences, the principles of sampling, design, analysis and probability theory have contributed a great deal to our store of knowledge. Similarly, the development of the reflective and interpretive approach to research investigation has thrown unparalleled light on aspects of human thought and behaviour. Both will continue to play a part in the creation and recreation of the world we inhabit, and both will benefit from the enthusiastic, disciplined and skilful commitment of students as they venture into their first research project.

15 Testing for statistical significance

The world is divided into two classes of people: there are statisticians and there are the rest of us. For statisticians, the language and mathematical logic of their trade run through their veins as surely as do red and white corpuscles in their blood. They find it hard to empathise with those who struggle always to understand how one statistical step leads 'self-evidently' to another. Sadly, though, number skills are not equally distributed in the human race, even among people of good intelligence.

This presents problems in research. You may be a successful student in your chosen field or really good at what you do for a living; you may be OK at carrying out a project based on the administration of a survey; and have experienced the pleasure that comes from finding an answer to your originally stated research question. But then comes the point when you realise that you need to engage with some statistical thinking in order to be sure that the conclusions you want to draw stand up to scrutiny.

Three things follow from this:

- You need to absorb some of the principles of statistical thinking (sampling theory, in particular) in order to plan your project appropriately.
- You need to understand what the concept of probability means.
- You need to be able to test the statistical levels of significance in respect of those parts of your data that require it.

In this book, we have already explored the first two of these, and it is time now to turn to the third.

My approach to this task is, perhaps, a shade unconventional. But it is driven partly by my experience that what quantitative researchers need is enough statistical knowledge to enable them to test their data for its significance, and partly by my awareness that an enormous proportion of undergraduates are required to carry out a survey in the course of their studies and that they can't all be expected to achieve grades of 60 per cent or better in statistical knowledge.

Student researchers should have access to guidance that tells them which significance tests to apply in any of the most common situations. They don't need to have turned themselves into ministatisticians in the first place. There are researchers and there are statisticians, and most student projects are designed to provide experience of research, with only secondary learning in statistics.

Even in the world of professional research – or, one might say, *especially* in the world of professional research – researchers, whether in the health sciences, criminology, policy analysis or urban planning, usually have access to a skilled statistician who will guide them or do things for them when they need it. Students often lack such guidance (although they should always seek skilled advice wherever it may be found), and so they need to be led by the hand to the right significance test for their needs. SPSS will usually do the donkey-work for you, but you need to know what to ask it to do.

It's no good statisticians being snooty about this. If every student who did a quantitative methods research project at whatever level had incorporated into their work the experience of getting a χ^2 result (and understanding it), had carried out an exercise to compare differences in means and test the significance level, and had delivered a correlation coefficient with a probability indication attached, most supervisors would be over the moon. Too often, students turn to spouses or partners, friends or friends of friends, or sons or daughters to do their statistics for them, and, as a consequence, deliver results which may or may not be right but which the responsible author of the project report doesn't understand (a fact that would be exposed in an oral exam) and that is often only too apparent from the text of the report.

In what follows, I outline eight ways of testing for probability. These are the statistical operations that you are most likely to find useful in the course of your data analysis. Each one is specific to certain circumstances, and your first task is to ask yourself which of them fits your own data set. (In fact, you need to give some thought to this at an early stage in your planning process, because, although it may smack a bit of the tail wagging the dog, there are occasions when you would be wise to plan the details of your data management and analysis so that they meet the criteria required for an appropriate significance test.)

Eight useful ways of testing for statistical significance

The test	When to use it	How to use it	Notes
1. The Chi-square test, giving the statistic: $\chi^2 =$	A test to use when you have a cross-tab and you want to know if the differences between (some of) the cells within it are statistically significant	SPSS, although I give guidance for calculation by hand in this chapter. For 2 x 2 tables, use Fisher's exact test and if your sample is small, employ Yates' continuity correction. SPSS will do this for you	This test tends to be most commonly used in projects that have their links to sociology, social administration or other subjects that use surveys and produce descriptive variables
2. The Mann-Whitney test, giving the statistic: U =	A test that enables you to compare the scores or ratings obtained from two unmatched (or independent) groups	SPSS	Frequently used in psychology-linked or similar projects that use rating scales
3. The t-test for unmatched or independent samples, giving the statistic: t =	A test that enables you to compare means from unmatched samples. The data must conform to strict criteria	SPSS	Only valid with scores based on interval or ratio levels of measurement. It is not suitable for use with rating scales based on respondent judgement or opinion
4. The t-test for paired samples, giving the statistic: t =	A test that enables you to compare means from paired or repeated-measures samples. The data must conform to strict criteria	SPSS	Only valid with scores based on interval or ratio levels of measurement. Not suitable for use with rating scales based on respondent judgement or opinion
5. The Wilcoxon signed rank test for paired samples	A test that enables you to compare outcomes from paired or repeated-measures samples. The criteria required are less rigorous than for a t-test, but the statistical power is more robust than in the sign test	SPSS	Commonly used in before-and-after studies or in inter-group comparisons that employ rating scales based on ordinal levels of measurement. It is based on the comparative rankings (plus, minus or unchanged) in the members of the two groups

The test	When to use it	How to use it	Notes
6. The sign test for paired samples giving the statistic: S=	A test that enables you to determine whether identified differences between two paired sets of data are statistically significant. The criteria required are less rigorous than for the Wilcoxon test	Easily done by hand	Can be used when comparing the performance of the same subjects in different settings. A simple exercise, but it has weak statistical power
7. Spearman's rank order correlation giving the statistic, Spearman's rho: ρ =	A test that enables you to check the strength of associa-tion between related scores. The criteria are less rigorous than for Pearson	SPSS; can be done by hand quite easily	Can be used with input–output studies, in which the paired elements are both subject to measurement
8. Pearson's product moment correlation giving the statistic: r =	To test the strength of association between related and paired scores. The data must conform to strict criteria	SPSS	Commonly used in pre-test–post-test studies, but it cannot be used with ordinal scales

Note: Clear guidelines for all the tests are to be found in most SPSS guides. They include Coakes (2005); Pallant (2005); and Kinnear and Gray (2004). You should, of course, use a manual that is compatible with the SPSS version you are accessing.

Testing for significance in cross-tabs

The Chi-square test

The Chi-square test (giving the statistic: χ^2 =) is the test to use when you have a cross-tab and you want to know if the differences between (some of) the cells within it are statistically significant.

If you have entered your data in an SPSS file, you can get a Chi-square result delivered by accessing the Chi-square check box. This will also provide you with a probability level without you having to access any tables.

exercise

Early in my research career, I found that one of the best ways of coming to terms with and understanding what probability theory means in social research is to learn how to calculate a Chi-square result by hand. Provided you are patient and can work accurately, it is astonishingly straightforward, more than you would ever imagine if you are one of the millions terrified by statistics. Let's try it in respect of figures based on another coin-tossing exercise. The results were these:

Coin	Heads	Tails
£1	9	11
20p	7	13
10p	11	9

The question in your mind is whether the difference that emerged from tossing the 20p coin might be statistically significant – suggesting that, perhaps, the coin used was in some way biased.

First, you have to create a total column, and then add another column to show the proportion of the whole contributed by the number of cases in each row.

Coin	Heads	Tails	TOTAL	Proportions of the whole
£1	9	11	20	0.33
20p	7	13	20	0.33
10p	11	9	20	0.33
	27	33	N = 60	1

There were 60 tosses altogether, and each coin (in this artificially simple exercise) contributes one-third of the results (0.33) to the total in the table. (Normally, the proportions in the right-hand column would be different numbers, but they will always add up to 1.00)

Next, you must create a grid with columns as shown below:

- O are the observed figures, that is, the actual results obtained in each of the six cells.

exercise *continued*

- Next is a slightly more difficult step. E are the expected figures – what the results would have been if they had been distributed in each column in exactly the same proportions as they are distributed in the Total column. Because each coin made up one-third of the total, you would have 'expected' each to deliver one-third of the heads and one-third of the tails. Of course, most tables are not as neat as this, and you get the E figure by multiplying the total figure at the foot of each column (here it is 27 for heads, 33 for tails) by the proportion in each row – and applying it to the cell where the row and column intersect. (Here the proportion in each row is 0.33. It is important to note that normally the proportion figure will be different for each row, so the multiplication result will not be – as it is here – quite so repetitive.)
- The rest is just simple arithmetic, using a calculator. First work out what the result is when you take E away from O; where E is bigger than O, the result will have a minus sign in front of it.
- Next, using your calculator, calculate $(O–E)^2$. This gets rid of the minus signs.
- Then divide each of the resulting figures by the corresponding E figure. You should then have a column of figures running to three decimal places.
- Finally, add them up to obtain your χ^2 calculation.

	O	E	(O–E)	(O–E)²	(O–E)²/E
£1 – heads	9	8.91	0.09	0.008	0.001
£1 – tails	11	10.89	1.89	3.572	0.328
20p – heads	7	8.91	–1.91	3.648	0.409
20p – tails	13	10.89	2.11	4.452	0.409
10p – heads	11	8.91	2.09	4.368	0.490
10p – tails	9	10.89	–1.89	3.572	0.328

So for our coin-tossing experiment, we would write at the foot of the table, $\chi^2 = 1.965$.

That, in itself, remains merely a mysterious formula. Two more steps remain:

- We have to quickly work out what are called 'the degrees of

exercise *continued*

freedom' (DF), and to do this you go back to your original table, look at it and in your mind's eye (mentally) remove one row and one column. How many cells are you left with? In our case, because it's a 3 x 2 table, you're left with two rows and one column, that is, 2 x 1 = two cells. And that gives you your degrees of freedom: DF = 2. (If it were a 2 x 2 table, you would have one degree of freedom; if your table had six columns and five rows, DF = 20.)

- You turn to a χ^2 distribution table, track down the row of figures against DF = 2, and see whether the result of your χ^2 calculation is greater or smaller than the figure contained in the first column. In our case, we hope it isn't, because if it were, it would have made the problem of writing this section very much harder.

We are now in a position to complete the entry at the foot of our table:

χ^2 = 1.965, DF = 2, Not Significant (normally written 'NS').

This means that the results obtained are not different from any that might be expected to have occurred by chance. Because we know that coins in good condition are evenly balanced and equally likely to come down heads or tails, a non-significant difference between the two columns is the result we would have anticipated.

But imagine that, instead of coin-tossing, a small scale survey had involved interviews with campus students and produced the following results:

What do you normally do on a Sunday afternoon?	History students	Law students	TOTAL
Academic study	9 = 33%	11 = 33%	20
Have sex	7 = 26%	13 = 39%	20
Watch the TV	11 = 41%	9 = 27%	20
TOTAL	27 = 100%	33 = 100%	N = 60

You might have wanted to draw some pretty firm conclusions

about the respective levels of (claimed) sexual activity in the two groups of students. At first glance, the results appear to show that history students prefer to watch the box while law students are more inclined to favour an active Sunday sex life. But applying the χ^2 test (as we have done) tells you to forget it: the difference is not significant. Therefore, the proper statement to make, in the absence of further investigation, must be that there is no difference between the two groups of students.

Student researchers (and others) find that very hard to do – but do it they must; above all, they should never ever use the phrase: 'There was a difference in the claimed activity pattern between history and law students, but it did not reach the level of significance.' To say that only reveals a failure to grasp the meaning of probability and it leaves it open to the naive reader to go away with the conclusion based on the first four words: 'There was a difference ... '. There wasn't, and it is your professional responsibility as the researcher to ensure that no reader is misled.

The critical level at which statistical significance can be claimed is set, by convention, at p<.05 meaning 5% or 1 in 20. At that level, your results could only occur by chance once in every twenty exercises, and that is regarded as a safe margin of error.

If, in an entirely different study in which again DF = 2, the χ^2 figure were bigger than 5.991 (the critical point shown by the table), then and only then could you claim that you had identified a significant relationship between two variables. The claim would be based on the statistical probability of such a finding only being expected to occur by chance on a 1:20 basis. If the χ^2 figure was bigger than 13.816, then you would have a finding which you could feel very confident about and your below-the-table indicator line would read:

$$\chi^2 = 13.924, \text{ DF} = 2, \text{ p<.001},$$

meaning that your findings would only occur by chance once in a thousand times.

Of course, the SPSS programme on your computer will deliver the

exercise *continued*

χ^2 result for you instantly once you tell it which parts of your inputted data to work on, and most of the time you will expect to use SPSS. But there are two advantages in 'doing it by hand' as an exercise: first, it helps you to understand the meaning of probability; and in any one particular case, by working with the data in this way, you get a sense of which parts of your data breakdown are contributing most to a high χ^2. As you become more sophisticated in the task of data analysis, you will be able to make use of this information in order to explore your variables more closely – and that can be of value as you think about your findings, write them up, relate them to other studies and plan follow-up investigations. One big disadvantage with SPSS is that, although it is of inestimable value as a tool, it can sometimes succeed in putting a mental barrier between you and your hard-earned data. But once you understand that the crucial contributor to a high Chi-square lies in the calculated difference between observed and expected values in identifiable cells, you can then visually interrogate the Chi-square data as it appears on your SPSS screen. It ceases to look like something only comprehensible to doctoral-holding scholars of statistics.

There are different ways of calculating χ^2 when your cross-tab is a 2 x 2 table. SPSS allows for this and offers you probability levels using either Fisher's exact test or Yates continuity correction – which is important with small samples.

Comparing differences between means

One of the most common student project data sets that require a significance test is derived from the award of scores or points on a rating scale to individual members of two samples. The researcher calculates a mean or median score applicable to each of the samples and needs to know whether the difference between them is greater than could have occurred by chance.

In any one case, the choice of the correct test to use is largely dependent on three factors:

1. Some tests require the two samples to be the same size, some don't.
2. If the samples are the same size, the data relating to the members in each of the two samples may or may not be matched or paired.
3. The measurements used to produce the scores will normally be based either on ordinal number-based scales or interval-based scales (see pp. 264–5).

In some instances, the two matched 'samples' may, in fact, be the *same* sample in which two sets of scores have been awarded to the same people. For example:

- the study might compare student grades for an essay on research methods with the grades awarded to the same students for a completed research project
- the study might record 'before and after' scores following some experience or intervention, for example responses to a stress scale before and after attendance at a yoga class, or body weights before and after attendance at a dieting clinic.

In all such instances, treat the samples as paired.

The following three tests are employed when you are comparing differences between means.

The Mann-Whitney test

The Mann-Whitney test is a commonly used test. You should employ it when you have detailed numerical data drawn from subjects in two groups. It gives the result: U =.

when to use the Mann-Whitney test

1. You have obtained measures, scores or ratings in respect of two groups which may be of unequal sizes.
2. The numbers that make up the scores must be of ordinal, interval or ratio quality.
3. You may quote either the mean or the median score to indicate the observed difference between the two groups.

when to use the Mann-Whitney test *continued*

4. It does not require the members of each sample to be matched or paired.
5. The test is commonly used when the rigorous conditions required for the t-test are not met.

The student project that compared differences in self-expressed spider-fear levels in men and women (reported in Chapter 8) is suitable for the Mann-Whitney test. It is possible for you to use the bar chart on page 126 in order to gain experience of the relevant SPSS program. The data should be entered into SPSS with sex as the categorical (independent) variable (M = 1, F = 2), and fear levels along the 10-point scale as the continuous (dependent) variable. This will give you 126 cases altogether. SPSS should produce for you a Mann-Whitney outcome of U = 703.5; a Z value of –6.314; and a probability value (p) of less than .001.

This result allows us to conclude from the study that the men interviewed were significantly less fearful of spiders than the women (Pallant, 2005, pp. 291ff.).

It is possible, although time-consuming, to carry out the Mann-Whitney test by hand (Clegg, 1990, pp. 75–7, 164–6), but SPSS will deliver it for you very satisfactorily and much more quickly.

The t-test for independent samples

The t-test for unmatched or independent samples is more powerful than the Mann-Whitney test but it can only be used when certain strict criteria are met. In the social sciences, it is quite common for these conditions to be unachievable, and the Mann-Whitney test is more frequently employed.

when to use the t-test for unmatched or independent samples

1. You have obtained measures in respect of two groups which may be of unequal sizes and whose members are not matched.

when to use the t-test for unmatched or independent samples
continued

2. The measures must be of interval or ratio quality. The crucial question for minimum t-test eligibility is this: is the interval between any two points along the scale the same as the interval between any *other* two points – as in a tape measure? This is not so with rating scales based on observer judgements or self-assessments.
3. Both samples must have a normal distribution.
4. The variances of the samples must be similar to each other.

The spider-fear data (from Chapter 8) does not conform to all the required criteria for the t-test for independent samples – making the Mann-Whitney test the correct one to employ and to base one's conclusions on. But, somewhat improperly, the data that you have inputted to SPSS for the Mann-Whitney exercise can nevertheless be used to try out the SPSS calculation leading to a t-test result for independent samples.

This will give you an outcome of t = –7.519 and a probability value of p<.001.

The t-test for paired samples

The t-test for paired samples requires certain criteria to be met. It is more frequently employed in studies that are in or close to the natural sciences than in social science-based projects.

when to use the t-test for paired or related samples

1. You have obtained measures in respect of two groups which must be of equal sizes and whose members are paired or otherwise related.
2. The measures must be of interval or ratio quality. The crucial question for minimum t-test eligibility is this: is the interval between any two points along the scale the same as the interval between any *other* two points?
3. Both samples must have a normal distribution.

when to use the t-test for paired or related samples *continued*

4. The variances of the samples must be similar to each other.
5. The difference between the paired scores should be normally distributed.

A common context in which the t-test for paired samples is employed is when the two 'samples' are made up of the same members who are scored on two separate occasions – perhaps after the application of some experimental or educational procedure. The requirement that only interval measures are eligible for t-test treatment means that the use of an ordinal numbers-based rating scale renders it inappropriate. Results using a thermometer, stop-watch, weighing scales or tape measure would give eligibility. It can also be used when the ratings are based on independently applied test scores – such as academic marking systems or personality or intelligence inventories.

Here is an example of a project suitable for the t-test for paired or repeated measures samples.

You have gathered together a random sample of 20 students. Having explained your intentions and secured their willingness to cooperate, you take them along to the university athletics ground where they carry out a single long jump. You measure the metric results. They have, at the outset, agreed to attend five training sessions with a long jump coach, and they all now fulfill this commitment. At the end of the coaching period, they again go to the athletics ground where they carry out a single long jump. You are hypothesising that there will be a statistically significant difference between their pre-coaching and post-coaching jumps. You enter the two paired data sets into SPSS. Before carrying out the full calculation, the program will check that the required criteria for a t-test have been met. If you follow the manual's instructions for the paired samples t-test you will be able, at the end, to access the details that you need for your result: the t statistic, the number of degrees of freedom and the level of probability achieved, with $p<.05$ the critical level.

Comparing pairs of scores in matched samples

The Wilcoxon signed rank test

The Wilcoxon signed rank test is for use with paired participants or in a repeated measures (before-and-after or pre-test–post-test). It is less powerful than the t-test for paired samples, but does not demand the same rigorous criteria. In the social sciences, it is common for the t-test criteria to be unachievable, with the result that the Wilcoxon test is more frequently employed. It compares the *relative* positions of paired participants – or the same participant on two occasions – and tells you whether the pattern is such as could have occurred by chance.

when to use the Wilcoxon test

1. You are comparing the measures, ratings or scores obtained either by one sample under successively different conditions (giving before-and-after measures or pre-test–post-test outcomes) or by two groups whose members must be matched.
2. Scores must be of at least ordinal quality, that is, they may be based on the results obtained from a rating scale reflecting respondents' judgements or opinions.

An example of when the Wilcoxon test would be appropriate can be illustrated by a project in which depressed patients in the community were invited to participate in a form of therapeutic groupwork. Before the groups began, all the patients assessed themselves in respect of physical and emotional symptoms; after the groups had finished, the self-assessment process was repeated. The relationship between the two scores in each case (plus, minus or unchanged) would form the raw material for a Wilcoxon statistic. Positive probability levels would be achieved if the pattern of change before and after was mainly in one direction.

The sign test

The sign test is, like the Wilcoxon test, for use when the

researcher needs to compare the respective qualities of paired participants in order to conclude whether the differences between them are statistically significant. It gives the statistic: S =.

The sign test has less power than the Wilcoxon test (that is, it will only identify a statistically significant difference if it is quite marked), and is therefore vulnerable to type II errors (see page 264). In a limited number of instances, it is a useful probability exercise, however, and it can easily be done by hand.

when to use the sign test

1. You want to compare the ratings or scores obtained by two groups whose members are matched (or paired) with each other.
2. You can use it to compare an individual's performance on a range of tests before and after some form of treatment or training.
3. Scores may be of nominal, ordinal, interval or ratio quality. In other words, even if the numbers involved have only symbolic value (for example, 1 = good; 2 = bad), the sign test can be employed. This is one of the sign test's principal attractions.

How to do the sign test calculation by hand
List the paired scores in columns side by side, and use a plus (+) or minus (–) sign to indicate the pattern of related numbers. If the numbers are equal, use the sign 0.

Here is an example. An independent judge was invited to rate two people in respect of 11 'positive qualities'. The scale ranged from 1 to 5 in which 1 = a low rating and 5 = a high rating.

	James	Jane	sign
Good looking	2	4	–
Good tempered	3	3	0
Energetic	4	3	+
Patient	1	5	–
Happy	2	4	–
Intelligent	3	5	–
Good at science	1	3	–
Good at languages	2	4	–
Well dressed	3	2	+
Tells jokes well	4	2	+
Good at sport	3	4	–

Method:

1. Calculate S. How often does the least frequent sign occur? The minus sign occurs seven times whereas the plus sign occurs only three times: S = 3.

2. Calculate N. How many signs are there in all (ignoring any zeros that reflect equal scores)? The answer in our example is: N = 10.

3. Let's say that you had specified a one-tailed hypothesis: that James would have fewer positive qualities than Jane. You look up the sign test table for N = 10 and find that if S is anything greater than 1, the results can't be claimed as significant at the 5 per cent level. So, despite initial appearances to the contrary, the conclusion has to be that the hypothesis is rejected. The sign test requires you to say that James and Jane are not significantly different in their possession of positive qualities.

Testing for significance in correlations

Instead of comparing the mean scores achieved by two contrasting or linked samples, another approach, again using arithmetic scores or measures of some kind, is to see whether there is a correlation (positive or negative) between them. SPSS will do this for you, and will apply appropriate significance tests, also offering you a diagram that allows you to represent the relationship visually. The two tests outlined below are two of the most frequently used for this purpose.

It is important to emphasise the two stages in this process: first, you compute a correlation; and then you calculate the level of statistical significance to attach to that correlation. It is not sufficient just to get an 'interesting' correlation coefficient. You have to check whether the probability of it occurring other than by chance reaches the critical level of $p < .05$; if it is not significant, you simply quote the correlation figure but attach the soubriquet 'NS' to it.

Correlation is a word sometimes used (wrongly) to describe the existence of a statistical relationship between any two different variables. It should only be employed in respect of arithmetic data that lends itself to the technical calculation.

An example of a positive correlation might be the relationship between the amount of rain that falls and the height of the water table in the ground: the greater the rainfall, the higher the water table level. A series of measurements would provide arithmetic data, and if the relationship was exact, we would say that there was a correlation of 1.

A completely random correlation would have a value of zero (0).

Correlations can be negative. If you start out each day with £20 in your pocket or purse, keep a record of how much you spend and note how much is left at the end of the day, you should obtain a perfect negative correlation. If you spend £19, you have £1 left, but if you only spend £1, you have £19 left. Using a scale of 0–20, a correlation measure would give you a figure of –1.

Of course, in real life – and in research projects – correlations tend to be more moderate or ambiguous, and the significance testing process that SPSS will do for you will tell you whether what looks like quite a promising figure (say a positive correlation of 0.63 or a negative correlation of –0.47) is strong enough to be relied upon.

Spearman's rank order correlation

Spearman's rank order correlation gives the statistic, Spearman's rho or ρ = . It is a test to use when you have been able to place the matched values achieved by two groups in rank order.

when to use Spearman's rho

1. You are comparing two groups of linked, matched or paired individuals, the scores they achieve or the ratings they are given, and their specific relationship one with the other.
2. The scores must be of ordinal, interval or ratio quality.
3. If entered into a scattergram, the linked scores should be more or less in a straight line.

Of course, Spearman's rho can be computed for you by SPSS, which will also deliver a precise probability level. But I can illustrate Spearman's rho by describing a modest student project (Tipple-Gooch, 2000) which asked the question, 'Do people of equal attractiveness marry?'

Tipple-Gooch selected five pictures of couples on their wedding day. She cut the pictures down the middle so as to be able to represent each man and each woman separately. She then asked 60 men to rate the women in order of attractiveness and 60 women to rate the men in order of attractiveness – on a scale from 1 to 5, where a score of 5 indicated the most attractive face.

The correlation exercise was focused on the pictures of the five married couples, not on the 60 interviewees, who were simply used in the process of computing an independent assessment of 'attractiveness'.

Tipple-Gooch emerged with average (mean) scores for each portrait and placed them in rank order as follows:

Married couple	Rated attractiveness of the man	Attractiveness rank of the man (R_1)	Rated attractiveness of the woman	Attractiveness rank of the woman (R_2)
D	4.48	1	3.98	1
E	4.12	2	3.53	3
B	2.85	3	2.10	4
A	2.10	4	3.86	2
C	1.22	5	1.30	5

To compute Spearman's rho, subtract each value in R_2 from its paired value in R_1, square the results and compute the total.

Married couple	$R_1 - R_2$	$(R_1 - R_2)^2$
D	0	0
E	−1	1
B	−1	1
A	2	4
C	0	0
Total		$\Sigma(R_1 - R_2)^2 = 6$

N is the number of paired scores in the sample = 5.

Multiply N by its own value twice ($5 \times 5 \times 5 = 125$) and then subtract its own value: $125 - 5 = 120$.

Always multiply $\Sigma(R_1 - R_2)^2$ by 6. In this case $6 \times 6 = 36$, and then divide it by $120 = 0.3$.

Subtract this answer from the number 1: $= 0.7$. The answer is your correlation coefficient and should always be between –1.00 and +1.00.

In the table of critical values for Spearman's rho, the level of significance required for a one-tailed test when N = 5 is, I'm afraid, a very tough 0.9, so the hypothesis was not confirmed: on the basis of the evidence produced and subjected to Spearman's rho, it cannot be claimed that people of equal attractiveness marry.

Pearson's product moment correlation

Pearson's product moment correlation gives the statistic, r = and is the test to use when you have precise data in respect of two variables. Although it is more sensitive and powerful than Spearman, it makes stringent demands on the appropriateness of the data and is often unsuitable in social science settings because of that.

when to use Pearson's product moment correlation

1. The items of data in each sample must be linked or paired off in some way.
2. It can only be used with interval or ratio numbers – not with rating scales based on human judgements.
3. It only works if within a scattergram your data follow a strict linear pattern.
4. The scores must be normally distributed.
5. The two sets of scores must have similar variances.

Pearson's correlation should only be employed when you have two sets of interval-based scores to compare: for example, IQ score and annual earnings, or body weight and number of days per annum spent dieting.

Statisticians argue that, before computing the Pearson correlation coefficient, you *must* plot the relationship between the two scores in a scattergram. If, by doing this, you observe a clear linear relationship between the two variables, then and only then will the Pearson statistic be meaningful. If you reach this point and emerge with a value for r, SPSS will also deliver a probability statistic to tell you whether the correlation, positive or negative, is statistically significant.

Some terms you need to know and understand

Type I and type II errors

The whole point about the idea of probability is that the findings that are based on it are never 100 per cent certain. If they were, we wouldn't call it 'probability'. This means that, despite all your best efforts, it is sometimes the case that one or more of your findings (and those of other people) may be wrong. Statisticians recognise this and have identified the two contrary ways in which errors occur.

They talk about *type I errors* when they are referring to positive findings (that is, findings based on a probability level where $p<.05$) where evidence emerges that the relationship so identified does not, in fact, justify the conclusion. The reason for type I errors generally lies in the research design or the process of the survey analysis – or it can just be that your finding is the one-in-twenty occasion that occurred by chance.

Statisticians talk about *type II errors* when they are referring to negative findings (that is, findings in which probability testing has led the researcher to the conclusion that there is no relationship between the tested variables and therefore that any apparent differences are 'not significant' or NS) where evidence emerges that the researcher had, for some reason, failed to identify a positive relationship. Type II errors are often the result of the researcher using samples that are either not big enough or not appropriately targeted; or using probability tests that are not sensitive enough to identify the relationship; or it may be that the named variables were, in some way, unsuitable for the researcher's purpose – perhaps because they failed to distinguish between subtle differences in the population.

Nominal, ordinal, interval and ratio scales

- *Nominal scales* have no arithmetic value. They are simply numbers used to categorise and differentiate between objects or people. For example, non-graduates = 1; people with first degrees = 2; people with doctorates = 3. Although, in this example, there is a progressive order implied, there doesn't have to be, and it has no numerical value.

- *Ordinal scales* reflect some sense of priority, value or choice, and are commonly to be illustrated in the use of Likert scales. These may involve a range of any length, with definitions attached to either end (good–bad, beautiful–ugly, sweet–bitter), but the measurements along the scale are imprecise, both in their strength and in the intervals between them.
- *Interval scales* reflect the presence of precision between the points along the scale, and crucially depend upon any one interval being identical in size to any other interval.
- *Ratio scales* are similar to interval scales except that they have an absolute zero, for example, time measured from a stated point in time. This means, for example, that 30 minutes is twice as long as 15 minutes (whereas, in the Fahrenheit temperature interval scale, 64° is not twice as hot as 32°).

Independent and dependent variables (IV and DV)

Independent variables in experiments are those which are manipulated or varied in order to assess their impact; in some settings they can be referred to as the 'treatments'. *Dependent variables* (or 'outcomes') are those which, it is hypothesised, may (or may not) be affected by their contact with the independent variables.

In descriptive surveys, the independent variables are those which provide the framework within which you plan to make comparisons. The dependent variables are those which you examine in order to observe similarities or differences.

'One-tailed' and 'two-tailed' tests

A *one-tailed test* is one in which the researcher has made a firm prediction (or stated a hypothesis) that one particular outcome will occur, for example that sample A will score higher than sample B. In other words, you have nailed your colours to the mast, bet on the outcome or stuck your neck out.

By contrast, a *two-tailed test* is one in which you have said only that there will be a difference in the results obtained from your two samples. You haven't stipulated which way you expect the difference to be.

Identification of one-tailed and two-tailed positions is important when you are reaching a conclusion about statistical significance and consulting the relevant tables or reading the SPSS printout.

If you asked me to recommend just one book on ...
statistics *it would be:*

Field, Andy (2005)
Discovering Statistics Using SPSS, London, Sage

Bibliography

Angier, C and Povey, H (2006) 'Storying Joanne, an undergraduate mathematician', *Gender and Education,* **18**(5)

Bales, R F (1950) *Interaction Process Analysis: A method for the study of small groups,* Reading, MA, Addison Wesley

Bales, R F (1999) *Social Interaction Systems: Theory and Measurement,* New Brunswick, Transaction

Bell, J (1999) *Doing Your Research Project,* Buckingham, Open University Press

Blaikie, N (2000) *Designing Social Research,* Cambridge, Polity

Bryman, A and Burgess, R G (eds) (1994) *Analysing Qualitative Data,* London, Routledge

Chavez, D (1985) 'Perpetuation of gender inequality: a context analysis of comic strips', *Sex Roles,* **13**, 93–102

Clegg, F (1990) *Simple Statistics,* Cambridge, Cambridge University Press

Coakes, S J (2005) *SPSS: Analysis without Anguish Using SPSS v 12,* Brisbane, Wiley Australia

Cohen, S and Taylor, L (1972) *Psychological Survival,* Harmondsworth, Penguin

Cornwall County Council (no date) – *A Guide for Using Focus Groups* – on the web: http://www.cornwall.gov.uk/index.cfm?articleid=12635

Denzin, N K (1970) *The Research Act in Sociology,* London, Butterworth

Denzin, N K and Lincoln, Y S (eds) (1994) *Handbook of Qualitative Research,* Thousand Oaks, CA, Sage.

Denzin, N K and Lincoln, Y S (eds) (2003) *Collecting and Interpreting Qualitative Materials,* New York, Sage

Eysenck, H J (1958) 'A short questionnaire for the measurement of two dimensions of personality', in Eysenck, H J (1973) *Eysenck on Extraversion,* Great Britain, Granada Publishing, pp. 31–7

Fawcett, M (1996) *Learning Through Child Observation,* London, Jessica Kingsley

Gladwell, M (2005) *Blink,* London, Allen Lane

Goldberg, D (1978) *Manual of the GHQ,* Windsor, NFER-Nelson

Greenbaum, Thomas L (1998) *The Handbook for Focus Group Research,* London, Sage

Interstate Commerce Commission (1949) *Table of 105,000 Random Decimal Digits,* Statement no. 4914, File no. 261-A-1, Washington, DC

Kinnear, P R and Gray, C D (2004) *SPSS 12 Made Simple,* Hove, Psychology Press

Marshall, C and Rossman, G B (1995) *Designing Qualitative Research*, Thousand Oaks, CA, Sage

Mason, J (1996) *Qualitative Researching*, London, Sage

Mason, J (2002) *Qualitative Researching*, 2nd edn, London, Sage

Mills, C W (1959) *The Sociological Imagination*, New York, Oxford University Press

Pallant, J (2005) *SPSS Survival Manual*, Maidenhead, Open University Press

Pallant, J (2005) *SPSS Survival Manual*, 2nd edn, Maidenhead and New York, Open University Press

Perakyla, A (2004) 'Two traditions of interaction research', *British Journal of Social Psychology*, **43**, 1–20

Rankin, I (2002) *Beggars' Banquet*, London, Orion

Robson, C (1993) *Real World Research*, Oxford, Blackwell

Roethlisberger, F J and Dickson, W J (1939) *Management and the Worker*, Harvard, Harvard University Press

Selltiz, C, Jahoda, M and Deutsch, M (1965) *Research Methods in Social Relations*, London, Methuen

Shaughnessy, J J, Zechmeister, E B and Zechmeister, J S (2000) *Research Methods in Psychology*, Boston, McGraw-Hill

Silverman, D (1993) *Interpreting Qualitative Data: Methods for Analyzing Talk, Text and Interaction*, Thousand Oaks, CA, Sage.

Silverman, D (1998) 'Analysing Conversation' in Seale, C (ed.) *Researching Society and Culture*, London, Sage, pp. 261–74

Stouffer, S A, Suckman, E A, DeVinney, L C et al. (1949) *The American Soldier*, Princeton, NJ, Princeton University Press

Thoday, C (2003) The experience of non-problematic illicit drug use by adult regular users, Ph D thesis, Norwich, University of East Anglia

Walliman, N (2001) *Your Research Project*, London, Sage

Weigel, R H, Loomis, J W and Soja, M J (1980) 'Race relations on prime time television', *Journal of Personality and Social Psychology*, **39**, 884–93

Whyte, W F (1981) *Street Corner Society: the Social Structure of an Italian Slum*, 3rd edn, Chicago, University of Chicago Press

Yablonsky, L (1967) *The Violent Gang*, Harmondsworth, Penguin

Student research reports

The following students, whose work is quoted in the book, were all third-year undergraduates studying for a BSc degree in Psychosocial Studies at the University of East Anglia, Norwich, 2000–2.

Austin, Joanna, 2001
What are the stereotypical implications of four styles of women's office wear as judged by samples of men and women?

Clark, Susan, 2001
Comparing younger and older people, is there a significant difference in mobile phone usage?

Cooke, Abigail, 2001
Are females more frightened of spiders than males?

Doggett, Louisa, 2002
Do men and women differ in their shopping habits?

Kensit, Jo, 2001
What gender differences are there in the division of labour in respect of six discrete domestic tasks?

Key, Georgina, 2002
Does the visible sign of pregnancy in a woman make it more likely that another person will defer to her in the competition for space?

Schofield, Jeanne, 2000
Are there differences between pre-school boys and girls in the way in which they dominate play of other children?

Start, Natalie, 2001
What are the factors which comparative samples of male and female students say make for a rewarding [intimate] relationship?

Tarrington, Emma, 2002
Why are men unfaithful in their sexual relationships?

Thoday, Caitlin, 2000
Are first-born children less extravert than later-born children?

Tipple-Gooch, Emma, 2000
Do people of equal attractiveness marry?

Verdon, Kay, 2002
What do students eat for breakfast?

Watts, Fiona, 2001
What does it mean to be an 'only child' at different points in the life cycle?

Index